2

GW00891771

REVERIE

REVERIE

an autobiography
by
ADELAIDE ROSS

ROBERT HALE · LONDON

© *Adelaide Ross 1981*

First published in Great Britain 1981

ISBN 0 7091 8822 6

Robert Hale Limited
Clerkenwell House
Clerkenwell Green
London EC1R 0HT

Photoset by Art Photoset Ltd., Bucks.
Printed in Great Britain by
Lowe & Brydone Ltd., Thetford, Norfolk
and bound by Weatherby Woolnough Ltd.

Contents

ILLUSTRATIONS

Foreword

The compulsion to write autobiographies is like cutting initials on trees and signing visitors' books. 'I have been here.' This volume is no more than initials carved on the Tree of Life, a name scrawled in the Book of Time. New bark will obliterate the one, a new book replace the other. Meanwhile I will forgo the pleasures of invention and exaggeration, and everything I tell will be true.

My father, who published over two hundred books, when asked in his nineties why he had not recorded his own life story said: 'I have many better stories still to tell. No biography or autobiography is true, because no one in his senses tells the truth about himself, and no one knows the truth about another. Whoever wants to know me can find me in my work.' In Rousseau's *Confessions* he wrote: 'I am not afraid of saying too much or advancing falsities, but am fearful of not saying enough, or concealing truths.' Though my bent is towards reticence I will be candid, and am fearful not that I shall conceal too many truths but shall retail too many trivialities.

Some wise people have decided that it is better not to be than to be: life is not worth its unavoidable suffering and inevitable extinction. I knew one honoured man who proclaimed that could he have planned it so he would have chosen not to be born. In my youth I could not believe that Thomas Hardy — it was he — meant this, for from my lowly standpoint I thought that in spite of his vision of pain and his own suffering, he must have received more enjoyment from literary creation, more pleasure from deserved renown, more satisfaction in a long life well lived, more delight in art, nature, and friendship, even more hope for the future of mankind, than if the sperm and ovum out of which he developed had not chanced to meet. But in my eighties I am sure that he and like-minded persons are sincere. And though I am too limited to concur, I know that according to their deeper insight, wisdom and compassion their convictions are genuine. Yet I dare to look forward to a time when it will be better for everybody to have lived than not to have existed.

All biographers are confronted with the problem: what shall be left out? What must love, friendship, loyalty, duty, decency leave unrecorded? Tell both good and ill, but judge not, is possibly the best advice. For I believe we have less choice than we think and others think we have to be what we are. In this testimony I may have told too much, or too little, or the wrong things. For our manifold shortcomings may my book and I be forgiven.

PART I

Parents

1

My paternal grandfather, Henry Phillpotts, born in 1828, joined the 15th Native Infantry of the Anglo-Indian Army and served through the 1857 Sepoy Mutiny, as the British called it, or as the Indians called it, the first war of independence against British rule. While Assistant Agent to the Governor-General of Rajputana he became ill and was granted fifteen months' leave, during which he fell in love with seventeen-year-old Adelaide Matilda Sophia Waters, eldest daughter of George Waters of the Madras Civil Service, who lived in Somerset. A beautiful girl with upslanting grey eyes, she resembled Dante Gabriel Rossetti's *Mary Virgin*. They were married and, after a London honeymoon, sailed for India, where my grandfather served on a remote station near Mount Abu—a granite spur of the Aravalli Hills, the country of the Jains—their home a bungalow standing beside Nun's Rock. Here, on 4 November, 1862, my father was born, a seven-months child and not expected to live, his mother having precipitated his birth by galloping bareback about the countryside. She could not suckle him, but thanks to a generous Indian woman who fed him as well as her own infant he survived.

Less than a year after Eden's birth Cecil was born, and my grandmother was carrying a third son, Herbert Macdonald, when her husband died, and she and her children sailed back to England, where her father received them in his West Country home. I think my father inherited his marvellous sense of fun and humour from that merry old fellow, who every Christmas morning woke his large family by playing the flute outside their doors and singing 'Christians Awake!'. When eighty-four he escaped from several grown-up daughters and returned with an elderly widow whom he introduced as their new Mama. My grandmother attracted many suitors but, a one-man woman, she refused them all.

2

While the Waters received the orphans lovingly, the Phillpotts clan, including Henry, Bishop of Exeter, were dutiful rather than affectionate. My father, even as a child, flashed into their midst like a changeling and, in so far as he was an artist, did not 'run true to type'.

In that narrow, class-ridden society, from early youth he possessed no sense of pedigree. Genealogy bored him, perhaps because he had what the rest lacked, his own creative gift, more precious than wealth or lineage, and could afford to be without the prestige those may or may not confer. Few of the race went into business, but one, Great-Uncle Abraham, had made a fortune in Jamaica, and for my grandmother's sake offered to adopt her eldest son and give him a university education, if at the age of twelve he would promise to enter the Church. Probably this rich, childless, pious and ambitious man foresaw another Bishop in the family, for young Eden was the brightest of the fatherless trio. His devout mother was overjoyed.

In his thirteenth year my father, to whom his good luck had been explained, was summoned to announce his decision — a foregone conclusion — yet to everyone's consternation he refused to become a clergyman. Forced since early childhood to attend services three times every Sunday and often on weekdays, to confess his sins to a High Church relative and endure other indignities in the name of religion, he revolted against organised Christianity, and neither threats nor maternal tears could force him to change his mind. To have defied even his pathetic mother whom he loved, my father must have possessed a good deal of moral courage and strength of character, and perhaps the dawning consciousness of his genius, for in those days few children were free to express their wishes.

The three brothers were educated at Mannamead College, Plymouth, and in 1879 moved to Ealing, where they and their mother lived with her spinster sister-in-law, my Great-Aunt Susan, a religious fanatic who felt it was her duty to have them. Eden at seventeen entered the Sun Fire Insurance Company, where he remained, an unwilling prisoner, for ten years. While working at the Head Office in Trafalgar Square his most vivid recollection was of political riots. In November 1887, he was watching John Burns, an Independent Radical and member of the Social Democratic Federation and Executive of the Engineers' Trade Union, orating on the steps of Nelson's Column — a big man with a magnificent voice who at ten had been put to work in Price's Candle Factory — when police arrived and my father, proclaiming himself a Radical, rushed out of the office to join in, only to get his topper knocked off by someone who took him for a 'bloody toff'. Asquith unsuccessfully defended Burns for his share in the affray and he was condemned to six weeks' imprisonment. Father had to buy a new top hat.

During these bondage years he spent the summer evenings running round Ealing cinder track and playing tennis and cricket at local clubs, the winter nights standing in Drury Lane queues to see Henry Irving and Ellen Terry in Shakespeare, and falling in love with Ellen. Inspired by these productions he, too, wanted to act and he enrolled at a drama school, where his first part was Bardolph in *Henry V*. But after two years he realised that his talent was mediocre and resigned. Meanwhile in the candlelit night hours he taught himself to write fiction; his short stories found a market, and he published a book called *My Adventure in the Flying Scotsman: A Romance of London and North-Western Railway Shares*. In 1889 he became Assistant Editor of a weekly journal called *Black and White* and thankfully abandoned insurance. It was then that he met my mother, Emily.

3

Emily Topham's paternal forebears were yeoman farmers in Yorkshire. One owned a snuff mill and a tannery on the Dee and became a Freeman of Chester. A cousin married the cartoonist 'Spy', who later made an amusing cartoon of my father, who was a great gardener, 'filling pots'. Her father, Robert, married Anne Okell, sister of a Liverpool merchant. They settled in Shropshire and had four daughters, of whom Emily, born in 1864, was the youngest, and two sons. She was eighteen when her father died and her mother accepted an unmarried sister-in-law's offer to share her Ealing home. Thus my widowed grandmothers and their progeny shared the homes of maiden sisters-in-law at Ealing, then almost in the country, near the pretty village of Perivale. Eden and Emily were introduced at the local tennis club, where they played a kind of patball, she in a stiff, high-necked white cotton blouse with tight sleeves, a long stuff skirt and petersham belt round her whaleboned waist, and a little forward-tipped sailor hat, serving underhand, he in white flannels, blazer and sporty cap, lobbing her easy ones.

They fell in love, but with family obligations it was a long time before my father proposed. Then knowing that like Oliver Goldsmith he could write better than he could talk, from Horrabridge on Dartmoor, where he was on holiday with his mother and aunts, he wrote to Emily's mother, explaining his favourable financial expectations, and also to Emily, setting out, amidst heartfelt expressions of love, his good prospects, his faith in his writing gift, and, with candour, confessing, as she told me afterwards, that it would have to come before everything and everyone else. For he knew that creative work can be more exigent than even a wife and family; at least it was to him. By return of post my mother accepted him.

'On top of the world', and of his beloved Moor, my father invited her to spend the rest of his holiday at Horrabridge and dashed to Plymouth to buy a sapphire and diamond engagement ring. The young pair spent hours courting on Pew Tor, a granite height above the village, and made a pact to lie there together in death; for even during this blissful interlude they knew that some day they must die and not even then could they bear to be parted. Whichever died first would be cremated and the ashes strewn on Pew Tor by the other, who, in his or her turn, would be scattered by their children. What happened to these arrangements, and it fell out extremely strangely, I will tell when the time comes.

Two years after their engagement my parents were married at Perivale and went to Guernsey and Sark for their honeymoon, before settling into a terraced Ealing house. My father had already published three novels and many short tales, had a play produced at the Grand Theatre, Leeds, and continued to pour out novels, stories, poems and dramas, including a comedy with his friend Jerome K. Jerome.

During a spring visit to Newlyn, where he was making notes for *Lying Prophets*, his first important book, my mother conceived, and in January 1895 bore a son, Henry Eden; and a year and three months later a daughter, Mary Adelaide Eden, on 23 April 1896. That it was the supposed date of Shakespeare's birth and death filled me as a child with inordinate delight. But I disappointed my mother, who had set her heart on another boy. How beautiful she was, with glossy dark hair, fine, arched eyebrows over deep, clear blue eyes, a rosy complexion and alluring dimple — so dazzling a face and perfect a form that every artist she met wanted to paint her. Two tried but failed to catch her elusive fascination, which relied on expression and personality, the one ever changing, the other difficult to penetrate; she had many masks. Modest, and fundamentally diffident, she was a pessimist. For though she shone in company and was a wonderful hostess, a faithful friend beloved by both men and women, amongst her own family she was often despondent and subject to dark moods and wayward humours — not without reason. In their youth my father called her 'Silvereyes' and wrote several beautiful 'Songs to Silvereyes', included in his early volumes of poetry: *Up-Along and Down-Along* (1905) and, I think, *Wild Fruit*. Our births were painless, but if our mother suffered she would not have admitted it. Her fortitude was extraordinary. I never heard her complain, unlike our father with his frequent attacks of gout and hypochondria. In his forties and fifties he often told me sadly: 'I shall never live to see another spring,' and with acute fear and sorrow I believed him. My brother inherited our mother's handsome looks and our father's artistic gift. I received a mite of his vitality, for when a week old, I am told, I was choking and turning black with whooping cough, clenching my fists and fighting for the breath of life. The doctor said: 'She can't possibly live,' whereupon my grandmothers sent Father, the only agnostic in the families, flying out to find a clergyman to christen me before I landed in Limbo. He bumped into a young curate and rushed him to the dying infant, who was splashed with water and named, and everyone relaxed, while she was left to die in peace, saved. Yet a strong inclination not to have made the journey down the birth canal in vain prompted me to survive, or was it something else — for someone else was there — a shadowy figure, about whom long afterwards Mother could tell me no more than that she was old, called Mrs Weedon, and 'came in to help'. 'She sat cuddling you hour after hour, night and day, till you were out of danger,' Mother said. It must have been she who saved my life and my soul.

A young woman of twenty-three, Lilla Hilliard Brewitt, said to be descended from the family of Nicholas Hilliard, the Elizabethan miniature painter, came to look after Henry and me in the nursery, where for several years we were brought up. We called her Nan, her assets being infinite good nature, strong sense of the amusing and the ridiculous, ready laughter and inexhaustible patience, besides willingness uncomplainingly to put up with a dwarf salary. She was much closer to us than our parents, whom we saw only intermittently.

After three more years our father's successful Cornish novel, and the first volume of his Dartmoor Cycle, *Children of the Mist*, enabled him to give up journalism and return to the West Country, and Dartmoor, about which he had planned a twenty-volume Saga, each to be set in a different area of the beautiful wilderness that he called his playground as a child and his workshop as a man. We moved to a small Torquay villa he named Cosdon, after Cosdon Beacon, where my memories begin.

Childhood

1

Life-story tellers are apt to dilly-dally over childhoods, because childhood seems far longer than subsequent spans of equal duration. Until
now my thoughts have seldom reverted to that opalescent period,
which can be beautiful and amusing, but also terrible, frightening and
sad, and is seldom the idyllic season depicted in art, yet, recalled and
purged of sorrow, may evoke nostalgia. Looking back to the start of
life the picture is foreshortened, and what has been a lengthy journey
seems curtailed, the longer part its beginning, the shorter its later
years.

Of Cosdon I most vividly recall the garden. A pine tree shed cones.
Hedgehogs lived in the shrubbery. The topsoil was red clay, and
brother Henry, more gifted and inventive than I, rolled it into balls to
make hedgehogs, stuck them with dead pine needles and dried them
in the sun. I copied him, but my hedgehogs were lopsided and fell to
pieces. I remember finding a mouse's corpse wriggling with maggots
and for the first time felt that uncomfortable sensation, pity; and I
recall on a walk with Nan spying a green, metal seat, climbing on to
the back and falling off, banging my head on the path — one of
countless impetuous actions. Her reiterated 'Do look before you leap,
Mim!' made no impression. Henry avoided risks.

I have only vague recollections of our parents at Cosdon—we
seldom saw them — but remember Father coming into the nursery
and chanting: 'Adam and Eve and Pinch-me went down to the sea to
bathe. Adam and Eve were drowned so who do you think was saved?'
I shouted 'Pinch-me!' and got pinched, while Henry kept mum.
Father's 'Think before you speak, child' went unheeded. He told us
stories about a fantastic creature called the Zagabog, who can be
found in his early book *Fancy Free*. Nan roared with laughter over
these games and tales.

I hear a distant echo of her songs: 'Comin' through the Rye'; 'Molly
Malone'; 'Oh dear, what can the matter be, Johnny's so long at the
Fair'; and a haunting ballad: 'Early one morning just as the sun was
rising, I heard a maiden singing in the valley below: O don't deceive
me, O never leave me. How could you use a poor maiden so?' (Thirty
years later, this piteous refrain was to become for her sadly appro-

priate.) Poor Nan, who longed for a home and children of her own, often sang 'Home Sweet Home'. She was never to have one, yet never envied those who had. Listening in to the past it is her voice I hear, crooning love songs and lullabies to put me to sleep.

We had to be silent when our father was working — all morning and after tea until supper. I recall being told to walk on tiptoe because he had a 'splitting headache', and visualised his forehead splitting open to reveal a red gash; and remember Nan's efforts to silence Henry's frequent screaming fits — his troubles so anguished me. Left-handed and destined to become a painter, he was forced to use his right hand and scolded if he resisted, which may have been one cause of his later terrible despairs. But my clearest remembrance of this elusive season is of being alone in bed, a nightlight burning on the mantelpiece in a little china house, when in came a stranger, who bent over my cot and smiled — a man with the most beautiful face I had seen, grey-eyed, with curly auburn hair. After that long, bewitching look and smile he said, 'Goodbye, little girl', waved his hand and left as mysteriously as he had come. He was Father's middle brother, Cecil, a wanderer, unwilling to settle in one place or to one occupation, roving the world and picking up a living where he could. He had just arrived from far away to bid us farewell before leaving for Australia, promising to bring his mother back a fortune, which only she believed he ever would. He was her favourite. His singularly attractive countenance, resembling the Hermes of Praxitiles, seen for those few moments is the first face I remember, before it vanished for ever.

Between the ages of three and four I taught myself to read, with help from Nan and *Reading Without Tears*, copied pothooks and hangers and learned to write; but before Henry could read or write or talk he began to paint and draw with astonishing ability. More real for him and me than real places and people were our fantasy worlds and in my case fantasy people — he did not need people. I never penetrated his imagined world, which was stranger than mine that was rooted in dreams of the night and day. I can still recall a nightmare of a girl with red hot hands rushing towards me and just as she was about to squeeze my throat with her molten fingers I woke. Father, too, as a child suffered from nightmares, of tunnels and trains about to run over him.

One episode during these nebulous years was a visit to Bude, where our father, who combined holidays and work, was making notes for a novel. I see sand dunes towering over me, sparkling in the sun, and feel hot sand trickling between my toes. The tide rolls in casting a misty spray. Mother fits us into bathing drawers with coloured stripes. Excitement is intense, though hidden, as I dash away to explore. I am alone which I like to be. Henry stays behind. I plunge into a pool and cold salt water envelops me. It is a new place, a new adventure, sun, sea, sky — which were going to play a big role in my minuscule existence.

I liked being read to and one line of a poem someone read was rooted in my mind: 'In a drear-nighted December . . . In a drear-nighted December . . .' I loved it.

Henry and I were six and five when we left Cosdon and moved to a larger house called Eltham, with a bigger garden.

2

Eltham abutted on to Oakhill Road which linked hills that descended to Torquay town and harbour. Next door at The Elms lived the Shackleton family, whose son Ernest was soon to set out in the *Discovery* for an expedition led by Robert Scott which, before turning back, reached within 465 miles of the South Pole: this began my passion for the Poles. Eltham's upper regions were lit by gas — naked jets like blue and golden fans — but we still went to bed with candles. The living-rooms were lamp-lighted by standards with ornate metal work, and glass and brass bowls with coloured shades. Twice a year fifty tons of coal were shot down a chute into a cellar, and every day Sharland the gardener brought up several scuttlefuls for the vast kitchen range, and in winter for the nursery and dwelling rooms. In another cellar stood iron racks for wine bottles. It was an adventure to descend into that coal-smelling domain, dimlit by gratings, where empty trunks, unused furniture and other lumber lay.

The back of the house was divided from the front by a swing door through which, every morning except Sunday, at ten o'clock passed our mother to meet Cook in the larder and arrange our huge meals, receiving a list of goods which Mother ordered at local shops, whence, were it but a pound of tea and half a dozen eggs, they were sent up by horse and van. A large kitchen garden supplied vegetables and fruit.

The room I preferred, the tower-room, where I slept with Nan, was the only one on the second floor, with thrilling views of sky, stars and sea and both sunrises and sunsets. Our day-nursery below overlooked the garden, the town, Berry Head and the bay. I stared out of its long windows, seeing what I could see. The World was out there. From the very first day of arrival I noticed on top of a cliff about a mile away a small columned building like a miniature Greek temple, about which I imagined all kinds of stories — it became an eldorado where lived the sprites and elves of my daydreams, an enchanted pavilion symbolising a magical world of beauty, like Bunyan's Celestial City in *Pilgrim's Progress*, the city that shone like the sun — but not, like it, within reach, rather, like Truth, for ever unattainable. Long, long I gazed. Nan said: 'Whatever are you staring at, Mim?' and I would mumble 'The sea.' No one must share my little secret gazebo.

Homelier memories are of being ill and sleeping in the day-nursery.

Dancing criss-cross shadows were cast by the fireguard on walls and ceiling, and in my fevered vision the end of the bed kept advancing and retreating. Nan bent over me, her long plait tickling my face, with a mug of Robinson's groats.

I recall winter afternoons in 'drear-nighted December' when she spread our thick bread and butter with demerara sugar, and for a treat made 'French toast', which dripped sizzling butter drops into the fire; and I recollect her endless darning of woollen socks and stockings with perfect wickerwork darns, snipping off the loops, and conjure up the song of her sewing machine, appropriately called Singer, which had a mother-of-pearl inlaid stand and steel-rimmed wheel, as she swiftly turned the handle and guided material for our clothes under its leaping needle through whose eye, after moistening her fingertips and dampening the thread, she pushed her cottons and silks.

My favourite books were *The Water-Babies* and Hans Andersen's and Grimms' fairy tales. Henry, who had no use for fairies, was too busy drawing and painting to read, and he would play only games he had invented. He searched waste-paper baskets for oddments of string, cardboard, torn envelopes and whatnot and turned them into toys. I remember once when nothing else was handy he bunched up a discarded newspaper, poked holes in it and dropped in a marble, the fun being to see where it would come out. He had surprised the grown-ups by his exceptional talents, especially Grannie Adelaide, to whom he gave pictures of trains, factory chimneys, and the tan-sailed Brixham trawlers we watched from the nursery window setting out to fish. Father, himself a gifted artist in pastels and watercolours, told me long afterwards that he had always hoped a son of his would be a painter. My chosen playthings were a wooden hoop with which I ran up and down Oak Hill Road, and a tin model of a dredger. We shared a microscope given by Uncle Mac, Father's youngest brother, through whose eyepiece we examined everything from snow to the mites in Father's Stilton cheese. Uncle Mac, who had been trained as a doctor at St Mary's Hospital, Paddington, practised in Ealing, where he and his mother lived together. When they came to stay, Grannie Adelaide loaded us with boughten toys, me with dolls which my soul rejected: they and I never got into touch. I loved a large black and silver plush teddy bear and wanted nothing else, except a piece of purple glass I picked off a rubbish heap, a brown stone, and a blue-rayed limpet shell, which I metamorphosed into three brothers, my secret playfellows. (Many children invent such families.) For me solitude was never lonely and very early in life I made a close companion of myself.

The nights of early childhood were full of phantoms: ladders appearing at the window, faces peering in; and to dispel these terrors I invented a continuing story about a black retriever dog which came to guard me and my imaginary family, and kept me so absorbed that the horrors subsided and I slept. But the dog was powerless to save me from a more awful dread at night of seeing my reflection in a wardrobe mirror near the foot of the bed. If I sat up I could see it glimmering, a weird white apparition, yet felt an irresistible compulsion to stare back at my *Doppelgänger*, appalled, with a menacing frisson.

Every morning Nan took us to a kindergarten to be taught by a tall, thin woman called Miss Poulton, and every afternoon for a walk, one being to a brickworks where clay was drawn in trucks up a steep hill through a tunnel to be tipped into a shed where machinery buzzed, driven by whirring leather belts, while an empty truck rattled down the incline to be filled. We could have watched for hours while the tumbrils came and went, but Nan dragged us away to resume the walk. Windmill Hill was another destination among wind-blown trees and old windmill stumps; and not far away rose the Rocks, above a valley in which were a marble works and a slaughterhouse. I can still hear the whine of marble being sawn, the squealing of pigs being knifed and feel a stabbing pity for the swine. One afternoon, rolling down the slope a bumble-bee stung the palm of my hand and the black sting which it left behind disturbed me much more than the pain, especially when Nan said 'Now the bee will die.' Henry and I found a deserted limekiln among the trees which afforded those thrills of danger children welcome — what fairylands and panic lands were at our feet!

Another delectable place was Chapel Hill, with a view of Torre Station's shunting yard and coal tips where Henry watched Mr Pack coupling and uncoupling trucks and sending them in all directions, waving a flag. Nan sat knitting and I slipped off to explore a squirrel haunted knoll on whose summit stood a medieval chapel. Nan readily fell in with our plans, though we guarded from her and from each other our special secret reserves. Many years passed before I learned, with what astonishment, *her* special secret.

My favourite walks were to the shore which even in summer we had almost to ourselves. To run on the firm red sand when the tide was low, pick up slivers of iridescent mother-of-pearl, dabble in anemone pools and find treasures in tide-wrack and wind-row, was very heaven . . . We would hang over a railing below which a local cobbler, a lean man with trousers rolled up, sculpted castles and ships in sand, to whom we threw pennies, aiming at his upturned cap, and he would look up and smile and pull his forelock. I was sad when the flowing tide melted away his masterpieces, but he did not mind: he could build new ones.

Sometimes Father joined Nan and us on our walks through the lanes and taught us the wild plants' folk names: Traveller's Joy, Grass of Parnassus, Star of Bethlehem, Sweet Melilot, Bouncing Bet,

Creeping Jenny and Gypsy Rose, Enchanter's Nightshade, Wake
Robin and Cuckoo Pint, Jack-in-the-Pulpit, Goldilocks, and hundreds more, and encouraged us to seek the rare ones. I left them for
Henry to find because I wanted him, so often scolded, to win our
father's praise and the barley sugar or butterscotch he fished from the
pocket of his Norfolk jacket. One hot summer afternoon we were
sitting in a meadow beneath a tree where red cattle with horns were
lying in the shade, when I glided off alone and found a nettle plant
hung all over with golden lockets glittering in the sunshine and
overjoyed, ran to fetch the others. Father said each little casket was
the chrysalis of a Red Admiral butterfly.

Once a week Nan and I went to a gymnasium run by a muscular old
man with a white moustache and pointed beard called Sergeant-Major
Tomney. Henry refused to go. The old man put a crowd of little boys
and girls through long jumps, jumps over the vaulting horse, high
jumps, and made us shin up ropes, climb horizontal and vertical
ladders and swing on parallel bars, which I madly enjoyed, showing
off in a way that would not have been tolerated at home, where the one
thing you must *never* do was to show off. And weekly, too, Nan took
me to a dancing class held in a large saloon, where Miss Hickey and a
young assistant called Aileen taught us polkas, gallops, two-steps and
other frolics. Henry refused to go. Of all the children I recall only a
flaxen-haired beauty of twelve called Agatha — (later Agatha Christie)
— wearing a blue silk accordion-pleated dress, who danced better
than anyone else and was prettier. She lived near us but we did not see
much of her until she grew up. One side of the saloon held a large
mirror and I recollect on my sixth birthday standing in front of it and
noticing my face for the first time. Then I caught sight of Agatha's
reflection: she was a thousand times nicer and cleverer than me. But I
never envied anyone.

At Christmas that year Nan took me to my first theatre, the
pantomime *Aladdin*, at the Torquay Theatre Royal. O, the rapture of
expectation, the transport of wonder as the curtain rose and a certain
indefinable aroma wafted from the stage into the auditorium, the
witchery of the painted scenery, the intoxication of beholding that
other world beyond the footlights and the unfolding of that splendid
story of the magical lamp! Though I have experienced dozens of other
theatrical adventures, both before the curtain and behind, that
production evoked something none other has inspired. There were
fairies with gauzy wings. I longed to possess a pair, and must have
betrayed my longing, for Nan revealed it to Aileen who said: 'You
shall have your wings.' A week later she gave me a parcel, saying,
'There are your fairy wings,' and I visualised a pair of sparklers. At
home I opened the parcel, in which lay a couple of limp brown canvas
'wings' decorated with purple spots smelling of oil paint and not quite

dry. O, crushing disappointment! But I should have known that mine was to be a wingless destiny.

A diversion which many nursery children must have shared in those days was to kneel behind landing banisters on dinner-party nights and watch guests arriving below, and walking arm in arm into the dining-room with our parents, the men with stiff shiny shirt-fronts, the women in elaborate gowns with low necks, Mother outshining the rest. Sometimes I heard snippets of conversation, of which the only one I remember, coming from a tall actor, was 'Beethoven is blancmange!' Beethoven — blancmange? Who was Beethoven, and how could anyone be like the least appetising of our nursery puddings? An actress who came, in an emerald green satin dress, was Lillah McCarthy with her husband, Harley Granville-Barker; another was Lena Ashwell; and a man, very stout, was the scientist Sir Edwin Ray Lankester, Professor of Zoology and Comparative Anatomy, on a visit to Kent's Cavern to see the fossil bones of a sabre-toothed cat. I begged Nan to take me to the cave, where excitement was tremendous, especially when the guide tapped a group of stalagmites that played a tune.

Not until Henry and I were in our teens did we meet visitors, many of whom never knew that our parents had children, so we grew up morbidly shy, reserved and undemonstrative. With our naturally introspective natures and hidden lives of the imagination, we spent most of our early lives in private worlds, remote from the grown-ups. But this secretiveness ran through the household. Father had his work, Mother her social life of tea-parties and paying calls, both with numerous admirers and lovers. Nan had her mother and siblings in whom our parents took no interest, or in the servants and their outside affairs and families. Even Gaffer the cat went his independent way, and Nan's fox terrier, Flip, kept in the background and was not allowed into the garden. There was no mingling of interests, no mutual communication, no general conversation and laughter. We were never allowed to interrupt our father's work. After all, his work *was* the most important thing, not only to him but to everyone else, the only part of the family that will be remembered.

Uncle Mac's Ealing practice had failed, and he and Grannie Adelaide were in debt; so Father, who had frequently come to their rescue, bought them a house called Eastcliff on Babbacombe Downs, where they took in paying patients whose families could not or would not support them. I remember a poor twisted woman called Ella, crippled with arthritis, who lay in bed wasting away, to whom I was taken to kiss her cheek and hold her thin bluish hand. I liked going to Eastcliff because I was allowed to open a cabinet full of shells, including huge clams and tiny cowries and a large conch in which, pressed to the ear, I could hear the song of the sea; and because

she scooped her huge ear forward with a wooden spoon, that I might shout into its hairy hollow, and would bellow: 'I can't hear you. Speak up, child! You're not dumb, are you?' By then I was dumb as a dodo.

They had an old maidservant, Charlotte, who cooked raisin gingerbread for tea. Grannie Anne made scrumptious brawns with brown sugar and vinegar for breakfast, and Aunt Frances had invented a marvellous toffee whose recipe she would share with nobody. During these visits I was taken to visit other members of the family — Henry would not go — including Great-Aunt Mary, on Father's side, a dear old woman with side curls and a mob-cap who lived with a green parrot in a Paddington flat. It was the parrot I looked forward to. It talked. And there was always a delicious tea. On one occasion a super meal had been laid and we were about to start when a thunderstorm broke and Great-Aunt, terrified, wept and called on God to stop it, screaming every time lightning flashed and thunder rolled. Tea was forgotten. The cakes were never eaten. The parrot screeched and bobbed up and down and Aunt Mary cried 'God save us! It's the end of the world. Cover Polly's cage!' Mother flung an antimacassar over it but the bird went on squawking. I could not help laughing and Mother was cross: 'Don't laugh!' Trips to London by horse-bus and tube, with a ride in a hansom cab and a visit to the Zoo, were magical. I remember stroking a kangaroo's nose and it bit my finger; and how Henry, mesmerised by giraffes and owls, yelled when he was pulled away to see the lions. I recollect the Tivoli Music Hall in the Strand and Little Tich, the Natural History Museum and a model of the gigantic diplodocus; and best of all Hale's Tours where one entered a realistic railway carriage and travelled all over the world.

Home again, it was Christmas, the only time Grannie Adelaide wore the Indian topaz set her husband had given her to celebrate Father's birth. As I was helping her to fasten the pendant cross of honey-coloured gems, hearing me admire them, she said: 'When I die all these will come to you.' It was like being drenched with icy water. I no longer wanted them.

Father published two or three books every year. And as the family prospered, my parents spent longer abroad in France and Italy. Mother had a passion for travel, but Father was always afraid of getting ill, though he wanted to see the great pictures and sculpture in Continental galleries. Once, when they and their friend Arnold Bennett were staying in the South of France, Aunt Frances came to look after us, which caused friction with Grannie Adelaide, who was jealous by nature, each declaring that *she* had been left in charge. I could not bear family strife, all too common in our household, and wanted everyone to love one another and be friends, as I loved everyone. Aunt Frances' attraction was her reading aloud about Brer Rabbit, Brer Fox, Brer Terrapin and Tar Baby. She tried to interest me in *Alice in Wonderland*, but when it turned out to be only a dream, for me it was ruined. One evening she was reading my favourite *Robinson Crusoe*, while I stared at a slab of peat smouldering in the nursery grate when a wisp of grey smoke shot through a crevice in the peat and swayed to and fro. Aunt Frances had seen it too and cried: 'Look! There's a witch dancing on the blasted heath!' and the grate become a wild moorland with a wild witch capering.

We were expecting our parents to return from Algiers when a telegram arrived. Something dire had happened. Grannie Adelaide was crying. Nan told us that Father was not well and they were staying on until he got better. Immediately I thought he was dying, and he nearly was. I heard the words 'double pneumonia'. Terrible days went by. At last everyone was smiling again, Grannie crying for joy. He was out of danger. One afternoon he came into the nursery, pale and thin, and told us how in his delirium he saw thousands of tiny camels stamping across his chest, and their feet hurt. I saw them too and felt their tiny hooves.

Mother took me to church, and in front sat two little girls who smiled at me. I asked Mother if I could be their friend and she answered: 'Their parents keep a shop in the town.' Apparently there was no more to be said. So I asked Nan why I could not be their friend and she said: 'Because their mother and your mother don't call.' Call? Why should they call? 'They don't leave cards.' Cards? There was something very odd here. It was all a mystery. I gave up. Yet there was something wrong.

Father's avocation was gardening. With a young gardener called Aubrey Sharland he transformed our plain acre into what a friend called 'this other Eden, demi-paradise'. For me it was heaven itself. From adult conflicts in the house, when voices were raised in anger and jarring words broke forth, Henry escaped to the tower room to paint, I to the garden to play with my invisible 'family' who never quarrelled, to that Arcadia of colours, forms, fragrance and wild creatures, to lean over the pond, turning back water-lily leaves looking for snail spawn, catching newts and frogs, watching water beetles, and dragonfly nymphs climbing reeds before bursting into dragonflies. The fat water-lily buds opened into crimson stars under the splashing fountain which caught rainbows, its voice the voice of summer afternoons. In dewy twilights toads plopped across the grass and above flittered bats, while humming-bird hawkmoths sipped the tobacco flowers.

People from all over the world came to see Father's garden, especially the rhododendrons his friend Reginald Farrer brought from the Himalayas. Every autumn he set me to pluck off their ripe seeds. There were limestone and red sandstone rockeries, pools, lilies, a rose border and shrubberies. Father wrote two books about it: *My*

Shrubs, and *My Garden* dedicated to 'The Lady of my Garden', Mother adored flowers.

The only time Nan went into the garden was before late dinner to pick a posy, which she tied and laid on Mother's dressing-table for her to pin on to her evening dress. Every morning Sharland fetched Cook a trug of fruits and vegetables for the much too opulent meals. During summer he would lift me in his fuzzy brown arms to pick apples, pears and plums from bending trees, and figs which were enclosed in a cage to save them from the birds. In the greenhouse ripened cucumbers, muscat grapes, peaches and nectarines. The hot section fruited orange and lemon trees, and over the roof rambled a Dutchman's Pipe vine called *Aristolochia elegans*. Garden frames contained netted melons lolling on slates. For over fifty years Sharland laboured happily for Father and would have begged, borrowed or stolen for his beloved Master, as he called him.

In the shrubberies grew dozens of trees, among them a mauve lilac with a swaying branch on which I sat, galloping round the world. Amidst the pines and horse-chestnuts outside my bedroom window cooed wood pigeons, and red squirrels leapt from branch to branch. Bats and cockchafers flew round my bed on summer nights, and in wafted the savour of white jasmine, honeysuckle and mignonette. Each autumn consignments of new plants arrived and were stacked in the coach-house until they could be planted. I recollect Father calling me to unpack a very precious tree: 'I want you to help me plant it because, though I shall not live to see it flower, you may. It will not flower for thirty, forty or fifty years!' It was a *Magnolia campbellii*, then rare in the British Isles. We settled it near the front gate and covered its roots with peat, watering and treading it in. That magnolia and I spent our childhoods together, but it soon outstripped me, and long before I was in my teens soared far above my head. But it did not flower.

I had a mania for caterpillars, moths and butterflies and began to scribble rhymes about them, which Nan made me copy out and give to Father for his forty-first birthday. His delight was astonishing. He went through each line and amended it. From that moment he encouraged me to write.

He had begun deeply to love me. I think he looked on me as an extension of himself, for he would take me into his bed and fondle me, compare my limbs with his and say 'Look! Your hands and feet are just like small editions of mine. You're so like me. And you're going to be a writer too.' He kissed me all over and said: 'You must never marry.' At six or seven that meant nothing to me, yet I did not forget those words, which all through my youth and afterwards were repeated. I loved him too, but only as a father, and for fear of hurting him I let him do whatever he liked.

4

It was 1903. Henry and I were taken from the kindergarten and sent to different schools, he to a local boarding-school for small boys, I to a high school for girls. Henry, withdrawn and hypersensitive, whose world revolved round his painting, was a ready victim for teasing and bullying. But our parents, who had found him stubborn and difficult, were determined that he should be disciplined and brought up like other boys until he fitted into the conventional mould. Of the high school I remember little except an older girl called Nelly with whom I fell in love, my first experience of that troubling state, at seven as delicious and painful as at seventy-seven.

My curiosity about people was developing, and on the walks to school with Nan I noticed those who were different: a 'mongol' woman, a man with a bunch of purple blobs instead of a nose—a pitiable deformity not then remedied—a seven-foot imbecile who helped a woman to carry baskets of laundry, a mentally retarded man walking vacantly beside an elderly mother, a young man with long blond curls, make-up, and a necklace, besides cripples in Bath chairs; and I saw a boy cycling downhill, carrying sheets of glass run into a wall; the glass smashed into his face, which someone covered with a coat. Blood where blood should not be was always a dreadful shock. Those poor afflicted people worried and haunted me for years.

Every winter we were invited to children's parties. Henry refused to go. Nan made me into a powder-puff, a poppy, a forget-me-not, and when it was time to get ready stood me in front of the nursery fire, her mouth full of safety-pins, and arranged me, wrapping me in a Red-Riding-Hood cloak she had made. We waited in the hall for an old cab, drawn by an old horse, and driven by an old cabby called Inch, who sat humped on the box like a beetle. I can still smell the leathery interior and the brown rug he folded over our knees. If it rained I felt dreadfully sorry for him and his nag getting soaked outside while we sat dry within. At those unenjoyed parties we played 'Hunt the Slipper' and 'Blind-man's Buff', 'Postman's Knock', 'Ring-a-ring o' Roses' and 'Musical Chairs', and sometimes there was a magic lantern or a conjurer. I recall dancing with a little old gentleman called Mr Frere who, like Lewis Carroll, loved little girls in fancy dress.

The diversions Henry and I most enjoyed were the Summer Fairs, to which we were taken by Nan or Grannie Adelaide and Uncle Mac. How the Fair people and their painted wooden caravans allured us, the glittering fairings, the gingerbread men, the nougat seller with long black ringlets whose pink and white nougat stuck to one's teeth. How the acetylene flares and coloured lights on the roundabouts thrilled us, the barkers shouting outside the boxing-booth, coconut-shies, and shooting galleries with celluloid balls jumping on water-jets, and the Freaks. Uncle Mac, who shared our addiction, took us to see the Fat Lady and pinched her colossal thighs, saying 'Don't mind me, dearie. I'm a doctor. No padding here!' And he slipped her a sovereign, He gave us handfuls of pennies, and while Henry saved his I spent mine on the Golden Gallopers, with its triple ring of chargers clanking round. Clutching my penny I climbed the steps and waited for a grimy youth to lift me on to a steed and hand my fare to a huge old man like a bloated spider sitting in the middle of the machine while the horses started to revolve. I loved the organ's gilded pipes spouting ear-splitting tunes, the mechanical ladies in bloomers and soldiers wielding batons, beating cymbals and jerking their heads from side to side. With ecstasy I hugged the twisted brass rod which rose and sank as the world below blurred, and I turned myself into one of the heroes who pervaded my daydreams: Richard Lionheart on yellow Fanuelle killed under him at Jaffa, King Baldwin of Jerusalem galloping into battle on his Arab mount Gazelle, Alexander the Great on Bucephalus, or Muhammad himself on Al-Burak ascending to the Seventh Heaven from the sacred stone under the Dome of the Rock at Jerusalem. But most often I became Bellerophon on Pegasus who sprang from three blood drops dripping from Medusa's head and was caught as he drank from the Corinthian Spring, hoofing the earth and causing to gush forth the Muses' Fountain on Mount Helicon. My head fumed with these tales. Father had given me stories from Homer, the Greek dramatists and Vergil, with pictures from Flaxman designs, and I grew so enamoured of those mortals and immortals that I drew up family trees of divinities and heroes. Goethe called Greek Mythology 'an inexhaustible mine of divine and human symbols'. To me the Olympians became close friends.

Annual visits to Dartmoor were a feature of our early years. Father's recreation was trout-fishing, but his chief purpose was to make notes for a new novel, tramping the district and letting it suggest the plot and the characters. I ran behind him, striving to keep up with his long legs, as his imagination hotted up until it boiled over and he stopped, pulled out his notebook and jotted down a description or some dialogue. If anything hooked my attention he would say: 'Write me a poem about it,' or he chose the theme: 'Write about those old weatherbeaten larches above the Cowsic Glen'. Sometimes he would lie in the heather, draw me into his arms and fondle me; or he would produce coloured chalks and make a picture: I recall one of a 'Joseph's Coat caterpillar', each segment a different colour, which I kept for many years, but, like so much else, it disappeared into the 'dark backward and abysm of time'.

One year we stopped in a furnished bungalow above Okehampton called Klondike, where Arnold Bennett joined us, though he never felt at home on the moor. He and Father had met in the 1890s after he left Staffordshire for London, and had in common a love of literature

and ambition to become novelists and dramatists. Together they had
seen Queen Victoria driving through the Park, and Gladstone walking
to the House of Commons; together they discussed their futures.
Father was already planning to leave the metropolis, but Bennett
resolved to win fame and fortune there and said: 'You are dedicated to
the moorland. I am going to dedicate myself to the Five Towns.' He
often stayed with us, and Father taught him a lot and helped him to
overcome his bashfulness and make him a man of the world. He
admired and cared for our mother, and in March 1902, sent her the
following verses, adding that they were 'originally composed by Lord
Jeffrey but very much improved by E. A. Bennett'.

> Why write my name midst songs and flowers,
> To meet the eye of lady gay?
> I have no voice for lady's bowers—
> For page like this no fitting lay.
>
> Yet though my heart may never bound
> At witching call of sprightly joys,
> Mine is the brow that never frowned
> On laughing lips and sparkling eyes.
>
> Take then, fair girl, my blessing take:
> Where'er on Devon's shores you roam:
> Or where, on further hill or lake
> You brighten a serener home.

In 1904, writing to Mother after a visit, he described Eltham as 'the
most perfectly appointed house I have ever stayed in', which enormously pleased her. Father told me in later years that while Arnold
liked sophisticated, *soignée* women who used make-up and wore
fashionable clothes, he preferred simple, fresh country girls.

Henry and I spent hours playing beside the tumbling rivers, I
leaping from boulder to boulder, he floating a stick Father had cut for
him down the currents and running to retrieve it before it sailed out of
reach. One afternoon he dared me to jump across a chasm above a
waterfall rolling into a boiling pool below; and I, knowing I could not
clear it, jumped, landed in the pool and was swept downriver. Henry,
who dreaded and avoided danger, plunged in, clutched me and
somehow we struggled to the bank. I ran dripping to our mother and
father who were some distance away shouting: *'Henry's saved my life!'*
Perhaps he had.

One night Father burst into our bedroom—we were staying at Belstone—crying 'Come quick! There's something I want you to see you
may never see again!' Arched over Cosdon Beacon shimmered a lunar
rainbow!

Arnold Bennett joined us again at Princetown. Father was planning *The American Prisoner*, and to get copy they asked the Governor to take them over the gaol. The grim structure, like a great wart on the fair face of the Moor, and the gangs of prisoners wearing ill-fitting clothes splotched with broad arrows, their heads shaved, guarded by warders with guns, haunted me. If I caught their eyes I smiled, meaning, 'Whatever you did you don't deserve this', and sometimes one winked and smiled. In the churchyard were mounds under which lay men incarcerated during the Napoleonic and American Wars for whom this Bastille had been raised. The whole prison system appalled me—and still does.

Arnold and Father were collaborating on a potboiler called *The Statue* and each morning set out for Nun's Cross, where they sat working. Arnold had difficulty inventing plots and envied Father his facility. 'I still reckon that you know more about constructing a novel than anybody else in the country,' he wrote. So Father supplied the plot and shape of *The Statue* and A.B. contributed dialogue and other matters. I would lie near them in the heather and heard one word over and over again—'Instalment'. What did it mean? The meaning of words had begun to interest me but I was too shy to ask them. So next time we were in the village I bought a sixpenny dictionary and an address-book and every time I read or heard new words looked them up and wrote down their meanings and every night learned them by heart. Years later Father told me that as a boy he had done the same.

Something happened, I never discovered what, to cause a rift between our father and Arnold Bennett and they parted. Arnold married, became famous and vanished from our lives, until long afterwards there was a dramatic reconciliation.

At the end of this tremulous era dire changes occurred in our little sphere. One morning I found Nan weeping: Mother had given her a month's notice. Henry was to go to a preparatory school, I to have a governess for a year until at nine I, too, went to boarding-school. For a parting gift they gave her a carriage clock. She accepted a post as nurse to a new baby at the other side of the town, and hoped sometimes to visit us, but Mother thought her visits would unsettle me and it was better that I should not see her again.

The pain of loss was excruciating, but I had one consolation. Mother loved music, and when she and Father returned from the Riviera, where they had attended concerts by Bronislaw Hubermann and Arthur Rubinstein, Father bought a pianola which he played for two or three hours every night. My bed was above the spot in the drawing-room where it stood and nothing could have made me sleep before the concerts ended. How void I felt when Father closed the lid, wound the grandfather and cuckoo clocks in the hall and came to bed. I wanted the intoxicating music to continue all night. For

years those nocturnal entertainments transported me to ecstatic
realms. To know that my parents were sharing the music consoled
me; it was wonderful to hear their laughter when Father played
Grieg's 'Trolltogs' Dance'.

One night new sounds ascended through the floor and I had frissons
of joy. It was Beethoven, and thenceforth other composers, though
not outlived, were outloved. I saw his hands on the keys, for I always
pictured artists at work. This night music partly satisfied a desire for
love and a passion for beauty.

5

Miss Morgan, the governess who superseded Nan, was of indefinite
age and seemed always to be afraid of offending somebody, doing the
wrong thing, and on the verge of tears. Soon after her arrival I found
her crying in her room and tried to console her. If, as Bernard Shaw
maintained, pity is the 'fellow feeling of the unfit' I was unfit indeed.
But I suspect that my agonisings about the grown-ups' troubles and
jealousies were rooted in terror that our fragile soapbubble of a society
would burst and spill me out to face the world alone. (Now I prefer the
definition given by Father's friend, Clarence Darrow, the American
defence lawyer: 'Pity is really pain engendered by the feelings that
translate one into the place of another.')

This was the age of the Entente Cordiale, and a young Mademoiselle
came once a week to teach me French. Chic, talkative, high-bosomed,
one morning she handed me a copy of La Fontaine's *Fables* and told
me to learn by heart and then translate *Maître Corbeau sur un Arbre
Perché*—pointing out that translations were printed at the end of the
book, but 'being an honourable little English girl I know you will not
crib'. Irked by this boring exercise—I wanted to be inventing my own
fables—I cribbed, hoping that a little poetical readjustment would
disguise my perfidy. On her next visit Mademoiselle asked me to read
my translation, after which she said: '*Bon! Très bon!* So you did not
cheat?' 'No.' I could never tell a convincing lie. '*Mon pauvre enfant!*'
she exclaimed. 'You are not artful enough to deceive a fly. To be a
good trickster one must be a lot cleverer than you. With your brain
you will never get away with it. For you, my poor child, honesty is the
only policy.' This was the most mortifying moment I had known. I
feared she would tell my parents, which she did not. Worst was the
ridicule, and that phrase about needing to be 'a lot cleverer than you',
though I knew I was not clever. The disgrace ended in tears,
whereupon she melted. 'Never mind, *mon petit chou*. The skies won't
fall because you cheated. But you will never cheat again.' I never did.

To wipe out the shocking impression I had made I thrust at her my
own rhymes, but she brushed them aside as if to say, 'Surely you don't
think you are another La Fontaine?' and I knew that to her I should

always be the horrid little creature who lied and cribbed. So I was glad when the year of Miss Morgan and Mademoiselle ended, and along with the pity inspired by the first and the shame occasioned by the second they disappeared from my life, and have not reappeared until now.

During the Christmas season of children's parties I was inserted as the Empress Josephine into *tableaux vivants* of historical couples, my Napoleon a youth of fourteen called Jack whom I loved, and prayed twice a day: 'Please God when I grow up let me marry Jack.' (He was killed on the Somme.)

Opposite our house lived Miss Helen and Miss Gertrude Ormerod, little old sisters devoted to children, served by two still older retainers who wore long black dresses and white aprons. I was taken there to tea, and sometimes caught a glance of their mysterious lodger, Edward Noake, who dined with our parents once a week. Why did those prim little ladies keep in their household that romantic-looking artist who painted an excellent portrait of our father, and a less successful one of Mother? He had a beautiful baritone voice and after dinner entertained them with Victorian ditties. The Misses Ormerod treated him like a nephew, and he made fun of them behind their backs—so Father told me long afterwards. One year he joined our parents on a voyage to Italy and, much to their annoyance, refused the captain of the liner's request to sing to the passengers, among whom a Sicilian prince fell in love with Mother and, finding her alone on deck, sank on his knees and begged her to elope when they reached Naples and fly to his castle in Sicily. Before she could decline, Father appeared and the lover scrambled up and fled. But they all ended as friends!

There was something appealing about Edward Noake, a pathos I felt but as a child could not understand—he was one of those extremely talented people temperamentally doomed to failure in their art or, as in his case, two arts, both painting and music, people who never reach the goals merited by their genius. Just before the First World War, which he foresaw, he vanished to Italy, to reappear after it ended, but only to collect his belongings, leaving most of his pictures behind, before returning to marry a middle-aged widow with a vineyard in Tuscany. The poor old sisters replaced him with a fox terrier, turned vegetarian and half starved themselves. The story went that on her deathbed Miss Helen murmured over and over again 'Roast beef and Yorkshire pudding! Roast beef and Yorkshire pudding!' Miss Gertrude died soon afterwards. Their house was pulled down and in the derelict studio were many beautiful but damp-ruined pictures by Edward Noake.

Twice a year Mother gave a tea-party for over a hundred people who lived in the big villas on the fashionable side of the town. Buzzard's

provided the elaborate cakes while our cook, Blanche, made the rest.
Mother was always afraid the party would not be a success: 'Suppose
nobody comes,' 'Suppose the cakes don't arrive in time,' 'Suppose
Eden gets gout.' But though Eden loathed these affairs he never let
her down, and she always looked wonderful in the new 'Ernest' gown
she had been to London especially to choose. In summer the party was
held in the garden and Mother would say: 'Suppose it rains!' I
watched from the spare-room window, and once saw Bernard Shaw
hide behind a weeping willow and leap out like a leopard, growling, to
amuse the guests.

This was the year Grannie Adelaide declared that she must go to
Uncle Cecil in Australia. 'I'm sure he needs me.' She needed him.
Father expostulated; but with that cast-iron obstinacy some weak but
sweet and determined characters possess Grannie prevailed. Father
made the arrangements. O, how I longed to go. Uncle Cecil met her at
Parramatta and took her to the fruit farm on the Murrumbidgee River
where he worked. Tall, slender and amber-haired, everyone called
him cornstalk. He brought her to his shack where to her astonishment
she found a pretty young woman with a baby girl, whom he
introduced as 'My love-girl and my daughter.' 'You're married!' she
exclaimed. 'Why didn't you tell us?' 'Not married,' he answered, 'just
lovers.' When Grannie got over the shock she tried to persuade them
to marry while she was there, if only for the sake of the love-girl's little
love-chick. But he said he would soon be leaving for Africa, and his
girl was going to work in a town and leave the infant with her mother:
'Gran will look after her.' Grannie Adelaide declared that she was her
Gran too, and planned to bring the child to Eltham to be brought up
with me. But this time she did not get her way, though I should have
been delighted to have a sister.

A long time afterwards a cable arrived to say that Uncle Cecil had
died of fever near the Zambezi, and from that moment Grannie bowed
her head and always wore black. Great-Aunt Susan, her husband's
sister with whom they had lived at Ealing and now settled in Torquay,
no sooner heard about Uncle's death than she hurried to Grannie to
tell her that he had not gone to Heaven, or was even on the way, but,
because of his fornication resulting in the birth of a bastard, had
undoubtedly been consigned to the Other Place. This pious old
woman, who spent much of her time on her knees, believed that
'whores and whoremongers' go straight to Hell. Grannie rushed to
Father, and he rushed to Great-Aunt Susan to tell her that *she* not
Cecil was bound for the gridiron, and he vowed he would never speak
to her again. But it was not long before Grannie forgave her, though
she let her know that Cecil was even then with his father in Paradise.

After this tragedy Grannie and Uncle Mac took a dislike to their
Babbacombe home, and Father, hoping a move might revive his

mother, bought them a house at Kingswear on the Dart, found a new paying patient for Uncle Mac, and Mother gave them a bull terrier called Chum. Mount Ridley stood on a hill overlooking the estuary with a glimpse of the open sea, and at Easter and during the August Regatta, Henry and I went to stay—bliss for Henry, surrounded by ships and Grannie whom he loved more than anyone else. She never scolded him, and for her he painted the view, and the eucalyptus trees. The paying patient was a demented old woman whom I was taken to greet every morning in bed, she wearing a frilled nightcap, twisting her fingers, mumbling, laughing, happy and smelling of old, old age. Uncle Mac did not come down until lunch time, because, said Grannie, he was 'poorly'. When he did appear he smelt of brandy and eau de cologne. Sometimes he would don a nautical reefer and stroll round Dartmouth Harbour in an old yachting cap dating from the time Father got him a post as a physician/secretary to an eccentric American Press millionaire called, I think, Joseph Pulitzer, who was planning a voyage in his luxury yacht in search of health and needed the presence of a doctor and amanuensis—a vain flight from death which occurred the following year. But being abnormally sensitive to sound he found our uncle's voice 'somewhat theatrical' and, for no other fault, soon dismissed him. I knew that something serious was the matter with Uncle Mac but no one would tell me what it was.

Like Goethe's grandmother and many another ours contrived to 'regale us with all sorts of nice morsels', and one Easter she stuffed me with so many chocolate eggs after breakfast that when we were visiting the grand people who lived at Kingswear Castle I was violently sick on the garden path, and for the first time secretly blamed our grandmother, when I should have had the courage to refuse, as Henry did, instead of being afraid to hurt her feelings.

I never tired of hearing about her life in India—how her Victorian mama made her promise that on her wedding night she would conceal her abundant and beautiful hair under a nightcap and take every other precaution dictated by modesty; and how she crammed her mane into an ugly cap her mother had provided, and when her husband entered the bridal chamber he looked at her and burst out laughing, pulled off the nightcap and said 'Never let me see you in that frightful thing again!' She told me that having babies could be painful though one did not mind because it was so wonderful when the baby lay on one's breast; and I felt a sudden thrill and held an imaginary infant to mine, hoping that one day I should have a nurseryful.

Back at Eltham huge crates arrived containing curios Uncle Cecil had collected on his wanderings, among the larger trophies elephant tusks and feet, the skull of a hippopotamus, a rhino's horn, a lyre bird's tail feathers mounted on red plush, and a stuffed secretary bird in a glass case—a melancholy creature which Father placed on the hall

mantelpiece but Mother banished to the housemaid's bedroom, she
having admired it. Smaller objects comprised green and golden
beetles, spears, knobkerries and shields, boomerangs and didgeri-
doos, antelope horns, and a spiral pair from a bull kudu that Father
got made into the support for a gong which for twenty years
summoned the family to meals. What most attracted me was a Zulu
girl's skull which was placed on our nursery mantelpiece. There were
also bead aprons and collars, necklaces and bracelets, and Uncle's
violin which I begged to learn but was not allowed. 'The sound of your
practising would drive your father mad!' The last item was a tin trunk
which when opened emitted a horrible stench and contained a
collection of bottled snakes, but the bottles had burst, leaving a slimy
mess of putrefying serpents.

Our father was perturbed by these pathetic relics of his adventurous
younger brother: perhaps he remembered their boyhood. I, too, was
upset by this last Hail and Farewell from the beautiful man who bent
over my Cosdon cot and said goodbye.

6

In 1904 our father was invited to unveil a memorial window to
Richard Doddridge Blackmore, author of Lorna Doone, in Exeter
Cathedral, the only time I remember him appearing in public. He
hated publicity. A year later he was asked to devise a motto to be
carved outside the Andrew Carnegie Library at Torquay and chose:
'Read Wisely, for a Good Book is a Faithful Friend'.

Shadowy Miss Morgan left as mutely as she had arrived. Henry,
protesting and miserable, was sent to a preparatory school run by
a clergyman at Tonbridge, and I was despatched to a local boarding-
school called Girton House.

Before our exiles, wonder of happy wonders, Nan returned. Father
had suggested to Mother that, to save the cost of having his increasing
piles of manuscript typewritten in London, Nan should become his
secretary, and look after us in the holidays. How gladly Nan agreed!
One of her first duties was to take me to the new school which, not two
miles from Eltham, seemed at the other end of nowhere. We were
received by the headmistress, Miss Guyer, a flat woman with an
unhappy expression and scraped-back hair. For a parting present Nan
gave me The Handy Shilling Atlas and World Gazetteer published by
George Newnes, and from the narrow world of school that little book
helped me to escape beyond the stars. After she left I felt like
driftwood washed on to an alien shore. I was told to play with the other
children but crept to my dormitory to unpack the books I had
brought: Coral Island, The Island of Pearls, and Mrs Molesworth's
Cuckoo Clock. I read the Cuckoo, with whose heroine I could
identify—a child called Griselda who makes friends with the cuckoo in

her great-aunt's clock—like our cuckoo at home. On one of their nocturnal adventures the cuckoo takes her to the Butterflies' Ball and commands the butterflies to embroider her nightgown with 'butterfly spangles which quivered with dewdrops'. I was far away at the Ball, quivering with butterflies and dewdrops, when a loud bell wrenched me from cloud-cuckoo-land to join the other children at supper, where Miriam, whose face glistened like melted lard, dumped before each of us a plate of half-cooked macaroni swimming in grease, and a cloam mug of lukewarm cocoa made with water. (All our meals were unappetising, the daily helping of cabbage always containing sodden boiled caterpillars—what a fate for my favourite creatures!) After thanking God for our good supper we went to bed, I to the misery of undressing before two strange girls, one of whom hoisted me on to her shoulders and jerked me up and down until I fell off. I was too supine to protest.

Miss Guyer taught the piano, and I recall her long, thin fingers with square-cut nails placing my clumsy hands in position for scales. The only lesson I liked was 'Composition', on a theme chosen by old Miss Downes. One day she told us to write about *A Journey I have made*, and I wrote *A Journey through my Brother's Head*, on which her justifiable comment was 'Not what was required.' The task I most disliked was Sewing, taken by another ancient woman, who doled out flannel squares on which we practised running, hemming, back-stitching and buttonholing. 'Be diligent! Be diligent!' she kept saying—a new word to me, so I added it to my home-made dictionary, and introduced into my essays as many other new words as possible. Miss Downes asked: 'Wherever did you hear *that*? You must use simpler words. Good writers never use words for the sake of using them. There's nothing clever about *that*.' I hated her sarcasm but knew she was right.

A general election was imminent and girls wore red, white and blue rosettes to denote that they were Conservatives, so I asked my mother to send me one. Back came a yellow and orange rosette with the explanation 'Father is a Liberal.' Believing that he knew best I wore my Liberal rosette, and when the Liberals won, Balfour being succeeded by Campbell-Bannerman, I felt triumphant. (Later, Father changed his allegiance to the Conservatives, and I to the Socialists.)

During my first term two things happened, one about religion, one about art. Our parents and Nan had never tried to influence Henry and me for or against religion: we were left to choose. Only Grannie wanted me to be a Christian and gave me holy books. I was nine years old when, kneeling beside my school bed to pray, like lightning came the question, is there anybody to pray *to*? For the first time I wondered; and the answer came 'No'. I felt quite sure; and it was

followed by relief, well-being, freedom and happiness, as if a lot of
difficult problems had been solved. Meanwhile a tiny birdlike woman
called Miss Finch arrived to teach us literature, and handed each pupil
a small dark-biue covered book on which was printed *A Midsummer
Night's Dream*, saying: 'This term we are going to do Shakespeare's
fairy play. We're going to do the *Dream*!' Fairies and dreams still
being my familiars, as the lesson proceeded there opened a new
Heaven and a new Earth—or rather a new heaven on Earth. For
homework she gave us 'How now, Spirit, whither wander you?' to
learn by heart. Thus began my lifelong love affair with Shakespeare.

The following holidays Henry and I caught measles, and while he
suffered severe earache, my temperature rose to 105 with delirium.
Nan nursed us night and day. When I was allowed to get up, Father
carried me downstairs and gave me a large blue china cat covered with
yellow hearts which I hugged joyfully. My first impulse was to show it
to Nan; I tried to run upstairs but my wasted legs gave way, I fell, and
the super-cat was smashed to smithereens—just one of numerous
awful moments of childhood.

Someone that materialises through the mist of those early years is an
aged harpist who trundled his instrument round the Torquay villas
and played on doorsteps, to be rewarded with a few pence. He came to
Eltham twice a year and set up his harp in the porch, hoping someone
would hear his music and open the front door, which if I were home I
did. Mother would give me sixpence for him, the signal to stop
playing. 'It disturbs Father's work.' I loved the harp music and
begged to be allowed to learn the instrument. How I wished the poor
man could be asked indoors. I wanted to say 'Come in!' but dared not.
Like all children I was constantly torn between loyalties. A pair of
Italian organ-grinders also came, to play in the drive. For them I was
given a penny, hoping I might stroke their tiny monkey in a red
flannel coat which took the penny in its paw, looking at me so
wistfully that I longed to hug it and have it for my own. On top of the
organ hopped two green love-birds in a cage. The handsome woman, a
red flowered scarf round her hair, smiled so kindly. Anyone from
'abroad' attracted me and I wanted them to feel at home in our
country.

A visitor to the back door was a knife-grinder to whom Nan took
her scissors and wood-carving chisels to be ground. And French
youths on bicycles came, dangling strings of shining onions. Sharland
disapproved and said his home-grown onions were better, and he
ballyragged Blanche for using them in her stews. 'You don't want that
there foreign rubbitch here!' Some years later the harpist and the
organ-grinders came no more. What we had missed I thought by not
asking them in.

The oddness of our household began to dawn on me. For instance:

while the maids ate in the kitchen, and the family ate in the dining-room, Nan was evidently not considered good enough to eat with the family but too good to eat with the maids, and had her meals alone in a small room between the fore and aft quarters of the house, where she typed, made and mended clothes, and, if she had a moment to spare, practised her wood-carving. In all the years she lived with us she never had one meal with the family; and Mother never called her by her Christian name. When I told her how sorry I felt she said: 'I don't mind, dearie—so long as I've got you.' But there was another reason which I did not learn until I grew up.

To revert to 1905, for me the chief event of that year was the arrival at Haldon Pier of a vast black hulk, an 'Exhibition Convict Ship', which was open to the public. Half scared, Nan and I descended to the holds, converted into dungeons divided into dim-lit cells containing gruesome wax manacled figures, so lifelike that I was terrified. It was a terror ship. The convicts, pinioned to walls, chained to iron balls, their faces contorted with pain, seemed to be half alive and to writhe. One, his back striped with blood, kneeled while a gaoler stood over him with lifted chain; another hung elongated and dying from a hook. These ghastly effigies haunted me for years.

What was the history of that frightful ship? Sixty years afterwards I found out. Sailing with my husband from Buenos Aires via South Africa and Singapore to Hong Kong and Japan, during a storm in the Indian Ocean I read a book from the cargo-liner's library in which there was an account of it. Built in Burma in 1790, she was named *Success* and roamed the seas for 156 years. At one time she belonged to the 'felon fleet' and carried convicts to Botany Bay; and when a tortured desperado murdered her captain, her sister ships were destroyed but she was spared, and twice was fitted with horrible waxworks, among them Captain Starlight the bushranger, Kate Kelly, and other rogues, while an aged man called Harry Power who had been imprisoned in her was hired as guide. But surrounded by his dead comrades preserved in wax he went mad, jumped into the sea and drowned. A crew brought the *Success* with her freight of dreadful dolls to London river for exhibition in Britain, and it was on this trip that Nan and I went on board. On the day the *Titanic* sailed she set out for Boston, Massachusetts, but like the *Titanic*, struck an iceberg and sank off Carrolton. Salvaged, show-people once more packed her with dummies of notorious rascals for display at the Chicago World Fair. In 1940 she was going to be broken up for her teak when, in Lake Eyrie Cove, she caught fire and the bizarre career of that old argosy culminated in cleansing flames.

In school one morning I was reading aloud when the print wavered and disappeared into a dazzling bow of light. I thought I was going blind. The teacher took me to an empty room and someone brought

me a glass of milk and left me. The dazzles got worse until vision was
obscured and I thought of all the things and people I should never see
again. But after half an hour bits of objects reappeared and sight
gradually returned to normal, followed by an excruciating headache. I
did not mention the experience at home, though similar attacks
occurred at intervals. Not until twenty-four years later, when the
headaches grew so ferocious that a friend consulted a doctor on my
behalf, did I learn that the trouble was migraine.

About this time Mother and Father were starting for Italy when a
telegram arrived to say that Henry was very ill and they went to him at
school. He had pericarditis and nearly died. When he could travel
they brought him home—a pale spectre I hardly recognised and
regarded with awe. Had he not stood on the portals of Death? The
thought was shattering.

Life changed. I was beginning to have a 'mind of my own', as
someone said, not as a compliment. But I did not want to grow up. I
clung to my beloved night music, my garden fairyland and my
imaginary family, to whom I had added a sister for my three brothers.

7

In the outer world suffragettes were becoming more exigent, shouting
'Votes for Women!' and growing violent. Father called himself a
feminist, but no one in our family except Grannie Adelaide, shocked
by these 'dreadful creatures', took much interest in the Cause. Even at
the height of hostilities, when a suffragette threw herself under a
racing horse and was killed, I was too bemused by poetry and
evanescent loves to care about female enfranchisement. Our beautiful
garden was my land of all delight, though instead of riding the lilac
horse I built a house in a tree and wrote a 'novel' there, copying my
father, as many another child has done before and since. But it soon
palled and the spirit of adventure drove me farther afield. So safe was
the neighbourhood that I was permitted to rove alone on Chapel Hill
where, accompanied by Nan's dog, my 'family' and a troop of elves as
magical as any in the Athenian Wood, I climbed precipices until I
knew every crevice and cornice, sporting with my mortal and
immortal friends. If there were human lovers on the benches I noted
them with pleasure and flitted by. When the weather was too stormy
for rambling I foraged among Father's books, my favourite game
being to invite Shakespeare and others, sometimes Beethoven, to a
party in my room.

During my tenth year Nan and I went to two lantern lectures at the
Bath Saloons which impressed me prodigiously, one about the
Krakatoa volcanic explosion in the Sunda Straight, whose sound was
heard for three thousand miles while dust rose to the stratosphere,
creating marvellous sunsets for years; the other, given by the

astronomer Robert Ball whose *The Splendour of the Heavens* was in my father's library, was so exciting that it opened not one new world but myriads, and for months I could read and think about nothing else. I found a second book, Camille Flammarion's *Astronomy*, its cover spattered with stars, and read it until I knew much of the letterpress and all the illustrations by heart. Uncle Mac had given Father a small brass three-inch refracting telescope which was set up in the garden and focused on the Moon. With what ecstasy I stared into its eyepiece, and how I coveted this new toy for myself, to turn it on to special objects mentioned by Flammarion. I asked Father to place it on a table in the tower room, where Henry now slept, so that he could watch the Brixham trawlers. A landing window at the top of the staircase opened on to a well in the roof where we were forbidden to go: it was an acrobatic feat to slither into it down the gutters. But late on starlit nights during the winter holidays, when the grown-ups were sleeping, by standing on a chair Henry and I managed to haul the telescope on to the sill and slide it into the well, where I set it on a tripod and procured a magnificent view of the whole sky. One night I turned it on to a large golden star and to my enormous wonder there was Saturn revolving in his rings. I cannot describe my joy. Henry did not share my mania for the stars and preferred ships in the bay.

Long after Mother and Father had discarded their old cantilever bicycles, we were given modern safety machines and rode about with Nan until she dropped out and Henry and I went different ways, he to the railway yards, I to the sea. I grew more and more reckless, flying down hills with hands off the handlebars, pushing through woods, tearing my clothes, trespassing, until I crashed on to a gritty road and scraped the flesh off the top of one knee. Afraid to mention it lest my adventures be stopped, I covered the wound with a rag and went on riding, until the sore festered and I was obliged to confess. My sprees were over.

We were due to spend a few weeks in Bude, for Father's work, and a Bath chair was hired in which, with indescribable mortification, I was drawn about by a boy leading a donkey. The thickly bandaged wound got worse, throbbed and bubbled with pus, so that I had to remain at the lodging while the others went to the sea. One morning I was alone, hot sun shining through the open window, when its beams touched me and I thought 'The Sun will heal me!' and stripped off the dressings, exposing my knee to its rays. In less than an hour the raw places glazed over and the angriness began to subside. From that moment it rapidly healed, and before we left I could walk again.

Meanwhile Father sat on the beach with the painter J. Ley Pethybridge, and Annabel Ley, his pretty hazel-eyed wife, who lived at Stratton. Mr Pethybridge had illustrated some of his early books, and also Charles Byles' biography of his father-in-law, Robert

Stephen Hawker of Morwenstow, Hawker's *Cornish Ballads and Other Poems* and *Footprints of Former Men in Cornwall*. Little did I foresee what an important part Hawker and Morwenstow were going to play in my life, and death.

One stormy afternoon we heard that a French trawler had run aground on a reef below Maer Point and hurried to the cliffs. The crew were being rescued by the Rocket Apparatus, and as each man reached safety the crowd cheered. I spied a young woman's profile, caught for a few seconds before she was hidden by onlookers, yet so blindingly beautiful that for the rest of my life at intervals it returned to memory's eye.

Again Henry and I were sent to new schools, he to Repton, I to Grassendale at Southbourne. To condemn Henry to a public school was a terrible mistake. He possessed to an exaggerated degree our mother's diffidence, our father's artistic susceptibility, and his own vulnerability which led to feelings of guilt and failure, amounting to self-dislike, and to fear of his father, sometimes causing hatred, alternating with a strong desire to please him, on whom he felt utter dependence but by whom he was often unfavourably criticised. As before, Henry became a target for school bullies; yet our parents were still determined that he should conform to the narrow standards of Edwardian middle-class society, education and morality, against which I had begun forcibly to rebel.

The school to which I was committed was in some ways worse than his—a school 'for the daughters of gentlemen'—'ladies and gentlemen' being a figment I refused to recognise; all 'classes' were one to me. Meanwhile my father had grown more and more affectionate and continued to draw me ever closer to himself. But love him as I did, deeply, I remained secretly averse from physical contact, though not for the world would I resist him. 'You must never marry. You must give yourself to your art.' Childhood was over.

Adolescence

1

My mother accompanied me to Grassendale, a stone-built edifice beside the sea in pine-clad countryside near Southbourne. We were shown into the headmistress's study to meet Miss Amy Lumby, stout and middle-aged, and when Mother left I was handed over to the Matron, a Fräulein of formidable appearance, who took me to the dormitory I was to share with two older girls. During the first term I was too shy to talk, and my room-mates asked me if I was dumb, which made me dumber. Most of the pupils belonged to wealthier and more aristocratic families than ours. After evening preparation we changed into evening dresses of which the others brought at least four and never wore the same one twice running. I possessed one far from new white silk, and one green shantung which I hated, leaving me nightly in the same frock, that had to serve also for the dancing class, for which the others had special creations. My shame was dire. Being the youngest in the school I was placed in the lowest class, where to compensate for my inadequate wardrobe I determined to shine at lessons, which were extremely elementary. Once a week we were instructed in deportment by an elderly woman in a floppy hat who attacked the piano with fingers stiff with rings, while we learned to curtsey, because 'Some day you will be presented at Court.' More congenial were singing lessons presided over by an old white-haired gentleman called Mr Moberly, who taught us Jupiter's beautiful Serenade from Handel's secular oratorio. *Semele*: 'Where'er you walk . . . Trees crowd into a shade'; and I visualised joyful aspens shaking their leaves and crowding round the lovely heroine. Every term each form read a Shakespeare play, my first part being Bardolph in *Henry V*, as it had been Father's first when he studied for the stage.

Miss Lumby guided us through Kings and Chronicles, Amos and Hosea, and the Gospel according to St Mark. Since earliest days I had explored the whole Bible and knew every fascinating character, as splendid a collection of individuals and stories as those in Greek Mythology and the Indian Epics; yet I was unhappy at Grassendale. I should have preferred a co-educational school; but my parents having considered the idea vetoed it, Mother because she feared I should become a tomboy, and Father perhaps foresaw danger for the child he had decided was never to marry. Games were compulsory: in winter hockey, in summer tennis and sports. I had no competitive instinct, in work or in play, and never acquired one; but though I had only average ability in lessons, I could run very fast and jump very high, thanks to Sergeant-Major Tomney at the Torquay Gymnasium. Knocking a ball about, however, was deadly and 'playing to win' a bore.

In the summer of 1910 a dramatic event occurred on our hockey field which ended in tragedy. It was let for a Flying Display at which the young pioneers would be exhibiting their skills. On the final afternoon the girls assembled at the ground, where an orchestra was playing Offenbach's 'Barcarolle'. We watched a small plane rise high above the crowd when suddenly its tail snapped off, it spun to earth, and crashed not far from where we stood. For a few moments the band went on playing the 'Barcarolle', and every time I have heard it since I see that little aircraft spiralling down and smashing before our eyes. The aviator who died was Charles Rolls.

To games I preferred Sunday afternoon walks, when the German teacher, Fräulein Hartmann, took up the rear of our 'crocodile'. An ageing, ungainly woman, most of the girls mimicked her and disliked her, partly because she was a foreigner to them. Nobody wanted to walk with her, but I, growing ever more interested in people from other lands, sometimes did. She took great pains to help me, especially with German composition, and on one of our walks said: 'Adelheid, you are going to be a writer. You may not succeed. Few do. But when you have left school remember what I say: *You will be a writer.*' I was astonished, that she could take it so seriously. She left before the outbreak of war and I know not what became of her.

The following year a young woman called Ethel Herdman, down from St Hilda's College at Oxford with an honours degree in languages, came to teach French Literature, and she, too, was giggled at and nicknamed Amos—'who was among the herdmen of Tekoa'. An art lover, especially of poetry, she was gentle and kind, and she also urged me when I grew up to 'write'. Yet though I appreciated her encouragement, embarrassed by her interest I avoided her, little guessing that forty years afterwards this unassuming woman, who rarely was seen without a little pile of poetry books under her arm, was going to play an extraordinary part in my life; and had she not come to Grassendale, or I had not gone there, I should have missed life's most wonderful and challenging years. But at fourteen how could I foresee that this unworldly young teacher would be the means of my experiencing both my deepest sorrow and my loftiest joy.

I did not need Miss Herdman or Miss Hartmann to drive me on to write. Every evening I rushed through my preparation and spent the time gained pouring out verses, which I kept in an exercise book hidden in my washstand drawer, where I thought it was safe from inquisitive eyes. But one night I returned from a bath to hear shouts of laughter and see the Head of my dormitory waving my rhymes aloft and bawling them out loud. I dashed at her and struggled until I got my mangled masterpieces out of her grip: no mother fought more fiercely for her kidnapped child. The commotion brought Matron, who mopped up my persecutor whose face I had scratched, reported me to Miss Lumby and I was punished. The outcome was comical. Deciding that I was using my head too much and my hands too little, and that my literary zeal threatened to take over at the expense of more suitable activities, Miss Lumby decreed that I must learn church embroidery, and I was taught to manipulate needlefuls of gold thread and coloured flosses that stuck to my rough, inky fingers, with which I made a hopeless botch; for I possessed no gift, manual or spiritual, for church embroidery.

Most of Grassendale's 'young ladies' were British, but two of my friends came from 'abroad': Rezzia from Italy, who subsequently married the Count of Ancona, and Odette, from Switzerland, the prettiest girl in the school, who married Frank Martin, the composer, and had one son. Though special friendships were frowned on, she and I wandered in the shrubbery arm in arm, reciting our verses, or strummed on an old piano we found in an attic. She gave me Heine's Poems. Sadly, she died young.

Then from France came Marie, a plain, warm-hearted girl with a sweet expression even as her nature was sweet. She lacked the power to attract friends, and gazed at me wistfully as a last hope. I recall her more clearly than all the fair, the witty, the clever, and otherwise outstanding characters, because she was the cause of an episode I feel ashamed, except in the cause of truth, to recount, and because some perfidious acts have a sufficiently cathartic effect to render one a changed person afterwards—to reveal one to oneself with all one's flaws.

A fancy dress dance was held at the end of the Christmas term, with a rule that we must improvise our costumes without spending money. I was a dolt at this kind of thing, but Marie said: 'If you'll let me I'll dress you and make you win the first prize.' Out of a sheet, pillowcase and other oddments she turned me so skilfully into *Alice in Wonderland's* White Rabbit that I longed immediately to run into the assembly hall and flaunt myself. But I had promised to assist her, with my red dressing-gown and some padding, to dress up as the Red Queen, so I must not yet go to the ball. Sensing my impatience she told me to run down and show myself and then come back to help her and we would return together. Vowing to be back in a jiffy I dashed to the ballroom and everyone complimented me, I was so carried away that I forgot poor Marie and danced every dance until the 'Sir Roger

de Coverley', without giving her a thought. To cap my brief glory I
won the first prize. Only then did I remember her. Where was she? I
could not find her in the crowd. Appalled, I rushed to her dormitory,
to discover her sitting on the bed reading the Douai Bible. 'Did they
like you?' she asked—not a reproachful word. I asked why she had not
fetched me and she answered 'I've been happier reading.' My success
delighted her, but for me it fizzled out like a live coal doused with
snow. And at the bottom of my wretched, rotten heart I felt a little
cross, if not envious, because compared to me she was so good, so
unselfish, so worthy of love, and yet not loved.

The happiest times at Grassendale were outings to Wimborne
Minster, and the New Forest whither in spring we drove in wagon-
ettes to see wild daffodils, when, like us, all the leaves were young.
Trotting back in the evening, mistresses and girls sang the latest song
hits, especially the Gaiety's 'Yip I addy I ay i ay . . . I don't care what
becomes of me when I hear that sweet melody!' Better still were concerts at Bournemouth Winter Gardens with Dan Godfrey conducting
the Municipal Orchestra and as soloists, Pachmann, Paderewski,
Backhaus—a Beethoven specialist—Kreisler, Jan Kubelik, Mischa
Elman and Eugène Ysaye. I fell in love with them all.

A soberer pleasure was inspired by University Extension lectures
illustrated by lantern slides, and recall one about medieval and Gothic
cathedrals, monasteries and abbeys which instilled in me a desire to
give up the world and live in a plain little cell, rising at midnight and at
dawn to kneel in the abbey church. The names of the Canonical Hours
and Offices fascinated me: Lauds, Prime, Terce, Angelus, and Sext,
Nones, Vespers, Compline, Matins—enthralling words. Pictures of
Chartres and Rheims, Canterbury and Cluny, appealed to some
obscure longing for peace, love, worship and serenity. Yet I had no
religious faith, only faith in mankind. Nevertheless I felt profoundly
drawn to that quiet life, which, to be good and valid, needed not
necessarily belief in the supernatural. The pictures of monks and nuns
in the cloisters, reading their breviaries, allured me, along with the
Brotherhoods and Sisterhoods who had created those glorious illuminated manuscripts and other striking images flashed upon a magic
lantern screen at Grassendale. I loved Héloïse and Abélard—Abélard
who wrote 'To live after thee is but to die'. I loved silence, darkness,
solitude.

To my passion for Shakespeare was now added a more intimate
relationship, with the poet as well as his poetry: Shelley. How madly I
adored him, and admired his love of freedom, his hatred of tyrants,
his belief in a united world. Daily I delved into his life and works,
until a classmate called Gwynneth declared that my hero was a cruel
man who had deserted his children and driven his wife to drown
herself. 'He's a murderer!' I was so furious that I fought her and

knocked her to the ground—a victory, however, without triumph; for was not my Beloved a pacifist? I asked her to forgive me, but she turned away and shunned me. A few days later, after our monthly shopping expedition to Beale's in Bournemouth, I found on my bed a volume of Shelley's Poems bound in green rexine stuffed with cotton wool, on its spine in gold letters *The Poetical Works of Shelley*, inscribed by Gwynneth: 'To My Dear Friend Adelaide Eden Phillpotts from G.E.T.'. I have it still, the rexine perished, the cotton wool bulging out all over, dozens of pages heavily marked and stained with pressed flowers.

For many years Shelley was my mentor who, in magical words and cadences, ethereal scenes, noble ideas, expressed my own ideals and searchings after Truth. Many a night I sat on a landing window-sill at school overlooking Hengistbury Head and the Needles, watching the moonlight gleaming on the sea, murmuring the last verse of *Prometheus Unbound*: 'To suffer Woes which Hope thinks infinite . . . This, like thy Glory, Titan, is to be / Good, great and joyous, beautiful and free; / This is alone Life, Joy, Empire and Victory'. And I would imagine a little skiff floating to the window, into which I stepped, to be greeted by the poet, and we sailed among the stars. His romantic portrait by Amelia Curran stood in an ebony frame beside my bed.

There was a penal system of Bad Marks at Grassendale known as Bees, read out before the assembled school on Saturdays after prayers. With nothing but regret I confess that by the end of term my Bees would have filled a hive. A few years after I left, Miss Lumby, fundamentally admirable, died of cancer and the school soon succumbed. Jesuits bought it and turned it into a seminary. Many years later I revisited it with a dearer companion even than Shelley.

2

School and home were two different worlds. Though Henry and I had grown a little apart and seldom referred to our schools, we were closer to each other than to others. I knew that the only ray in his darkness at Repton was his painting, which Father told me had been recognised as extremely unusual by the art master, Mr Clarke, who wrote so enthusiastically that he was invited to stay. One day I heard him say that Henry displayed genius. But when I told my brother he poohpoohed it and said that Mr Clarke was only saying it to please our parents, and that he would not let Henry paint as he wanted to, and was academic and conventional.

Appreciation from higher sources should have encouraged him, but I doubt if it did. Father's friends, the artists Frank Brangwyn and George Clausen, who also came to stay, prophesied for him a glorious future; but he scoffed and did not believe they meant it. His favourite subjects were cities with docks and tall factory chimneys under smoky

skies, full of movement, colour and atmosphere. He was as solitary as
ever. One or two Repton boys tried to make friends and wrote to him,
but he never answered their letters: he did not want to be diverted
from his art and his visionary world. No adult had yet called forth that
sociable, generous, kindly and appreciative side, that sympathy,
which was not to appear for many years; but, from the first, I sensed
and cherished it. Even in childhood he revealed it to me. In all our
lives we never quarrelled or exchanged one unfriendly word. If he was
unfairly crossed, as he often was, if those in authority unreasonably
scolded and criticised him, unjustly as he thought, he would either
rage or sink into severe depression, with the certitude that he was 'no
good'. And I would always take his side and suffer too, hoping to help
but not being able to.

Unlike Henry I was full of restless spirits which I worked off roller-
skating on the pier, rising before dawn and dragging poor Nan to see
the sunrise from Petitor cliffs at Babbacombe, and cycling further and
further afield. One afternoon I was walking my bicycle across a
narrow railway bridge at Newton Abbot when a dray drawn by two
huge cart-horses loomed in front at the moment a whistling express
train tore underneath, steam rising in a thick cloud. The frightened
animals reared and for a second I saw their steel shoes just above my
head. I ducked and they missed me by half an inch.

I set myself arduous tasks and drove myself to the uttermost, as I
had read Arctic explorers did, an indulgence which provoked a sort of
selfish gratification. And I yearned for I knew not what. The sound of
church bells affected me to tears. Many years later I came upon a
passage, in Rousseau's *Confessions*, about his youth that expresses
these typical emotions better than I can: 'The ringing of Church bells,
which ever effects me, the singing of birds, the fineness of the day, the
beauty of the landscape . . . altogether struck me with an impression
so lively, tender, melancholy, and powerful, that I saw myself in
ecstasy transported into that happy time and abode, where my heart,
possessing all the felicity it could desire, might taste it with rapture
inexpressible; nor did a trace of sensuality mingle with these dreams. I
never recollect to have enjoyed the future with such force of illusion as
at that time.'

I kept a journal into which I poured my sentimental longings for
sublime achievement and romantic love, and kept it in a chest of
drawers. Meanwhile I resolved to do what I could to abolish capital
punishment, and war. I suffered from what Goethe called 'The
beautiful dream of mankind that things will be better some day'. I
longed for equality, justice, brotherly love, and questioned whether
there should be servants, even daring to raise the matter with my
mother, who said: 'If we didn't employ them somebody else would
and might treat them badly, or they might get no more work and

starve.' Why, then, I asked, did they not live with us as equals and friends? Irritated, Mother confided in Father, who could be devastatingly sarcastic. 'Don't be such a prig!' In short, this was a time of awakening, and of prejudice against prejudice. In a more characteristic moment Father told me now much he disliked his own 'smug middle class', and preferred to write about the folk of Dartmoor.

He dedicated to me a fairy story called *The Flint Heart* about the Pixies' Holt near Dartmeet, a woodland glen where I had often played. How proud I was, and still am, of that charming and amusing book. With it he gave me a flint arrowhead set in gold as a brooch, which I wore constantly, until it was stolen in Spain.

I now fell passionately in love with a member of the local Municipal Orchestra at the Torquay Pavilion, to whose afternoon concerts my music-loving mother took me during the holidays. The conductor, Basil Hindenberg, then twenty-seven, had studied under Joachim and played with the New Queen's Hall Orchestra. He visited us at Eltham, and when the war broke out changed his name to Basil Cameron. It was not he, however, to whom I gave my heart, with more abandonment than to anyone else before—it was to the co-leader of the violins, a dark young man called Roderick. Sometimes during concerts we exchanged a smile. But the only time we almost met was in a gale of wind and rain outside the concert hall when suddenly my hat blew off and landed in his arms. He returned it with a laugh, but not a word was uttered. In my daydreams it was not my hat which flew into his arms! My old wish to learn the violin recurred, and I would take Uncle Cecil's old instrument out of its case and stroke it with the bow, whose horsehair had long since perished.

Those concerts drew Mother and me closer together. But there were times when I, careless of appearance, shutting myself away to write blank verse tragedies, puzzled her, and I knew I was not what she wanted me to be. We were returning from a visit to Grannie Adelaide, walking home into a beautiful sunset, to which I kept calling her attention, when she sighed and said: 'Oh, Adelaide, you make me feel so worldly.' I was shocked, startled, ashamed, and I could not forget it. To please her I tried to become more grown-up, considerate, more womanly, and nicer to her friends, but I failed.

Still fond of exploring, I discovered Aladdin's Caves and Ivory Towers of old second-hand bookshops, stacked to the ceiling with volumes, and tattered out-of-date newspapers and magazines, novelettes, and portfolios of ancient prints and steel engravings of balloons and castles and sailing-ships—caverns and eyries of treasure where one might find the very book one was hunting. In such lairs for a few pence I picked up Bohn classics, complete editions of Schiller and Goethe, and sometimes leafed through dead romances, reading the love scenes and skipping the rest. Rummaging in Father's study I consumed Plutarch's *Lives*, Balzac and George Eliot; Thomas Hardy, who was Father's friend; Dickens and Nietzsche. But nothing excelled *Don Quixote*, illustrated by Gustav Doré: that was my favourite.

Father belonged to the Rationalist Press Association, and among fellow free thinkers who came to stay were Edward Clodd, and Joseph McCabe who had spent ten years in a monastery. The RPA publications switched me to science, which I gobbled, bent on solving the mysteries of the universe. I yearned for a vision of the Whole, an explanation, not in mystical sense, like Plato and Plotinus and other God-oriented thinkers, but a scientific exposition of the All, and decided that instead of being created, the universe, or universes, if more than one, had always existed—Eternity and Infinity—and would never end. That seemed the most satisfying hypothesis. I read Newton, Einstein, Faraday and others, alive and dead, searching for answers to the bewildering questions which have never been and may never be answered. Grannie Adelaide said: 'Surely you don't want to be a *bluestocking*?' She had a widowed friend with a red-headed son whom she kept thrusting at me, as she used to thrust unwanted dolls, trying to entice me from dry books and my own scribbling to his youthful flesh and blood; for she was as anxious for me to marry young as Father was that I never should.

Meanwhile Uncle Mac's health deteriorated and he and Grannie could no longer look after a paying invalid. Their finances were precarious. Mount Ridley was sold, and Father bought them a smaller house at Paignton, where Henry and I spent the annual Fairs; but our uncle was sadly changed, and no longer patronised the Freaks, though he took me to my first film.

When I was fourteen we went with mother to Paris. After a night at the Charing Cross Hotel, when Henry, intoxicated with delight, sat up watching traffic on the river, we boarded a Channel steamer at Dover, and his happiness increased. I, too, had a memorable experience. Standing alone in the stern I was watching smoky wraiths from the funnel streaming over the wake, seagulls swaying above, when from the waves came the song 'All men are brothers! Every land is home!' And I was filled with joy. 'All Men are Brothers!' I sang to myself. The sea-borne voices proffered the sublime faith I had been yearning for. Henceforth there would be no more barriers, no frontiers between races. Every journey would be from home to home. There would be only world-people. And again I felt the deep relief I knew when I ceased to believe in the supernatural. Many problems, including that of evil, were solved. The universe became more sublime. Thenceforth I lived in two worlds, equally real: an ideal world—all its peoples united—and the actual world, with its enmities and conflicts, hatreds and fears, its irrational antagonism, its wars. I strove to love everybody. And joined to this affinity with human nature I felt a strong attachment to non-human nature, even at its most destructive and violent. Hiding my revelation I rejoined Mother, and Henry, who was scanning the sea for ships. That was his vision of reality and thrilled him as much as my wave-singers transported me.

On the first Paris morning, Mother, noting the smartness of French girls, bought me a raffia-embroidered hat, and Henry said: 'That's certainly an improvement!' We had grown more self-conscious, and even I wanted to leave my long hair loose instead of tightly plaited and tied with a black ribbon. But so well had I been drilled against vanity that I dared not display one curl. (The only compliment I had received from Mother was: 'If your nose was smaller you would be quite nice-looking, but you've got the Phillpotts' nose'—and I saw myself with a beak like a toucan! She meant to be kind.) Now in Paris I perceived that several men stared admiringly at her, and heard one whisper as he passed *'La Belle!'* But when I drew her attention to it she frowned and said 'Nonsense! It's you they're looking at'—which was sweet of her, though she must have known I was not deceived. Compared to her I was plain as mud. She took us to the Maison Rumplemayer, where Proust drank tea, and we gorged on rum babas; and to the *Folies Bergères* to see Mistinguett and Maurice Chevalier, where I was surprised to observe fat elderly gentlemen stroking the thighs of cocottes, and noticed Henry's eyes riveted on the naked bosoms of the *Folies*.

During winter holidays I sat in my bedroom composing plays with grandiose plots, until Mother, resigned to these silly activities, bought me a paraffin heater, which melted my heart. Martin Harvey and his Shakespeare Company had been appearing at the Theatre Royal in *The Taming of the Shrew*, *Richard III* and *Hamlet*, and with his actress wife called at Eltham with free tickets for anyone who wanted to go. Nan and I went, and immediately I composed a piece of blank verse nonsense which I hoped Martin Harvey would produce. Of course he did not! Soon afterwards came Frank Benson with his Richard and his Hamlet. Both these actors thrilled thousands of youngsters like me. Much later I saw John Barrymore as yet another Dane. I thought they were all wonderful.

Mother took us to Ealing, where Grannie Anne, Great-Aunt Margaret and Aunt Frances were ageing; but Mother never seemed to change. Arthur Bourchier, another actor friend, had sent us tickets for Beerbohm Tree's ornate production of *A Midsummer Night's Dream* in which he played Bottom; live rabbits hopped among real plants, and there were real pools into which extremely unreal fairies splashed. Mother preferred *The Arcadians* and the Russian Ballet, with Pavlova dancing the Dying Swan, and partnered by Mordkin in *Le Spectre de la*

Rose. To please Henry she got permission to see the Ivory Warehouse at the docks, and I recall the creamy blue light shed by huge stacks of elephants' tusks, all that remained of countless murdered beasts, which added to my Causes the Abolition of Big Game Hunting.

Against Mother's advice Father sent Uncle Mac and Grannie for a change to the South of France, and they had not been gone long when Grannie telegraphed: 'Mac very ill. Come at once.' Mother rushed to Cimiez, but when she arrived Uncle was dead. The local doctor insisted on showing her the poor man's body punctured with injection jabs. Grannie was shattered, but Mother settled everything and got them and the coffin home.

Our Uncle was buried in Torquay Cemetery, where an adjacent plot was reserved for our grandmother. Mother sent Henry and me black ties to wear at school, and mine bestowed a strange sense of importance: I was a mourner. Death *was* important. I thought about it more and more. Looking back, I think Uncle Mac resembled Eugène Marais, the poet and naturalist who was also a morphia addict, for thirty years, and wrote: 'It is to those temperaments in which pain is a predominant element of consciousness, and in which some quality of suffering is inseparable from thought, that alcohol and joy-creating poisons constitute the greatest threat'. Grannie never got over this loss of the child of her sorrow, the posthumous son, now again sorrow's child and child of her woe. From that time she stooped more and her black clothes seemed more densely black.

Whatever happened, nothing interfered with Father's work. In 1910 was published *Wild Fruit*, the second of over twenty volumes of poetry, and what he thought was the best of his Dartmoor cycle, *The Thief of Virtue*. In 1912 appeared *The Iscariot*, an epic about Judas, which he judged was his finest poetical work. Meanwhile two tragedies adapted from Dartmoor novels had been produced at the Liverpool and Miss Horniman's Manchester Repertory Theatres: *The Shadow* and *The Mother*. At Manchester he met young Sybil Thorn-dike and her husband Lewis Casson, who became his and later my friends. But none of his plays had succeeded in London. In 1911 a play founded on his novel *The Secret Woman* was accepted for production there, if it passed the Censor; but because of two sentences it was banned. If Father would delete or change them the production could be licensed, but he refused to do so. (Later he told me that he regretted refusing.) This affair caused such a stir that, in February, 1912, literary colleagues, including Joseph Conrad, H. G. Wells, Henry James and Bernard Shaw, signed a group letter to *The Times*, and as only commercial productions were subject to censorship, subscribed enough money to mount a private one, managed by Granville-Barker. Arnold Bennett was abroad and his signature arrived too late to appear with the rest.

Touched and grateful, Father could not refuse to attend rehearsals, and he and Mother stayed in Victoria at the Grosvenor Hotel. Unfortunately, the production was bad, with an ill-chosen cast none of whom had the slightest idea how a Dartmoor farmer and his family looked, dressed or spoke. Sickened by the whole affair and loathing London, Father bought Mother a splendid mauve picture-hat trimmed with ostrich plumes and begged her to let him go home. How could she refuse? He went! She stopped for the first performance, which was not well received. Of it Father wrote to his brother-in-law: 'The play has been highly approved by artists and creators, but little liked by reviewers. I am doing a better one.'

Our school careers were ending: Henry left first. Father told him that he was to go to the Slade School of Art, his wayward talent to be disciplined. 'You must learn to draw. You must learn draughtsmanship. You'll find Henry Tonks a good Master.' Poor Henry, sent off once more whether he would or no to another academic institution—his reluctance was only slightly mitigated when he heard that he was to live with Aunt Frances and Grannie Anne. My fate was to be equally unacceptable.

There had been talk of my going to Oxford and I went there to take a preliminary examination; but Miss Lumby, who was glad to get rid of me, suggested that I might benefit by being 'finished' in Paris, where she knew a Sorbonne Professor called Rémy Perrier with wife and three daughters, who had taken some of her ex-pupils and turned them into charming young ladies now gracing adult society with becoming manners and perfect French accents. By coincidence, she wrote to my parents, Madame Perrier had just written to enquire whether she knew of another delightful young lady who would care to live with them for six months. Might not dear Adelaide be the very one? Reasonable terms were mentioned, and perhaps I would be willing to help with the younger daughters of eleven and nine? My parents decided that this was the very thing, and without asking me agreed to the project. Mother felt convinced that after six months in Paris all that nonsense about Causes and that bookish scribbling would cease.

Well do I remember the last train journey from Bournemouth to Torquay after my last school term. I had been warned never to travel in an empty carriage, even for Ladies Only, or one in which there was not another woman, *never* with only a man! That day I chose an empty compartment where I could be alone with my make-believe 'family', who were still my companions. The day was full of sunshine, the summer landscape gilded with ripening corn, the sky flecked with cirrus clouds, and the train's shadow ran over the fields, passing through horses, sheep and cows. Along the horizon marched trees, and elms and oaks stood in green meadows to give shade. This

recurring scene, between Hampshire and Devonshire, still reappears
to my mind's eye as if it had never changed—those sunny cloudlets,
those distant trees seeming to keep pace with the train, the checker
pattern of grass and grain, and I sense a faint, faint echo of my feelings
on that liberation day. Neither past nor future mattered: the present
was so ravishing. I sang to the empty carriage and was steeped in such
an upsurge of joy, such a rapture of hope, as I had not known since the
drive to Kingskerswell with Grannie Adelaide over ten years earlier.
Everything was beautiful, the view, the hot sunshine streaming
through the open window, the freedom. To be alive was beyond
words wonderful, and I pitied anyone not young and joyful like me.
But, as always, by exultation was not to last.

When I reached home Henry was in trouble again. Father had
heard from Professor Tonks, enquiring why his son had given up
attending the Slade: he had been to only two or three classes before
vanishing. Aunt Frances had reported that he was well, going out
every day, she presumed to the School of Art. But when Henry,
ordered home, was confronted, he confessed that having found the
Slade insupportable, with no opportunities to paint what he wanted to
paint, in the way he wanted, he spent his time at Limehouse and the
Docks, where he could sketch and study the spritsail Thames barges
he loved, of which there were hundreds working the river, trans-
porting cement and sand, coal, grain and hay, so rigged that one man
and a boy could handle them. He showed Father his sketches, but
Father was too angry to look. Mother wept, and in an agony of distress
I took Henry's part and defended him. To revenge himself, he
dragged from its frame a boyhood painting our parents particularly
valued, tore it into four pieces and stuffed them in the dustbin. I
wondered how he could ruin and destroy his own work, which I could
not have done to my much lesser achievements. Luckily, the torn
pieces were found before the dust-cart arrived, and Father had the
picture so skilfully restored that no one would guess what it had
suffered. It hangs before me now.

Henry was overwhelmed by a sense of failure and self-dislike, in
such a miserable state, that I feared he would destroy *himself*. Every
evening he would go out to avoid sitting with the family and wander
the streets or hang about the harbour until after midnight. I felt so sick
with worry that I could not sleep until I heard him go upstairs to bed.
However, he had a faithful ally in Grannie Adelaide. After Uncle
Mac's death Father bought her a small semi-detached house at
Babbacombe, near a church she liked, and there Henry often joined
her. Was she not, like him, lost, grieving, needing comfort and
sympathy, and able to give them to her grandson, as he gave his to
her? He had always sympathised with the sick and sad, and now he
alone could console her and she alone consoled him. Art meant

nothing to her, but she loved him for himself, and knew what course would have been best for him, though the others did not agree.

I, too, visited our grandmother, sometimes for a weekend, accompanying her to Sunday Evensong. I liked to watch an acolyte with a taper ignite the altar candles which shed a soft illumination and were reflected in brass candlesticks, creating shadows in the roof. I liked the singing of the Magnificat and the Nunc Dimittis, and was impressed by the elderly vicar, who was kind to our grannie and assured her that she would be reunited with her husband and sons through Eternity, and in spite of his atheism, Father would be there too. During Evensong I suddenly conceived an idea for a long epic poem about the brotherhood of man, and directly I got home began it, into it pouring all my heart and soul, and called it Illyrion.

Mother and I still went to Pavilion concerts, and I still adored Roderick, and confided my devotion to the journal I concealed in my chest of drawers. One day I came in early from a ramble to find Mother standing in my room reading it. Which was the more shocked? For a moment we were transfixed. Not a word was said. She closed the book, handed it to me with a Mona Lisa smile and left the room. Neither of us ever mentioned the encounter. It was commendable that she took an interest; but at the time this did not occur to me.

With troubled spirits Henry and I parted, he back to London, I to prepare for Paris. Perceiving how down-daunted I was, Mother and Father promised that when I returned I should learn the violin, which took the edge off my unhappiness. A few days before leaving England I was strolling up and down Oakhill Road, reading Shelley, my supreme Comforter, when an old man came along, smiled and said, 'May I kiss you, my dear?' I disliked kissing, except in daydreams, but the aged fellow seemed so pathetic that I offered my cheek and hastily withdrew, hoping he would not follow. So little did this unimportant meeting signify that I jokingly mentioned it at the luncheon table, while the maids handed round potatoes and greens. (Father ate cabbage twice every day.) An uneasy silence fell until they had left the room. Then Father burst out: 'How *could* you let that old lecher touch you? Haven't you been warned over and over again *never* to speak to strangers!' and unable to contain himself he stormed out of the room. ('Lecher'—a new word. I must look it up.) 'But he was only a doddery old man,' I said to Mother, and she replied: 'They're the worst! Didn't you realise he was mentally undressing you?' That did jolt me. Whatever did she mean? She explained and added. 'You might have caught syphilis.' (Another new word!) 'What's that?' I asked. She told me. I was aghast and enquired how long it would be before I knew if I had caught it. 'In about six weeks,' she said. 'I'll be in Paris—' 'We must hope for the best,' said she. So I was left with not only the ordeal of entering a strange family, but the torture of waiting six weeks to find out whether I had contracted that shameful, horrible, disfiguring and perhaps fatal disease, which could make me mad. I fled to Nan. 'Nonsense!' she tried to reassure me. 'They're frightening you—for your own good. Don't believe them about syphilis.' But I did.

France and the First World War

1

I most regretted leaving Roderick and the Pavilion concerts, and decided to wear a heart-shaped locket which someone had given me and not remove it until I saw him again. Mother conducted me to the Perrier family, who lived in an apartment at 6 rue Nansouty, overlooking the Parc Montsouris. A young maidservant admitted us and led us to Monsieur and Madame Perrier in the salon, who introduced us to their eldest daughter and her two little sisters. I was gripped by a paralysing shyness, and only with the children did I feel at home. As none of the family understood English, Mother no French, and my accent was atrocious, conversation lagged, and when Mother left I felt close to despair.

Madame Perrier, who decided that I should be called Adèle, had recently broken an arm and was in a nervous state. I soon realised that, though she meant kindly, I mystified her. She frequently mentioned her previous boarder, Vera, who was so jolly, talkative, helpful and amusing, and made me feel painfully inferior, which indeed I was. Monsieur Perrier, Sorbonne Professor of Entomology specialising in Lepidoptera, wore his grey hair *en brosse*, had a square-cut beard, and was jovial and friendly, a typical French *père de famille*. Jeanne, aged twenty-four, a pianoforte pupil at the Scola Cantorum, studying under its co-founder Vincent d'Indy, had been badly crippled in early childhood by poliomyelitis, and dragged her sadly twisted legs. She had just become engaged to a violinist, now doing his military service, and they hoped eventually to found their own music school. The children, Geneviève and Guilhen, were little beauties with cream complexions and large brown eyes. Marceline the maid cooked, cleaned, and did a score of other jobs.

One a week a stout woman instructed me on Jeanne's piano and gave me Daquin's 'Cuckoo' to learn. But knowing how superbly Jeanne played, and conceiving for her one of my airy fairy admirations, I was too bashful to practise, and my 'Cuckoo' was the sickest cuckoo that ever cuckooed on the keys.

Madame's indisposition led to an unexpected bonus: I was let loose on Paris alone. Had my parents heard they would have been horrified and furious, but I had learned to keep my mouth shut, and was only too thankful for this windfall of freedom. During that long unhappy French interlude, had I not been allowed to wander at will, many aspects of humanity might never have been revealed. I had not forgotten Mother's threat of syphilis and was glad when, after six weeks, no symptoms appeared. Meanwhile relevant enlightenment began. On my first bus-ride to the Louvre a man sitting beside me kept pinching me so that I was obliged to alight, still far from the goal, and walk. I had not gone far when another man from one of the ornate Parisian urinals saluted me in a most unexpected fashion; and another, on foot, accorded the same greeting. Somewhat shaken by these unfamiliar displays, I went into a shop to buy stationery and the salesman fumbled me. At seventeen I was not innocent, not prudish, not disgusted, not afraid, and certainly not indifferent; but by nature I was extremely modest, and these startling demonstrations troubled me exceedingly. I felt sorry that I, naturally responsive and ready to return most manifestations of attraction, could not respond to these, though I hoped the poor creatures would find others who would.

Unlike my generous parents, the Perriers were frugal and abstemious. Madame was the very soul of thrift, and at meals I dared not ask for a second helping even if offered one, so I frequently felt hungry; and if, after buying stamps, fares and writing materials, I had any money left from the five francs weekly pocket-money Madame was supposed to give me, I spent it on chocolate and gingerbread. Sometimes for two weeks running she forgot my five francs; but I feared to remind her in case it made her feel negligent. So I walked everywhere or sat in the Parc Montsouris, scribbling rhymes.

The Louvre was nearly always my destination. I would enter it, trembling with anticipation, and first salute the Victory of Samothrace, then linger in the long gallery with its ancient statues of Hermes, Apollo, Pan, a hermaphrodite, and a boy's bronze head I loved, leading to the Venus of Melos, where I sat working on my epic, *Illyrion*. Then I would seek Michelangelo's Captives and, if time allowed, sped to the Buddhas and Goddesses of Mercy. For five months I haunted that magnificent museum and picture gallery: it was my real home.

Once a month the family attended a family dinner party at the house of Monsieur's famous biologist brother, Edmond Perrier, Professor of Zoology, and their old and intimidating mother. Thirty or forty members of the clan forgathered and I had to be taken too. I dreaded these occasions, when political affairs were discussed. Hatred of Germany was always the theme, stemming from mortifying memories of their 1870 defeat, with the loss of Alsace-Lorraine. One heard bitter references to Prussian lust for more territory, and her envy of Britain. The Perriers would gaze at me. What had I to say? Nothing. My predecessor, Vera, had apparently said a great deal. If only I was like her, I thought. Why could I not be more intelligent? I was shocked by their hatred and feared it more than imperialistic portents from Germany. Like Clemenceau, every Frenchman seemed to be possessed by the lust for revenge. At last, incensed by a remark made by a Perrier nephew, I was stung into speech and told him of my belief in universal brotherly love, proclaiming goodwill and peace—that there was only one race—at which he shouted with derision and mirth and called everyone's attention to my lunatic sentiments: 'We have a nihilist amongst us, or are you an anarchist?' whereupon they set upon me and strove with their logic and common sense to disillusion me. I never mentioned the subject again, and was not disillusioned.

Rémy Perrier owned most of the French Classics and pressed them on me to read, which I did with pleasure, and picked up bargains on the Seine and Odéon bookstalls, where for a few *sous* one could acquire almost any masterpiece. Though still loving Roderick and Shelley, now I loved Jeanne Perrier too—the poor lame girl who played Beethoven so movingly; and I yearned for her to become my *amie intime*; but was she not dreaming about her own beloved, and her divine teacher, Vincent d'Indy? I saved my pocket-money to buy her a bronze bust of Beethoven but was too abashed to present it, and planned to leave it for her to find when I departed.

Meanwhile Madame Perrier became quite maternal and realised that in spite of my *gaucherie* I wanted to be affectionate. On my eighteenth birthday the family gave me a silver necklace of ginkgo-leaf sprays that deeply touched me and amazed.

At Easter who should call but my Grassendale teacher, Ethel Herdman, with a bunch of lilies of the valley and the inevitable little bundle of poetry books, and ran me all over the city to the Cluny and Carnavelet Museums, the Bastille, Napoleon's Tomb and I know not where else, until even her phenomenal vitality began to wane. When she had left, on my own I explored Père-Lachaise Cemetery, to find the tombs of La Fontaine, Molière, Abélard and Héloïse, Corot and Daumier; but Chopin's grave most affected me. Leaning over the headstone, suffused by that joyful sadness, or sad joy, which pervades the resting-places of those one admires or loves, some of whom left immortal works, I felt a first stirring of *volupté*, desire; and looking back it seems strange that in this realm of death should occur a faint awakening associated more with birth—the universal impulse towards perpetuation. But there was no intuition that next time I stood there would be with my husband.

Throughout these solitary pilgrimages I was still accompanied in imagination by those fantasy boys and girl conjured in early childhood from a piece of glass, a stone and a limpet shell, who had grown up with me; but one murky evening, rain beginning to fall, I was standing under a lamp standard in the rue Bonaparte, the lamplight casting

mauve patterns on the mist, when those faithful comrades forsook me.
I distinctly saw them walk down the street, turn, wave and disappear,
and knew they had gone for ever—a sorrowful and inevitable parting.
With them vanished part of myself, faded into not only the wet
oncoming night but into that limbo from which I had summoned
them. And though for a time I missed them I soon outlived them, and
for over sixty years gave them not a thought until now.

2

The Perriers spent part of the summer in Corrèze, near the beautiful
Limousin-Dordogne country where, beyond the village of Peyrel-
vade, they owned a cottage called Chaunac, surrounded by a small
garden above a river valley, with long views of chestnut forests, wheat
fields and small farms tilled by peasants with the same primitive type
of tools used by their forefathers. The first evening we supped on the
terrace to the music of nightingales, cicadas and croaking frogs, while
the sun set, glow-worms gleamed, and after a long twilight sparked
innumerable stars.

I spent the mornings trundling Vevette and Guilhen round the
garden in a *charrette*, and after *déjeuner* took them on rambles, sometimes to a wild area of waterfalls, or to call on neighbours who gave us
cherry tarts made from the abundant wild fruit bowing laden trees; or
we visited peasants in their tiny cots, where the little girls fried *crêpes*
mixed with chestnut flour in iron pans over burning wood fires. But
when the magical landscape was shrouded behind mist and rain I sat
in the living-room listening to Jeanne practising Debussy's 'Deux
Arabesques' and Beethoven's 'Waldstein' Sonata, which, to this day
when I hear it, I am in that little parlour with the girl at the piano, the
children playing on the floor, Marceline sewing, Monsieur rolling
cigarettes, and Madame brooding over her eldest daughter's poor
deformed body, with so sad an expression that I longed to comfort
her—a scene imprinted for ever on my mental eye, changeless as the
figures on Keats' Grecian Urn. As the sun went down, the afterglow
sometimes shimmered with sheet lightning and distant thunder
boomed. Then Marceline would fetch the oil-lamp and close the
shutters. And when the little girls had gone to bed I read Victor
Hugo's *Les Misérables* or Père Dumas' *Comte de Monte-Cristo*, recommended by Père Perrier.

Towards the end of July ominous news appeared in his *Figaro*. The
assassination of the Archduke Franz Ferdinand and his wife led to an
Austrian ultimatum to Serbia, followed by a declaration of war, and
Russia mobilised. War was in the air. The Perriers' talk about this
dreadful possibility horrified me. They seemed to look forward to it.
Since that spiritual experience on the Channel crossing, for me all
people belonged to one family. So when a young neighbour hoped that

war would spread to France that he might go off 'to fight and kill our enemies', I was scandalised. And when Madame Perrier cried 'O, that I had a son to fight for France and slaughter Germans!' I was appalled. Jeanne wept silently: her fiancé would be called up.

On August 1st Germany declared war on Russia, and in France the general order for mobilisation was pinned on every door: *République française—Mobilisation générale.* Unable to bear the atmosphere at Chaunac, I went out, miserable and afraid. I was watching the blue-bloused peasants, many my friends, threshing corn with wooden flails on a granary floor, others reaping with hooks and sickles, when a man in uniform appeared and they dropped their implements and crowded round. He had brought the mobilisation order and explained what it meant: all able-bodied men were called up. Women, who had run from cottages, cried and moaned. With old men and children they would have to complete the harvest. Their husbands and sons, transformed into *poilus*, were to be herded into the army to fight. The men accepted their fate with fortitude. The women wailed.

On August 2nd, Luxembourg was occupied and German troops crossed into France. A Note was delivered to Belgium. On August 3rd, Britain mobilised, and Germany declared war on France and Belgium. The Germans had refused to confer with the British, who, under Sir Edward Grey, were trying to effect a settlement. The question was: Would Britain declare war on Germany? The Perriers looked at me with dubious, pleading expressions, as if the choice were mine.

It was August 4th, Shelley's birthday. Since girlhood I had always written him a poem on that day. This year, to escape from Chaunac, with Jeanne crying and Madame repeating 'O, that I had a son to fight for France!', Monsieur damning Germany, and everyone, I suspected, blaming me for my pacifism, and England for not entering the contest, I sought the fields, wondering how, when, and if I should get home again, and trying vainly to compose something worthy of my poet on his natal day.

Madame Perrier had begun to hoard, giving all the food she could spare to her husband and children, so that I ate the minimum and was always ravenous. That blazing afternoon I found an ungleaned cornfield and rubbed handfuls of grain between my palms, blowing away the husks. Farther on, I came upon an orchard and picked up hard little apples fallen before their time. How delicious that sour green fruit and ripe, unground wheat tasted.

Next morning the Professor squashed me against his watchchain and kissed me on both cheeks, praising my country and telling me that Britain had declared war on Germany! All was well! Reading from his newspaper he announced that two thousand Germans had already been slain, but only two hundred Frenchmen. I was aghast: so many already dead—the shock of that news never subsided.

One evening two peasants, Joiny and Péra, came to Chaunac dressed in their uniforms to say goodbye before leaving for the front. One told me that he did not want to go to war because it meant leaving his sweetheart Miette, 'who is very much like you'; but the other seemed glad to go because '*Ça nous promènera*'. They were pleased that my land was fighting alongside theirs, and kept shaking my hands. We all embraced, and the Professor and I promised to come to Tulle to see them off.

How harrowing it was to watch the troop train puff out of the station, and, oh, how I hoped they would survive, and that the war would soon be over, as most people prophesied. We returned with the women, several carrying small babies, some soon to give birth. I often went to see these courageous people in their shacks, to comfort and be comforted. Old Miette, young Miette's grandmother, fried me chestnut flour *tortues*, which she could little spare. '*Mange! Mange, ma petite! Tu as faim!*' she would say.

A telegram came from Mother: 'Keep Adelaide with you', and my heart sank, as I am sure did the Perriers', for they must have longed to get rid of me. Passenger ships to Bordeaux had ceased to run and Paris was expected to fall. I felt marooned, perhaps until the war ended. The heat was tremendous. Seeking shade and solitude in the woods I got stung on the ankle by ferocious ants and my foot swelled enormously. Lightning flickered all night. Fretting, with throbbing foot, and famished, picturing the war, the wounded, dying, and wanting to be with them, I could not sleep and crouched at the open window, watching shooting stars stream across the sky.

Monsieur Perrier longed for the *Grande Bataille* to begin, and poor, worried Jeanne continued to play Debussy and Beethoven, yearning and praying for her betrothed, now in the fighting-line. The terrible weeks crawled on. In September, when German troops were on the doorsteps of Paris, which was being raided, a telegram came from Father asking the Professor if possible to get me there, where a young American would meet me and bring me back to England. I felt a sunshaft of hope, but everything depended on whether Monsieur Perrier would escort me. Madame naturally did not want her elderly husband to risk his life in a raid, or to be interned; but he could not hide his eagerness to return to his beloved Paris in her dangerous hour, and insisted on taking me. The anxious wife and children wept and begged me to refuse to go. 'We will take good care of you. You will be *our* daughter,' said Madame, 'until we can return you safely to your parents.' I was desperately anxious to get home, yet how could I urge the Professor to risk the journey? I said I would stay. He overruled us all and told me to pack: we would start in the morning.

Before we left I placed on Jeanne's bed the Beethoven bust I had

Nun's Rock, Mount Abu, India, birthplace of Eden Phillpotts

Adelaide Phillpotts (Grannie Adelaide), mother of Eden Phillpotts

Lilla Hilliard Brewitt
('Nan')

Eden Phillpotts and
daughter Adelaide at
Cosdon

lacked the temerity to give her, and hoped it might console her as her music had consoled me. After wild embraces and *au revoirs*, the children and mother wondering what would happen to their dearest papa, he and I departed to board a northbound train to Tulle. It kept stopping and not until midnight halted at the junction, where we got out to await the Paris express. While standing on the platform in the blacked-out night, a string of cattle-trucks bound south drew up opposite, packed with German prisoners, some with bloody bandages. The people on our side of the line, including the Professor, rushed across, shaking their fists and screaming in fury, spitting at the poor wretches and sending them to hell. This was my true initiation into the fears and hatreds latent in the whole of mankind. And I, too, began to boil with anger, though not against those miserable prisoners in the cattle-vans. These primitive emotions existed just as outrageously and dangerously in me! We were indeed all one brotherhood, all prejudiced, violent, unjust and unreasonable, all cruel, all mad—yet all human, all one race, all capable of loving the others, all one family.

After many tedious hours we reached Paris where, at the Grand Hotel, the Professor handed me over to my American Perseus: a blond, blue-eyed young man of twenty-six, Sinclair Gluck, stepson of Hughes Massie, my father's literary agent. Gleeful at being back in Paris, unencumbered by his family and me, Monsieur Perrier hurried off to his University, while Sinclair and I awaited the ten o'clock night-train for the coast.

Many people seemed scared, expecting to be overrun by German troops, or bombed. A bomber had just flown overhead and reconnaissance planes were droning. We lunched at a Duval restaurant and talked of many things, drifting into an affectionate relationship. The train in which we traversed the north of France was so crammed that we took it in turns to share half a seat until we reached Dieppe, where thousands of people swarmed on the quay, waiting to board the steamer for England. Crushed into the jam we could not move until at last the gangway was lowered and we were borne along in the crowd. By late evening we docked at Folkestone, and after another mob, got one seat in the London train.

How wonderful it was to reach Victoria and the Langham Hotel, where Mother was waiting, and next day to be reunited with Father, Henry and Nan in what, compared to France, was a land of idyllic peace.

(After the war I heard from Madame Perrier that Jeanne's betrothed had survived and they were married. All the family were prospering. But Joiny and Péra, and other Chaunac peasants had been blown to pieces or drowned in Flanders mud, and their bodies were never found.)

3

For two years I worked as a VAD in the kitchen of a Red Cross hospital, and took lessons in Nursing and First Aid. But as this shift work engaged only five hours a day, my parents decided that I must devote most of the rest to Great-Aunt Susan and other aged members of the family. Acting as unwilling Companion, I did what my Aunt ordered, one duty being to groom Pansy, her Yorkshire terrier, the only creature who loved her or whom she loved. To cook and clean she employed an aged widow called Mrs Cawse, and one day I arrived to hear Mrs Cawse crying, Aunt Susan shouting, and Pansy howling like a fiend. *'Thief!'* Aunt bawled, and turning to me: 'She's been going to my drawer and stealing a shilling a week!' She pointed to a desk drawer where she kept her purse. Lying on top was a piece of cardboard on which she had written 'GOD IS WATCHING YOU', and the sight of this warning had so confounded the old woman that she screamed, alerting Aunt Susan, lurking behind the door, that her trap was sprung, whereupon she marched in for the kill.

Soon afterwards she fell ill and stayed in bed. I sat holding her hand as she moaned: 'Dear God, take me home. Take me home,' over and over again, and at last she died. Only Pansy mourned, and she was almost immediately sent to the vet to be destroyed. Aunt Susan left her estate of five hundred pounds to Grannie Adelaide, and after Grannie's death to me.

My father and mother kept their promise to let me have violin lessons, which I fitted in with the new leader of the Municipal Orchestra, Barry Squire. I had not forgotten Roderick but heard that he had left, to fight in France. I removed the locket I had worn since the last time I saw him, wondering why I felt so little sad. To avoid disturbing Father with my violin practice I sawed away in the saddle-room, a narrow space leading out of the stables, but there was little time for practising. Mr Squire suggested that I learn Handel's 'Largo', with Father accompanying me on the pianola, which we tried, with such excruciating results that Mother implored us to give it up. So I dropped the lessons, but had acquired just enough skill to play second fiddle in the Red Cross Kitchen Band, consisting of a few genuine instruments and several comic ones, like a fish-kettle drum, saucepan lid cymbals, and a triangle made with skewers. We gave concerts to the wounded men, playing 'Tipperary', 'Pack up your Troubles', There's a Long, Long Trail', 'Mademoiselle from Armentières', and older favourites like 'Auld Lang Syne' and 'Home Sweet Home'. I wished Uncle Cecil could know that his violin had come to life again.

All through the war patients from the Red Cross Hospital took it in turns to visit Eltham once a week, where Mother and Father gave them as good a meal as possible and afterwards drinks and games.

During the first few months France had lost a million soldiers, Russia two million in one year; and during the Battle of the Somme Britain, France and Germany lost a quarter of a million men. No one realised the enormity of this suffering more than my brother. To him as to me, in almost whatever cause, organised killing, torture, maiming and imprisoning were evils. But our father, who had offered himself for war in any capacity, disagreed and expected his son immediately to enlist. If anyone young delayed doing so he was apt to have a white feather thrust at him and to be branded a coward. Henry was not a coward, or a conscientious objector, and the question of his enlistment was delayed because he had to have an operation, and by the time he was well conscription had become law. So he was called up and drafted into the army. The experience in camp was drastic and so unbalanced him that he was soon pronounced unfit for combat but fit for non-combatant service. Unwilling to face our parents he fled to Grannie Adelaide, who willingly took him in. Meanwhile Father, distraught by these events, appealed to a friend of their journalist days, Robert Murray Gilchrist, a novelist, who lived with parents and sisters at Holmesfield in the Peak District and was engaged in work for Belgian refugees. With the family lodged George Carfitt, head of a Sheffield cutlery factory which had been taken over for munition making, and he offered to take Henry to work there for the war's duration. And though Henry loathed the idea of making lethal weapons, he was too shocked to protest and spent the rest of the war operating a lathe. And as that war broke thousands of other non-combatants, as well as combatants, it broke Henry, and destroyed his genius.

I continued, when I could trap time, to work on *Illyrion*, which I gave Father on his fifty-third birthday, and so pleased was he that he arranged for it and other verse to be published by a young publisher who had brought out Father's own poems, *Delight*, and the first of his many prose fantasies which he called fairy stories, *The Girl and the Faun*. My book was published in 1916 and received friendly reviews.

During that year a writer called Anthony Ludovici came to lunch with us, and during the meal described the delights of literary London so glowingly that suddenly I felt a powerful hankering to leave home and work in the capital. I was twenty—more than time to wing from the nest—and was not the war a perfect opportunity to escape into the classless society I thought prevailed in the metropolis, where I could earn my living and take part in that exhilarating world described so temptingly by Anthony Ludovici?

My parents did not take my plans seriously, and both Nan and Grannie Adelaide were hostile. However, I cajoled Nan into agreeing that as my heart was set on London to London I must go. To humour my mother and father I enquired about joining the Women's Services, but Father was not in favour, and though I was most drawn to nursing, that, too, was vetoed. At last Father, realising that I should soon be of age, extended feelers and heard of a woman who edited a non-militant suffragist journal called the *Common Cause* who wanted a secretary. Would I come? The salary was thirty shillings a week. I accepted.

No one asked me where I was going to live, so I looked up advertisements in *Bradshaw's Guide to British Railways* in the Reference Room at the Carnegie Library and found the address of a boarding-house in Claverton Street, Victoria, to which I wrote. By return came a letter from someone I will call Miss Lark, saying that she had a bedroom to let with breakfast and supper. I took it. Nan wanted to come with me to find out what kind of place it was. (She was afraid the White Slave Traffickers would get me.) But I overruled her. Was I not grown up? Henceforth I must fend for myself.

London I

1

The year 1916 had been a prolific one for my father. Besides *Delight* and *The Girl and the Faun*, he published *The Green Alleys*, a novel about the Kentish hopfields, for which Henry designed a jacket; and his Devonshire comedy, *The Farmer's Wife*, was produced by Sir Barry Jackson at the Repertory Theatre, Birmingham.

Nan came to see me off to London and her last words were 'Be careful of strange men!' My euphoria lasted until we reached Paddington, where I could not secure a taxi: people kept shoving me aside; until one of those 'strange men' of Nan's fancy grabbed me a vacant vehicle and vanished before I could thank him. The driver stopped beside a tall house in Victoria, dumped my trunk and departed. A middle-aged woman, Miss Lark, jewelled and scented, with a pleasant rouged face, opened the door and exclaimed 'You're only a juvenile!' 'Oh, no, I'm twenty,' said I, and she helped me in with the trunk, surprised by its weight—books—and, leaving it in the hall, conducted me to a cold attic, saying 'I'm afraid you'll have to unpack below. Supper at eight. Call me if you want me,' and ran downstairs, her bangles rattling on the banisters. I relayed my belongings and set Nan's parting gift of an owl clock with swivelling green eyes on the clothes chest, banking my books on either side, then, wrapping my neck in a voluminous woollen scarf she had given me, went out to explore.

How different London looked from its pristine appearance in my childhood. Embedded in the roadways were nuts and bolts and other metal objects, which suggested a short story about a small boy who grubbed them up. I would call it *The Grubber*. Back at Claverton Street Miss Lark handed me a box containing beautiful white orchids sent by a schoolfriend who lived in an Inigo Jones mansion where I had stayed and these flowers had been grown. They proffered such delight that for more than sixty years they have floated through my memory like *Immortelles*, and reappear here for the last time.

Next morning I walked to the office of the *Common Cause*, and after a long wait was interviewed by two formidable women before whom I felt like a wisp of hay. They did not know what to do with me, and it dawned on me that they must have expected a quite different, older, and more experienced female. Miss Meredith said that if I shaped well I might take her place as Editor of the journal; but the possibility filled me with such misgiving that I stared a denial, and felt them summing me up as a dud. I was. Though my duty was to take and send telephone messages, several days passed before I could nerve myself to use the instrument; and Miss Longley failed to understand how anyone presuming to be a secretary could be intimidated by a telephone, or had never used one before. When she heard that I could not do shorthand she declared that without shorthand I should be quite useless to the *Common Cause*, or any other cause, and I must learn it; whereupon she made arrangements for me to attend an Institute in Holborn to acquire the swiftly mastered method called Sloan Duployan. How thankful I was to get away from that office, and travel on an exciting tramway which ran along Victoria Embankment, rumbling under Aldwych and Kingsway and emerging opposite the shorthand school—a thrilling seven-minute ride.

One day Miss Meredith directed me to call on the President of the National Union of Women's Suffrage Societies and fetch a consignment of Union Jacks on pins to sell in Victoria Street for the Soldiers' and Sailors' Families Association—a charming old lady called Millicent Fawcett, sister of Elizabeth Garrett Anderson, the first woman doctor, and widow of Henry Fawcett, the remarkable statesman who conquered blindness to become Postmaster-General. She offered me biscuits and tea, and gave me a large bundle of miniature pennants insecurely tied in brown paper, to convey to the *Common Cause*. I boarded the wrong bus and had to dismount in Trafalgar Square, and while hurrying towards Whitehall, got mixed up with traffic; the string on the parcel slipped, it burst open and spilled hundreds of flaglets over the crowded Square, and they were crushed under wheels or whirled away by the wind. Trying to retrieve them I was nearly run over and drivers cursed me—so, in less picturesque language, did Miss Longley and Miss Meredith.

Next day I was ordered to stand in Victoria Street and sell the few flags that survived; but I was never a good pedlar and lacked the guts to rattle a tin and beg for alms. The Office Ladies let me know what they thought of my general incompetence, and I slunk to my Claverton eyrie and wept. That inhospitable attic was nearly as disappointing as the *Common Cause*: moreover Miss Lark had become too friendly, and when I gave her a copy of *Illyrion* introduced me to her very odd lot of lodgers as 'my little singing bird'! Her breakfasts and suppers grew thinner and thinner, like me, and when the weekly expenses were paid I had little if any of my thirty shillings left, though Nan sent me an occasional postal order, with a cherry cake, incorporating her own rations. I felt obliged to share it with Lark and the others, and if a cherry remained I was lucky. To still the craving for something sweet I stoked up on threepenny college puddings at the Express Dairy in Victoria Street, and now and then a quarter pound of nasty chocolates which I munched in the evening at one sitting, while composing my story of *The Grubber*.

Perceiving that as a future editress I was a rope of sand, Miss Meredith called me to her room, suggested that I might be more useful to the war effort in some other capacity, and advised me to call on the Women's Service Bureau in Victoria Street, where suitable work for women could be found. Thankfully I hurried there, to be interviewed by a woman resembling a Pre-Raphaelite heroine, and having filled in a form was preparing to leave when, without consulting it, she smiled and said: 'How would you like to work for me? I need a new secretary.' Amazed, I felt bound to tell her that the *Common Cause* had disposed of me as a secretarial failure, and she laughed and said: 'That's all right, then. Can you start on Monday at half past eight? We'll pay you two pounds a week. Half Saturday and all Sunday free.'

I shared a back room with a fellow clerk and an office girl, and my work was to take letters from the Pre-Raphaelite lady and type them for her to sign. She dealt daily with dozens of applications from individuals and institutions needing war work and workers; and typing particulars, posting lists of suitable jobs, and answering letters kept me busy until six o'clock, with half an hour for lunch at the Express Dairy, or walking by the Thames. Before the war ended our Bureau placed thousands of women in useful work. (But I wished I had been a nurse at the front.)

I had not been there long before I caught German measles. Miss Lark got in touch with Aunt Frances, whom I had avoided, wishing to be entirely FREE; and suddenly I was on the doorstep again, a tearful Lark singing out: 'I will never forget my little singing bird'! and Aunt Frances and I were on our way to Ealing, where I was put to bed. Great-Aunt Margaret had died and Aunt Frances and Grannie Anne were living in a smaller house, Grannie as little and light as a child. Her voice never rose above a whisper, and all day she sat in a wicker armchair, her tiny feet on a footstool, dozing and dreaming of the past. In her melodious voice my aunt spent hours reading aloud to me, *Wuthering Heights* and *Tess of the D'Urbervilles*; and Emily's novel so exalted me that I determined to write a novel too, and was pleased to learn that, according to Emily's Diary of July 30th, 1841, the family had a goose called Adelaide, so my name had been on her lips. Aunt Frances seemed to belong to both Hardy and Brontë-land. She begged me to stop on with them, but the fear of losing liberty was so keen that I told her truthfully that I could not afford the fares; and when she offered to pay them I refused to let her. Sadly she gave up, but I promised not to return to Claverton Street.

On my walks to the office I passed a building with an oak door, brass fittings and a plate stamped with the letters GFS. Would the Girls Friendly Society befriend me? It did. That little hostel room became my first real London home. I went out and bought a folding card-table, with money Aunt Frances had given me, at the Army and Navy Stores, and set it up every night and began the novel inspired by *Wuthering Heights* and *Tess*. Meanwhile from some obscure journal whose name I forget I received first earnings of a guinea for *The Grubber*, and spent it on what I was told was a silver Georgian mustard pot, for Mother, and other gifts for Father, Nan and Henry. Mother was pleased, even though it turned out to be neither silver nor Georgian.

On the first GFS evening I sat at supper next to a War Office worker called Ethel who instantly became my dearest friend. Tender-hearted, she treated me as a younger sister, but her real love was her own younger sister who worked at Woolwich in a munitions factory. One night there was an air raid with din of bombs and anti-aircraft fire and Ethel feared that her sister might be in danger: Zeppelins had already bombed Woolwich and thirty-three people were killed. So I ran out to a telephone box at Victoria Station, dialled a Woolwich number at random and asked if the raid was there. A voice answered 'no'. In fact, it was the first aeroplane raid, dropping bombs between Brompton Road and Victoria, and as I ran back, shrapnel was tinkling and spurting from the ground.

On Saturday afternoons I tramped via the Isle of Dogs to Lime-house and Dockland that I might tell Henry about his favourite places; and one scorching summer day I had walked through Stepney and Poplar, along Commercial Road East to the East India Docks, which I hoped would lead to Gallions Reach, when I encountered a tall steel barrier guarded by a policeman, who looked down on me with annoyance and surprise. 'What are you doing here, miss? Where do you belong?' I could think of nothing to say, not feeling that I belonged anywhere in particular, or else everywhere, and he com-manded me to 'Go home at once! You've no business here.' I felt crushed and hurt and never got to Gallions Reach.

Another day I was roving in the West End for a change, and while standing under a glass roof above the entrance to Dover Street Tube Station a deafening explosion occurred, the roof was shattered and glass spattered over me followed by a tremendous weight like a sack of coals which hurled me to the ground and landed on top of me. I thought it was an air raid, which in a sense it was: a huge charwoman, leaning out to clean the canopy, had overbalanced and fallen through the glass. Acting as a cushion I may have saved her life, for she was only shocked, and people crowding round helped her to recover. They were so concerned about her that nobody noticed me, still flattened on the pavement. So I got up and walked away. All through that year there were many air raids by Gotha planes and thousands of people were killed.

As often as possible I saved up for a theatre or a Promenade Concert at the Queen's Hall. I would tear away from the office and wait in gallery queues, entertained by buskers, who stirred one's compassion. I went to the Royal Opera House to hear *Samson and Delilah*, deeply moved by the love duet. A young African sitting beside me told me that he was a flautist but it was now very difficult to get work. Could I help? Alas, no. Into whichever pit or gallery I crowded, my neighbours usually spoke, so friendly were people in those wartime days. One, a Jewish writer called Coleman Phillipson, wanted me to spend a day with his wife and daughter, whose photographs he showed me to prove that he was 'respectable'; but I never accepted invitations.

One day a colleague at the office asked me to join her at a lecture in the Essex Hall, chaired by H.G. Wells, to hear Headmaster Sanderson of Oundle speak. Both men were sitting on the platform, and Wells was introducing Sanderson, when that vast man suddenly toppled off his chair, dead.

My most glorious experiences were Shakespearean productions at the Old Vic, where a gallery seat cost sixpence. Sometimes I got there early enough for the front row and would lean over to watch that wonderful woman, Lilian Baylis, greeting celebrities. From 1898 she had laboured to turn her Aunt Emma Con's slummy old Royal Victoria Hall and Coffee Tavern into 'The Home of Shakespeare', and also to revive Sadler's Wells and found a National Opera House and Ballet. Many people think Shakespeare owes more to her than to many subsequent persons who now produce his plays. To me those Old Vic presentations were well nigh perfect and leave the modern ones nowhere.

The cast included Father's friends, Lewis and Sybil Casson: I watched Sybil as a delightful Beatrice, a gay Rosalind, a moving Imogen, and a harrowing Constance. One night during *Cymbeline* I was smitten with acute abdominal pains and obliged to search for a lavatory. No one could direct me until, doubled with agony, I appealed to an attendant, who told me there was 'a privy in the basement'. I staggered down dozens of stone steps into the cellarage and at last ran to earth a foul-smelling hole in the ground. Fifty years afterwards when Lilian Baylis died and a biography was written, I read about those 'medieval lavatory facilities' and how, when challenged, she blamed God and said: 'He really has made a very bad arrangement and He'll have to do better.' When the Old Vic was rebuilt I was glad to hear that better had been done.

During these years I met Martin Harvey again, at His Majesty's, in

Richard II and *The Taming of the Shrew*; and at the Savoy I saw
Hamlet, with Father's friend H. B. Irving as the Prince; and *Romeo
and Juliet*, in which his first love, Ellen Terry, whom forty years
earlier he adored as Juliet, played Juliet's Nurse.

On Sundays I joined young friends in their bedsitters, where,
according to our lofty standards, we set the sad world to rights. Alas,
how many of them are dead, some killed in that war, some in the next,
and some of old age. I mixed little in the literary world, though
Father, who kept out of it himself, planned meetings for me with his
acquaintances and would say: 'You must be willing to meet more
writers and to *assert* yourself more.' Once, under duress, I did accept
an invitation to a reception and dinner given by the publisher, William
Heinemann, whom I had met when he stayed at Eltham, to celebrate
the publication of E. M. Delafield's first novel, *Zella Sees Herself*. I
had nothing suitable to wear, only an old white muslin with a blue sash
which must have made me look younger than I was because the
waiter, instead of filling my glass with wine, passed me by and
returned with lemonade. After dinner Mr Heinemann introduced me
to a grandfatherly old gentleman with white hair who said: 'So you are
Eden Phillpotts' daughter! How do you do, my dear. I'm Edmund
Gosse.' I had never heard of him but was grateful for his kindness and
did my best to respond by asking him if he was a writer. He told me
that from 1904 to 1914 he had been Librarian to the House of Lords.
(I discovered later that in 1907 Heinemann had published his masterpiece, *Father and Son*.) He took me to greet his artist daughter, Sylvia,
with flaming red hair. But after the *Common Cause* I was scared of
intellectual women, and feeling that I had done my duty I slipped
away to my perch at the GFS.

2

Soon after coming to London I had met Cecil, who lived in a Chelsea
studio, to which he invited me to supper. His older brother had just
been awarded the Victoria Cross for gallantry on the Western Front,
and I was touched by the younger's fraternal pride, and regret that he,
too, could not serve in the army. To return his hospitality I took him
to the Opera to see Mussorgsky's *Khovanshchina*, and was moved to
receive his confidences during the interval. He was a publisher and
promised to publish a verse play I was writing, about that victim of the
envious Muses, Arachne, and eventually did so. I recollect a midnight
stroll in Hyde Park, and a day when he brought me a bunch of wild
flowers. One evening we were talking in his studio when he said he
would like to marry me. I was astonished. He confessed that he was
lonely and anxious to be married and have a family. Would I be the one?
I, who felt only friendship, replied that I was very sorry but I could not
be, and I felt sure that he would soon find someone else. (I'm glad to

say that he did.)

Meanwhile, on a weekend visit to Aunt Frances I had mentioned our friendship and how we walked in green places by starlight. What a trusting fool I still was. She immediately wrote to my mother to warn her. Mother told Father and he was furious, though this was before the proposal, which I did not mention to anyone. The upshot was that I was summoned home and told to wind up my work at the Bureau. 'Your Mother needs you,' wrote Father. 'Father needs you,' wrote Mother. 'Father and Mother need you and so do I', wrote Nan. I was not averse from leaving London, which had palled, and now thirsted for the country. The terrible war continued. Everything I deplored was happening every moment of the day. To see Nan, parents, countryside, seashore, would be a temporary solace; but I planned soon to procure other work, and try to stop the war.

Father sternly rebuked me—in a letter, when I got home. To my bewilderment he would not meet me face to face and left me the letter to find. He guessed that Cecil had offered marriage and set forth all the disadvantages of *any* matrimonial alliance: I must devote my life when the war ended to my art. I was hurt and mystified that he chose to write instead of talking. And I told him again and again that I had no intention of marrying anybody, though I knew my mediocre gift of art was not worth sacrificing children for; I wanted to have them. I was under no illusions about my work's insignificance. Poor Father— he seemed so pathetic and unreasonable—he, the apostle of reason. Yet even then I doubted whether my work was the sole reason for his attitude. But what other could there be? His admonishment turned my mind from marriage for a long, long time, and with relief I flew to the blessed wild places associated with childhood. They had not changed. But I had.

Cambridge

I do not remember how my father initiated my next enterprise: perhaps he appealed to Anthony Ludovici, who was a friend of C. K. Ogden, Editor of the penny *Cambridge Magazine*, who wrote to say that I was welcome for two pounds a week to work for him, and sent my parents the address of a lodging. With that address, and boundless hope, I set off on another adventure.

Having reached Cambridge I took a taxi, and was driven to an old house near the Round Church and admitted by an ancient woman who had mothered generations of undergraduates. Mrs Olde, as I will call her, showed me to a large, low-ceilinged room on the first floor, brewed a pot of tea, said I could have a hip-bath in front of the fire, and hobbled off to her kitchen, where she snoozed most of her life away.

After a wakeful night I walked to Mr Ogden's house in Jordan's Yard—a magical Castle of Books: every passage, staircase, and room was crammed, and in their midst sat the Knight of the Books, C.K. himself. Charles Kay Ogden, then twenty-nine, struck me at first sight as a cold, well-glutted bookworm and super-intellectual. How wrong I was. I learned later that he had won a classical scholarship to Magdalene College, and left it to live in this house, one of several he turned into bookshops, offices, and libraries. He bought books in bulk, most of which were pulped to procure paper for his magazine. Skilful businessman as well as scholar, he manoeuvred in both house-market and book-mart; and he collected masks and musical boxes, mechanical toys, clocks and gramophones, but especially books.

C.K.—to his friends—received me with a nod and explained the magazine, which he had founded, in 1912, as a penny University Journal. (The first number announced that 'The frank statement of a point of view, any readable contribution, whether ultra-academic or verging on the horsy, will be gladly received . . . We have secured the services of many leading representatives of the various movements and interests, academic, athletic, political or religious . . .') In its early days G. K. Chesterton, Gordon Craig, Quiller-Couch and Gilbert Murray contributed. Now, with a circulation of 25,000, it reviewed the foreign Press and reported their different attitudes to the war, and included anti-war articles. In 1915 Thomas Hardy had written: 'I read the magazine every week, and turn first to the extracts from foreign newspapers, which transport me to the Continent and enable one to see England bare and unadorned—her chances in the struggle free from distortion by the glamour of patriotism. I also admit a liking for the lighter paragraphs.'

The *Cambridge Magazine*'s humanitarian and internationalist attitude, balanced, just, and of Faustian range, became to many people highly suspect, even seditious and treasonable—a 'red rag' to right-wing bulls. There had been several rumpuses, as C.K. called them: he was accused of flagrant pacifism and an effort to influence young people against the war. As I learned long afterwards but did not know at the time, in March, 1917, Mr Ogden received the letter, reproduced below, signed among others by my father, which C.K. printed in the 36th Vacation Extra Number of the magazine under the caption:

Fighting with the Right People
The undersigned have read with surprise and regret a letter which appeared recently in the Press signed by Sir Frederick Pollock, Sir Francis Younghusband and others, as representatives of the Fight for Right Movement, making what we regard as an unjustified attack upon the *Cambridge Magazine*.

While perhaps none of us is in agreement with all the views expressed in that paper, and some of us differ strongly from its general attitude, we desire to record our opinion that the *Cambridge Magazine* has done useful service during a time when it is specially difficult to preserve a well-balanced judgment; and in particular that its extracts from the foreign Press do fairly achieve what they profess, viz., to correct any one-sided views that may be engendered by the extracts published in other English papers.

The freedom of the press is an old and valuable heritage; and we resent the victimization of the *Cambridge Magazine* for an honest attempt to preserve the high tradition of independence and originality of thought associated in our minds with the name of the University of Cambridge.

EDWARD V ARNOLD	H H JOHNSTON
HAROLD BEGBIE	GILBERT MURRAY
ARNOLD BENNETT	PARMOOR
ARTHUR CLUTTON BROCK	EDEN PHILLPOTTS
J B BURY	ARTHUR QUILLER-COUCH
COURTNEY OF PENWITH	H B LEES SMITH
THOMAS HARDY	J C SQUIRE
JANE HARRISON	GRAHAM WALLAS
C H HERFORD	JOSIAH C WEDGWOOD
LAURENCE HOUSMAN	REBECCA WEST
JEROME K JEROME	ISRAEL ZANGWILL

During our first interview, Mr Ogden was careful to emphasise that his magazine *did* excite disapproval and controversy, not only among the academic, fanatical, patriotic and ignorant, but also among plain, simple, ordinary folk. What did I think? It was very important to have a point of view. I said that I agreed with his ideals and was ready to defend them against the deadliest opposition, and he repeated: 'The great thing is to have a definite point of view.' Unsure of mine, which was not fixed, and apt to waver, in spite of my avowals, C.K. did not seem to know what to give me to do. I realised that, like the *Common Cause* women, he had expected a wiser and more intellectually gifted person, as most of the people in his circle were. Anxious to proceed with his own work, he scooped up a bundle of books, circulars and tracts lying about and told me to read and review them for the magazine. Being entirely devoid of the critical faculty, which I greatly admire in others, I was dismayed, but tried to assess them, uninteresting as I thought they were, and returned them with my reviews. He neither mentioned nor printed them, or offered me anything else to criticise. Instead, he dictated a few letters; but the typewriter was so worn that it took me longer to type one letter than it would have taken him in long-hand to answer ten. I felt as out of place as a prawn on dry land.

I had never before nor have ever since met anyone resembling Charles Ogden. He seemed both very weak and vulnerable and very courageous and tough. And though he had many male and female friends, some very devoted, I doubted if human beings were more important than his principles, his ideas, his visions of the future, or even his thousands of books. I was wrong. Later I discovered that he was by no means all brain and no sentiment, but was as human and insecure as the rest of us, more sensitive than most, easily hurt and disappointed by adverse criticism, and had certain blind spots. Who has not? Nevertheless, he possessed a rare, almost superhuman quality. And to his diverse friends of every age—he was secretive in trying to keep them apart from one another—he was loyal, kind and helpful, going out of his way to do good turns, ready to give all and take all, or whatever they were prepared to receive and accord. He could be roguish and witty, with a mordant sense of humour and irony; but he was never cruel. A staunch feminist—in 1915 he had written, under the pseudonym Adeline More, *Militarism versus Feminism*, and *Fecundity versus Civilisation*—he supported women's suffrage, trade unionism, agnosticism and birth control. A champion of Father's friend, A. R. Orage of the *New Age*, and G. D. H. Cole, who campaigned with Ivor Richards for Guild Socialism, he advocated extended education for all. In short, he was a man of vision who looked forward to a democratic and international world.

Sometimes when C.K. went forth to visit friends he took me with him and left me in the car until he returned, it might be not for two or three hours. At first I was tempted to alight and walk back to

Cambridge, until I realised that he was only thoughtless and time meant nothing to him. When he reappeared he would say: 'I haven't been long, have I?' and I reassured him. I thought, mistakenly, that he must be missing much of the joy of life and of youth; but he may well have thought that I, with my greater limitations, was missing more.

In 1909 at Magdalene College he had founded the Heretics, who forgathered over the Pepsyian Library. Now they met every Sunday evening at Top 'Ole—called after an 'Old Bill' war cartoon—the book-lined attic at the summit of his home, to which many well-known people came, whose ideals I shared: Bertrand Russell, J. M. Keynes, whose brother Geoffrey, the Blake enthusiast and scholar, I met, George Moore of *Principia Ethica*, Dr M'Taggart of *Studies in Hegelian Cosmology*, and people from other lands. They discussed anything from religion and philosophy to aspects of the war, not disdaining more frivolous matters. Feeling like a strayed cat among a pride of lions, I listened to those brilliant minds playing with the most abstruse problems of war and peace, ethics, linguistics, and other topics, tossing the subjects to and fro, so that nothing said was unduly solemn, but often illuminated by C.K.'s special brand of wit and wisdom. I wished that I could have joined in but lacked the powers of expression and reflection.

These meetings often lasted into the small hours—C.K. never seemed to sleep—and I could hardly keep my eyes open. Scintillating discussions and flashes of conversation faded into darkness and sometimes I did drop off.

At Father's command I attended lectures on the Art of Writing at one of the colleges, given by his friend Professor Arthur Quiller-Couch, 'Q', and excellent they were. I recollected him telling us never to use the word 'case' 'unless you mean case, that is a receptacle. Never write "In any case". Case is Jargon's dearest child'. And he quoted from a cigar merchant's letter: 'In any case let us send you a case on approval.' I strove never to err, but sometimes lapsed. In any case I enjoyed those lectures. Meanwhile the war turned in the Allies' favour.

On November 11th, at 11 a.m., C.K. and I were in his office when suddenly long-silent bells pealed out, followed by the roar of running feet careering down Jordan's Yard, the shouting of menacing voices, as a horde of young students reached the Castle of Books and hammered on the King of the Castle's door. C.K. turned paler than usual and told me to go back to my lodgings as quickly as possible, 'They've come to burn down me and my library!' I refused to go but he pushed me out of the back door and opened the front door to face the mob. I returned. The war was over. An armistice had been proclaimed. The jubilant undergraduates, medical students among them, to express their scorn for C. K. Odgen and his perfidious magazine burst into the house, tore down his original paintings and hurled them and hundreds of books into the street, trampling them and setting them on fire. The place was wrecked and looted. He stood ashen, though fortunately unmolested, making no protest, outwardly serene, but inwardly how he must have suffered. His friend I. A. Richards and others were soon at his side.

I saw Charles Ogden only once more, when he came to tell me that I must return to my family. He did not blame the students, and I think he was prepared to be sacrificed, and remained, in the best sense, 'above the battle'. Precipitated by that days's doings he decided to leave Cambridge for London, and turned the magazine into an intellectual, psychological, philosophical and linguistic quarterly, advocating feminism and birth control, encouraging rationalistic and scientific contributions, until in 1921 it came to an end. The same year, with I. A. Richards, he wrote *The Meaning of Meaning* and edited several series of learned and less learned books, of which one series was The International Library of Psychology, Philosophy and Scientific Method, to which Adler, Jung and Wittgenstein contributed. With Richards and James Wood he wrote *Foundations of Aesthetics*, and with the help of Frank Ramsey translated Wittgenstein's *Logisch-Philisopsiche Athandlung* and called it *Tractatus Logico Philosophicus*. In 1926 he went to the United States and edited *Forum*, and in 1927 founded the Orthological Institute.

He is best remembered for his and Richards' collaboration in the invention of Basic English: a 'minimal English capable of serving all purposes', which many people hoped might become a universal, international language: both Churchill and Roosevelt were interested. But Basic English suffered many misfortunes, which greatly disappointed C.K.O. However, he must have discovered that the pleasure and satisfaction of working on something in which one believes counts more than any other reward, and mitigates failure—if failure it was; and failure can be more rewarding than success. He died in 1957, still hoping that Basic or some equivalent language would one day become everyone's second language, as everyone with the good of future generations at heart must hope. Charles Ogden has been called a Polymath, an Outsider, an Eccentric, a Financial Wizard, but also 'One of the few universal men of this century'.

The end of the war which had destroyed so many millions filled those who were left with sorrow, not triumph. And the few of them who are left still brood on what their lives might have been, and in losing them what the world lost. Their numbers were increased by an influenza plague which struck every country, costing at least twenty million more lives. To justify my escape from death, and from the loss of anyone close and dear, I resolved to try to make beautiful things.

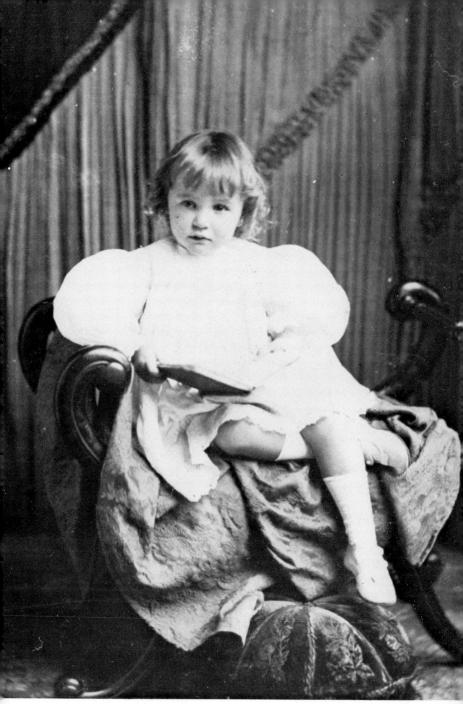

Adelaide Phillpotts in childhood

Eden and Emily
Phillpotts with Arnold
Bennett and (standing)
Mrs C. Williamson,
photographed in the
South of France

Eden Phillpotts in his
garden at Eltham

Interlude

1

In June 1919, the Treaty of Versailles was signed, incorporating the Covenant of the League of Nations, the first halting step towards loosely uniting all countries. Most people prophesied that the League would fail, and, handicapped infant that it was, it did. Yet I hugged the defective nursling to my heart with hope and joy, and thought it would achieve more than previous covenants for the future of mankind. But though this first-born possessed the will to live it lacked the vital spark.

The war had brought people from many lands to Britain, and I wanted to befriend any who strayed into my ken. One wanderer did arrive—Marie Gromoff, a Russian girl who had fled the revolution, sailing from Archangel with her family's heirlooms, now doing domestic work in a third-rate Torquay school. The headmistress forbade her to keep her treasures there and she was searching for a safe store. I asked my parents if I could keep them at Eltham until she returned to Russia, but though Nan was co-operative Mother and Father were not. Mother said: 'If you must do it *you* must look after them, but don't ask her here.' I arranged a meeting with Marie at a teashop and told her to bring her possessions and I would care for them.

Twenty-one, with a round red face and short brown hair and brown eyes, Marie was ill-clad and neglected, but her relief at finding a friend was affecting. To our tryst she brought an ungainly bundle wrapped in a tablecloth which I lugged home and hoisted to the top shelf of the airing cupboard, over which Nan presided, where it would be safe. Realising that insurance might be required, with Marie's permission Nan and I opened it, expecting to uncover gold and precious stones. Inside was a pathetic jumble of cheap metal plates and dishes, kettle, teapot, cutlery and a few other articles, valueless, except to Marie and her family, but to them precious enough to have been sent with her on that precarious voyage from Archangel that they might not fall into Bolshevik hands.

She was piteously grateful, and I felt ashamed that I could not ask her to Eltham and introduce her to my family. On her rare afternoons off duty we met in the town. Mother and Father called me quixotic, declaring that it was imprudent to get entangled with doubtful strangers and their property. Marie's fardel lay in our airing cupboard for two years until she decided to chance a return to Russia: she missed her family, her sister Zenaïda, her little brother, her beloved parents and other relatives, of whom she used nostalgically to speak. On Torre Station Nan and I reunited her with her pack and she wept for joy to have it safely in her arms again. Months later she wrote to say she had married a childhood sweetheart, and thanked us over and over again for guarding her valuables.

About this time Agatha of the dancing class, married to Colonel Christie of the air force, came home to have her baby, and two days after the birth I called to see her and hold little Rosalind. The infant's body gave mine such an indescribable thrill that I told myself: 'You must have as many of these as possible!'

I finished *Arachne*, a verse play published in 1920, and acted by pupils of a grammar school built on the site of the Shackleton's demolished house. The scenery was painted by our friend and neighbour, Sybil Heeley, daughter of the Pre-Raphaelite William Heeley, and friend of Rudyard Kipling with whom she had been brought up. During winter evenings I often walked past her house— where she lived with her mother and thirty grey Persian cats— watching constellations between the branches of trees, and felt a desperate yearning to write something worth while, such as I had promised as a thank-offering for being spared. If my boundless imaginings could have found expression I might have succeeded, but while the vision was present, I lacked the gift and my striving was in vain. However, I did write two one-act verse dramas: *Savitri the Faithful* after an episode in the *Mahabahrata*, and *Camillus and the Schoolmaster* from Plutarch's *Lives*, sometimes acted by boys' schools, both of which were published in 1923 by Gowans and Gray. And every year by invitation of J. M. Barrie's secretary, Cynthia Asquith, I wrote a story for a children's annual. I was also planning *Man: A Fable*, published by Constable in 1922, and completing a novel, *The Friend*, published in 1923 by Heinemann. Father's literary agent, Edmund Cork, a kind and generous young man, who superseded the late Hughes Massie, helped me into the publishing world.

Every morning I joined Father on his 'constitutional' to Chapel Hill, where for an hour we walked up and down a shaded alley, discussing plans for future work and work completed. What a long way he had come since 1888 when his first book was published. What a long way both he and I had still to go. He had broken off his Dartmoor series to write tales about British industries: pottery, rope-winding and paper-making, hop-growing, nursery gardening and slate quarrying. But he longed to get back to Dartmoor, and was about to add three volumes to his moorland sequence; *Miser's Money*, *Orphan*

Dinah, which he dedicated to me, and to conclude the saga with *Children of Men*. Meantime, Nan collected *One Hundred Pictures from Eden Phillpotts by L. H. Brewitt*, an excellent anthology of descriptive passages, published by Methuen. I remember with gratitude those excursions to Chapel Hill, for Father was then at his most helpful and paternal, lavish with literary encouragement. (That terraced walk in the woods, shaded by dark ilex trees, unchanged for over fifty years as I recently discovered when retracing our footsteps, reminds me that Wordsworth, whom we both revered, also favoured terraces, like the sheep-tracks between Grasmere and Rydal Mount where he composed much of his finest poetry.)

Father and I spent four or five summer weeks at Princetown, where he hired a suite in the Duchy Hotel that he might work undisturbed. After lunch we tramped to Foggintor quarry or Nun's Cross, or rested beside the Meavy brook which ran past boulders hollowed by Elizabethan tin-streamers into moulds, where they poured the molten metal and left it to set. Here in the hot sunshine Father would stretch out amidst the bracken and heather and cuddle me. I can see him now, his crooked nose, broken at school and not set, scarlet with sunburn, his light blue eyes reflecting the scenes to him so dear. I can hear the spurt of matches as he lit and relit his pipe, reclining in perfect contentment. But I felt as restless as the bounding bubbles on the river, as the trout flickering out of the water to gobble up leaping grasshoppers and other insects, and wanted to be off exploring, dreaming, roaming for miles as I roamed in London, but how much more happily in the wild. Yet I could not spoil my father's joy. These untranquil moods when my parent was tranquil made me feel guilty, not for desiring solitude but for not responding to his heart's desire, though he thought I did. I loved him with my heart and soul but not in any other way, and I used to wonder: Did he ever think 'I can't keep her for ever'—I do not think so. (Long afterwards Nan told me that when I was a schoolgirl he had told her: 'If Adelaide ever loves anyone more than me there will be trouble.')

The conscientious objectors had left Princetown Gaol, and the villagers were glad to recover their 'grey birds' as they called the convicts. One morning seven escaped and there was a great hue and cry. The desperate men, who had sunk themselves in a bog, were caught and carried through the town on stretchers—a sight which filled me with seering ruth. People were so ready to condemn. But how much were they responsible for the misdeeds which had brought them here?—a question that had troubled me for years. How much is anyone responsible for being what he is? Was incarceration, often in dreadful conditions and even in solitary confinement, one answer to crime, and to the problems of retribution, restitution, redemption? I knew that it is not.

2

Henry returned from Sheffield, his spirit broken, as scathed as many who had fought, feeling a burning culpability because the best of his generation had been killed while he was left alive—a torment nothing could assuage. Father was determined that he should 'justify his existence'; but first Mother said that she wanted to go abroad again, and he planned for us to visit Venice and the Dolomites. On the way we called at Schaffhausen to see the Falls of the Rhine, but missed the rainbow which inspired Goethe's *Theory of Colours*, of which he wrote: 'The rainbow appeared in its greatest beauty: it stood with unmoving foot in the midst of the tremendous foam and spray, which threatening forcibly to destroy it, were every moment forced to create it anew.'

Henry was staggered by the wonder of Venice, where he painted pictures which, though lacking his pre-war genius, were beautiful. While he sat sketching in the fish and fruit markets, Mother and I roved among churches and galleries, leaned over bridges, and were borne through canals by smiling gondoliers who complimented her on her beauty. One morning I rose before dawn to watch sun-up, and searching for the hotel doorway stumbled upon prone members of the staff asleep on the floor of the entrance hall, where one sleepy youth, who must have cursed me for disturbing him, unbolted the door, presuming that it was not sunrise to which I was furtively creeping but an assignation—as it was, with the Sun. In the foreglow, gondoliers began to polish their brass ornaments, and when the star rose and the water sparkled they sang. Boats laden with wood glided past. A water-rat bobbed out of the Grand Canal and stared at me. Mother and I spent the day at a Murano glass factory where a workman, who was making a chandelier for Rudyard Kipling, nipped off a piece of molten glass and fashioned it into a little dog, which I still possess.

When the time came to leave for Bozen and Innsbruck, Henry was so distressed, as if he were abandoning an adored person, that I wished we could have given up and stayed in Italy, but Mother wanted to see the Dolomites. True it is as Goethe wrote in his *Italian Journey* when quitting Rome: 'In every parting there is a latent germ of madness, and we must beware not to tend it and let it ripen in our minds.' Parting from Venice ripened in Henry's mind until it made him mad. So did he pine that afterwards on any old slip of paper he drew plans of its canals and buildings, as it might be a loved woman's countenance. Venice was the face of Henry's beloved.

Father was pleased with his pictures, but soon inquired how he proposed to earn his living, a problem which Henry evaded; so Father asked Barry Jackson if he could employ his son as a scene-painter. My heart ached as my poor brother departed on another ordeal.

3

Like most young people I was interested in sex and wanted to find out more. When Henry had gone to Birmingham I used his turret room as a study, and looking through his bookcase, concealed at the back I found some French paperbacks he must have bought in Paris, and Krafft-Ebing's *Psychopathia Sexualis*, which he probably purloined from Uncle Mac's medical books. What a remarkable world was revealed! I was immensely surprised by this unexpected knowledge. Why should something so interesting, important and fundamental be secreted and considered unmentionable? I had no idea how varied sex could be, and for the first time realised that it was, in a sense, the mainstay of our existence and continuance, the means of calling us into life. Why, then, hide it as if it were a thing of shame? This book listed other relevant works, only one of which my father possessed: Balzac's *Fille aux Yeux d'or*, which I read, and procured through book catalogues and in second-hand shops Diderot's *La Religieuse*, Gautier's *Mademoiselle de Maupin*, and Wilde's *Picture of Dorian Grey*. I kept my new knowledge to myself, knowing that my friends and relations, who never mentioned sex, might be shocked if they found out in what territories I was exploring, and intended further to explore.

Among many friends who visited our parents at this period was Israel Zangwill, author of *Children of the Ghetto*, who during the war founded the International Jewish Territorial Organisation. Friend of Theodore Herzl, with Max Nordau he promised support for a Jewish National State in Palestine, but dying in 1926 never saw the fulfilment of their dream. He gave me a copy of his play *The War God*, produced in 1911 and 1914, of which the poetess Alice Meynell wrote: 'It is a very great tragedy, full of genius.' Looking back on Father's friends, he whom I found most noble was the great American internationalist, attorney and defence counsel, Clarence Darrow, defender of Loepold and Loeb, and in 1925 of John Scopes, denounced by William Bryan for teaching evolution against the law. His wide sympathies as he asserts in his autobiography 'always went out to the weak, the suffering, and the poor'.

4

Grannie Adelaide, who had recently lost an eye through glaucoma, had gone to stay with Anglican nuns at a convent a mile from Eltham, where I sometimes joined her and stayed to Compline. She was not happy and longed to be near us so that she could see Father. I wanted her to live with us—extended families struck me as the ideal way of living—but my parents disagreed. So Mother found her a lodging in the house where Henry and I had attended Miss Poulton's kinder-garten. One afternoon I had taken her for a stroll when she had a stroke and soon became disabled. Her sisters, Alice and Georgina, with the latter's daughter, Lucy Robina, took her into their house at Lympstone near Exeter, where she rapidly grew worse. Mother and I found her stretched on a narrow bed over which a muslin curtain had been arranged to keep off the flies, her long grey hair spread on either side of her white face. She was dying. She did not know us, though her sunken eyes were looking in our direction. That night she died.

Grannie was buried next to Uncle Mac, and the graves were united under a slab of white marble and enclosed in a single kerb. After the burying I went into the dining-room at Eltham, where Father was at his desk, holding his mother's Bible, which the Aunts had brought him. He wiped tears from his eyes, the only time I saw him weep. She was the most endearing of grandmothers, who indulged us as only a grandparent can. She left me the topaz set she used to wear at Christmas, a small mourning ring in memory of her husband, and Aunt Susan's legacy.

Father was moved by the way his young cousin Lucy Robina helped to nurse her, and how she sacrificed a pair of white silk stockings to clothe his mother in her shroud—a gift which he often mentioned with feeling and which first attracted him to her.

My grandmother's death increased my restlessness and desire again to leave home, and an appropriate opportunity occurred. A friend from the Women's Service Bureau had completed the first year of a Social Science course at Bedford College, London, and suggested that I should join it for her second year and take the two years' course in one year. Mother and Father were agreeable; so once more I picked out an advertisement for a bedsitting-room, this time in Coram Street, Bloomsbury, engaged a room and prepared for a second encounter with the capital. At the last moment Mother touched me to the heart by giving me a folding Corona typewriter, which I used for the next twenty-six years.

London II

1

As the train approached Paddington its environs appeared more sordid, my project less enticing, than on previous occasions, and a feeling of apprehension prevailed. The taxi scurried along Praed Street and Euston Road, where houses still stood in ruins, and dropped me beside a shabby house at the end of Coram Street. A sluttish woman showed me to a back room which looked as if it had been empty for some time, gave me a key, and without a word closed the door. The dressing-table drawers, which smelt of stale scent, were full of dust, face-powder, soiled cotton-wool and a stub of lipstick. The mattress was stained, the carpet frayed; the lace curtains were torn and the windows had jammed, the glass was blurred with dirt. Any sensible person would have left at once. I started cleaning the drawers with a handkerchief, unpacked and arranged my books; but that unresponsive room seemed to reject me.

No meals were served so I went out for fresh air and a cup of tea. In the hall two women wearing tawdry clothes and a lot of make-up, laughing together, passed without greeting. Chilled, I wandered about the neighbourhood, past dreary squares, surrounded by rail-ings with gravel plots and soot-blackened trees, open only to house-holders, where unwilling children were dragged to play and pet dogs exercised. I noticed that on the corner of Coram Street and Hunter Street stood a double-fronted house with a glass door over which was illuminated MINERVA CLUB, and saw people at small tables in a restaurant, served by a pretty little woman wearing a velvet-topped dress and a long string of orange beads. I wished I could transfer there but knew that it would be too expensive, little guessing what an important part it was going to play in my future.

I walked round Brunswick Square, peering through uncurtained windows, a habit acquired during previous London evenings, and on the south side passed a hostel at numbers three, four and five where people were having supper in number four, then returned to Coram Street and ate a bar of chocolate Nan had given me.

After two days it dawned on me that I had landed in an inferior rooming-house for less affluent prostitutes; and though I was anxious to make friends I could not put up with my filthy room. Moreover, I felt something of an outcast, not 'one of the band'. I was passing the Brunswick Square Hostel, wondering what to do, when I decided to knock at a venture on number three, whose door was opened by a stout woman in a black wig who asked me what I wanted. 'A room, please, if you have one to spare.' She regretted that all the rooms were let. I explained my predicament but she repeated, 'I'm afraid we're full up.' I was leaving when she called after me 'Wait! There's a slip of a room you could have until there's a better one free.'

I hurried back to Coram Street, packed, and said goodbye to the slatternly woman who had been so unwelcoming. She smiled wanly saying: 'I didn't think you'd stay.' I said I was very sorry but something had turned up. 'Of course,' she sighed. I shook her hand and paid for a month, wished her good luck and she threw her arms round me with a kiss.

My refuge, an overgrown cubicle, led out of a larger room occupied by two young women in love, and the propinquity of love was heartwarming. At this hostel one had a good breakfast and supper and if in at teatime a free tea. The boarders ranged from an old woman who told fortunes at the hectic society parties and balls of those days, at which I sometimes acted unsuccessfully as her tout, to students, including two Irish girls from Dublin University who became my friends, one of whom was Kitty O'Brien with whom I spent many an evening exchanging dreams and aspirations. Though far more gifted than I and a year younger, she asked me to help her to write, so I set her tasks, and one night she brought me a promising short story called *Lagoon* about a Venetian vase. Then I knew that she would become a writer, which she did, as Kate O'Brien, and made her name with a remarkable novel, *Without My Cloak*.

I was on friendly terms with several others there, including a medical student who took me to a dissecting-room at the top of the London School of Medicine for Women, founded in the 1870s by Elizabeth Garrett Anderson. Whole corpses and parts of corpses—or cadavers as they were termed—were lying on slabs being, or about to be, dissected. The smell of formaldehyde and corruption was strong. I recall a young woman's arm and hand, the fingers curved, from which the flesh had been stripped, the nerves exposed and the bones were visible. It had not been pickled and reeked of death, yet looked in some weird way living. Why had it not been buried with her to whom it belonged? I pictured it alive and warm, shaking other hands, dandling a baby, sewing, washing up, lying inert in sleep, clasped in love. It looked so piteous.

A better room was soon forthcoming at the top of number three, its windows overlooking the Foundling Hospital, from which I watched processions of little orphans hand in hand. This Foundation, now moved to Berkhamsted, had been started by Captain Thomas Coram and incorporated by Royal Charter in 1739, 'to prevent the frequent murders of poor miserable children at their birth, and to suppress the inhuman custom of exposing newborn infants to perish in the streets'. In less than four years 15,000 babies were found in baskets hung outside the building. Handel's *Messiah* was often sung by the blind foundlings, in whom he took an interest and to whom he bequeathed a manuscript of his oratorio. Hogarth's portrait of Captain Coram and Handel's bust by Roubillac were kept there, and exhibitions of pictures were held, which in 1768 led to the founding of the Royal Academy.

2

Before the Social Science lectures began I spent several hours in the British Museum Reading-room, where I procured books, recommended by Arthur Weigall, concerning the Life and Times of Pharaoh Akhnaton, about whom Father had urged me to write a blank verse play—a splendid theme which I had promised to attempt. Opposite me one morning in the huge circular chamber sat a woman in her mid-thirties, a pile of volumes beside her, writing diligently. Her light brown hair was wound in a thick plait round her head, and when she looked up I observed that her blue eyes were singularly beautiful, and her personality unusual. Serenity streamed from her, and she so distracted me from Akhnaton that those beings of the past receded from my mind and to regain them I moved to another seat.

I was allowed to take the full course at Bedford College in one year instead of two, and fitted myself into the curriculum. Our studies included lectures on Philosophy, Psychology, Theory of Government, Social Economics, and Hygiene, with visits to hospitals, youth clubs, schools, a town hall, the Walwark Women's Welfare Centre, and a Mothers' Clinic for Constructive Birth Control opened in 1920 by Marie Stopes, besides meetings with probation officers and others engaged in welfare work. I looked forward most to the lectures on philosophy with Doctor Susan Stebbing, Reader at London University. Imagine my surprise when in walked my remarkable neighbour of the Reading-room. I felt that I already knew her. At the conclusion of her first lecture she told us that if anyone liked to send or hand in a question she would make time to answer it after the second lecture. Her expression was kindly; her brow glowed with intellect, her mouth breathed generosity, her bearing suggested tranquillity. A student told me that she was a friend of Russell and Wittgenstein, a member of the Aristotelian Society, and contributor to *Mind* and other abstruse publications; that she had published books and was now engaged on one about Logic. I soon discovered that far from being remote and superior she was modest, gentle, unsophisticated and delighted in fun.

To keep in touch I posted a question, something like: What is the *real* size of things? A man sees an object one size, a horse or cat sees it another size, a magnifying-glass can alter the apparent size. What is the actual size? What is size-in-itself? And so on—I feared Dr Stebbing would think the question too trivial, if not meaningless, but was ready for a snub if I could get to know the woman. When her second lecture was done she came and sat beside me saying: 'Did you know that your question is a philosophical one?' and proceeded to expound. That was the beginning of a close friendship which lasted for twenty-two years, until she died. Sometimes she invited me to visit her at Hampstead, where she lived with a sister and two friends who kept a girls' school; and how I enjoyed those evenings! After supper we went to her study and debated not only philosophy but the whole field of science, art and sociology, including crime and punishment which so worried me. I found it extremely helpful to discuss these questions with an understanding woman, wiser, further-sighted and more tolerant than I, who enlarged my knowledge and sympathies. She confided in me, and I marvelled at her fortitude, and acceptance of mental and physical suffering. Nobility was the keynote of her character; and besides being a profound and disinterested seeker after abstract truth and non-utilitarian knowledge, she was simple, humble, cheerful and unassuming, ingenuous and full of humour.

During visits to institutions what wretchedness I saw. In one hospital we were shown a padded cell into which violent 'lunatics', as the deranged were still described, were interned, often in strait-jackets; and one day I felt so sick that to avoid collapsing I had to leave.

Sometimes I spent the lunch interval tramping, and once, saunter-ing in Euston and watching children playing among the ruins of bombed houses, I saw a tiny boy run up the steps of a battered porch and, striking an attitude, shout to his companions: 'This a big golden castle and I'm the King!'—a scene that, I know not why, persists in my memory, like the beautiful woman on Bude cliffs, and the foaming white clouds on my last journey home from school.

3

My father had told Sybil Thorndike that I was in London, and several times she and her husband invited me to sup in Chelsea with the family. On my first visit she was teaching her younger daughter Anne the piano, while the elder boy John jumped in on a pogo-stick. A feeling of utter delight suffused me: here was my ideal family, even to the presence of Sybil's mother, who lived with them. One evening Sybil took me to see her act in Grand Guignol: she could play any part with distinction, from farce to *Medea* and Shaw's *St Joan*.

On the third anniversary of Armistice Day I was walking down

Southampton Row when at 11 a.m. the two-minutes' silence began, so eerie, there in the middle of silent, frozen London, that I shivered with a cold sweat, as thousands of us, all traffic halted, in a silent world, recalled the dead. Had that war really been the 'war to end war'? I doubted it.

One evening Kitty O'Brien asked me to join her and her fiancé John at a club for homosexual men in Soho, to meet a young musician who had been obliged to sell his violin; and knowing that I had one at home she asked me if I would lend it to him until he could afford a new one. She and I were the only women at the club but everyone was friendly and bought us drinks. I promised John's friend to send for my violin and he was welcome to play it until he could buy another. He promised to return it then. A long time later I asked Kate O'Brien to enquire about it, but she had lost touch with the club and did not wish to resume it. I was sad to lose that last link with Uncle Cecil, who had smiled so bewitchingly as he bade me a first and last farewell. Farewell now to his violin—I wonder what became of it.

I met many other unusual people, and felt concern about the women prostitutes who traversed the Bloomsbury streets. I recall one in her fifties who seemed so haggard, hollow-cheeked and unhappy and must be finding it hard to make a living that I wanted to make friends with her and try to help. Alas, I never did so—one of many craven withdrawals from people which I regret. My often harrowing experiences of those days, sometimes into the lower depths, or 'underworld' as some called it, to be found in all great cities, made me understand the strange allure which those of us beyond good and evil—outcasts, convicts, criminals, drug addicts, drunkards, victims and perpetrators of violence, who, beaten and rejected, in their turn reject and rebuff all proffered help and care, preferring to live and die alone in some derelict den or on the streets—the hopeless, forlorn, rootless, so-called 'inadequates' and 'down-and-outs', often handicapped mentally and physically who through no fault of theirs have become the flotsam of huge centres of population—the strange allure these have for artists, both small and great, like Dickens and Dostoevsky, Baudelaire, Hugo and Genet, Turner and Goya, to mention a few. 'Beyond Good and Evil'—words that call up Nietzsche, whose works, and all Dostoevsky's, I read at this time. But the 'real thing', unmetamorphosed by the magic and glory of art, was often excruciating in its horror and misery.

During this year I met two worthy women: Mrs Holyoake Marsh, daughter of George Jacob Holyoake the Co-operative pioneer and free-thinker, imprisoned for blasphemy; and the living free-thinker, Mrs Bradlaugh Bonner, daughter of Charles Bradlaugh the fighter for freedom of thought and expression who won the right to make an affirmation without taking the oath—two old ladies who in their widowhood seemed very moss-grown and worn—quite unlike another old lady, still good-looking and lively, called the Baroness von Hutten, whom I met, and did not know whether to feel flattered or vexed when her first words to me were: 'You have the face of an abbess!'   Ethel Herdman took me to tea with Wilfred and Alice Meynell, he a friendly man of seventy, she, rare poet and essayist, whose work had been praised by George Eliot, and Ruskin, Browning, Rossetti and Meredith, so unsubstantial-looking as to seem unearthly, halfway to heaven—as indeed she was. She died the following year. For nearly half a century these twain had been married—'fifty years of heaven on earth', as Wilfred described their union. Of their seven gifted children only Viola was there that day, and I recall no word that was spoken, and never suspected that Ethel's friendship with the Meynells was going to influence my whole future life.

I was invited to spend a weekend at Max Gate with the Thomas Hardys. Some mistake about the time of arrival at Dorchester occurred and no one met me, so I started trudging along the Wareham road, lugging a suitcase of books my father was sending to Hardy, when a workman on his way home overtook me and offered to carry it. 'Ah,' he said hearing where I was bound, 'you'll be the new servant, then. They're always changing.' Touched and amused I did not disillusion him and at the gate he wished me luck and said goodbye.

The creeper-covered dwelling, called after an old tollhouse, had been designed by Hardy, who lived in it on and off until his death. He felt a strong attachment to plants and animals, and soon after my arrival we explored every corner of the shadowed garden, Florence Hardy carrying a kitten called Cobweb, Wessex the rough-haired terrier gambolling round. I remember nothing of the conversation during the next few days, but recollect Thomas telling me how when a child his mother used to give him a penny for a bun, and he found it difficult to decide whether to buy one big penny bun, or two smaller halfpenny buns, usually choosing two for a halfpenny each because two seemed to contain more substance than one. He was simple and kind, but one felt that underneath his benign exterior he was extremely complicated and, like my father, full of contradictions. His parsimonious and morbid sides were not evident on his countenance which was calm, distinguished, and sometimes humorous. Outwardly Florence was quiet and sad, her expression melancholy in repose. To Mother, whom she deeply loved, and to me she was a loyal friend. During one of their visits to Eltham, she told Mother how passionately she had wanted children, and that had she not been driven into marrying Thomas, she might not have done so, hoping to meet someone young enough to give her a family.

Many years later Miss Ellen Titterington, parlour-maid at the time of my visit, wrote in her *Afterthoughts of Max Gate*: 'Once we had the daughter of Eden Phillpotts the writer staying, and it was a pleasure to see the old and young taking an interest in each other. Mr Hardy seemed to come out of his shell when talking to younger women as if a light was suddenly breaking through and he could see them in one of his books . . . About Miss Phillpotts, when she was staying Hardy's wireless broke down, and it was fun to see her and Hardy crawling on the floor, testing the wires, to see if they could get it to go, Hardy giving her useless advice and laughing like a boy.' Florence kept in touch with me until she died.

4

Home for the vacations I renewed the fraternal bond which since babyhood had been so strong. Unable to fit into screen-painting at the Repertory Theatre, Henry had returned to Eltham, and Father, defeated in that and several other projects for his dear but difficult son, gave up trying, and wished him to pursue his art at home in peace. Sharland chopped down our old fig tree which had outgrown its cage, and in its place a studio was erected. Henry still brooded over the war, unable, as Father was able, to wipe out the past and feel neither remorse nor regret. His original spark and supreme gift, the rare power to express a unique vision, never returned. Yet I still hoped it might revive, and was so desperately anxious for him to succeed that when I returned to London I hawked examples of his work round all the artists' agencies, studios, and exhibition-rooms, climbing to mysterious lairs high and low where I tried to persuade people, some very weird, to use them, if only as greetings cards. A few said they liked his work but none would exhibit it or order copies. At last I had exhausted every possibility and, cruelly disappointed, had to tell Henry I had failed. He said he was not surprised and had expected it. Long ago he had made up his mind that he was a hopeless failure.

5

One morning in the summer of 1922 Mother was shopping on Torquay Strand when who should come towards her but Arnold Bennett. His yacht, the *Marie Marguerite*, was anchored in the port. Overjoyed, Mother begged him to dine with us and hurried home to prepare Father for the meeting. How thrilled we were! When he arrived he hugged us, exclaiming at Mother's enduring beauty, and praising Father's work; and I realised how simple-hearted and benevolent he was. He invited me to lunch alone with him on the yacht, and was extremely sympathetic and helpful, as with all striving youth. Father had given him my *Man: A Fable*, recently published, and after useful criticism of the gentlest sort, he urged me to improve my 'style'. I was never one to search for the right word, the perfect phrase, the unimprovable sentence, or to ponder over a paragraph. He kept pushing the conversation away from himself and asked me about my ambitions—taking them more seriously than I did, for I put work last and people first. When the time came to go home he said: 'Come and see me next time you're in London. And don't worry about anything. *You'll be all right!*' I felt a sudden premonition, that *he* would not be all right. Before continuing his voyage he took Mother to an old curiosity shop and bought her a gold and amethyst seal and a beautiful millefiori paperweight under whose crystal dome clustered purple flowers with dewdrop centres, a bauble that delighted her. But what pleased her more were his parting words: 'Your household runs without motion.'

After this dramatic reconciliation, Arnold, who had recently published *Riceyman Steps*, often came to stay, and collaborated with Father in a comic operetta, set in Italy, called *The Bandits*, for which E.P. supplied the plot. He told Father that he wished he could invent plots 'as you do. But God in his wisdom has decided otherwise!' Though they completed *The Bandits* and Frederic Austin composed the music, it was never produced. As of old, Arnold confided his problems to our parents, including his love for the actress Dorothy Cheston whom he wanted to marry. But his Catholic wife refused to divorce him. The following summer he sailed into Torquay with Dorothy, and brought her to Eltham to dine. The night was balmy. The pretty young woman wore a simple black dress, and when Father picked her a truss of pale yellow rhododendron the colour of her hair, she tucked it into her shoulder band. This return into their lives of a long lost friend gladdened our parents.

6

During my last term at Bedford College an unexpected invitation reached me from Father's second cousin, Bertha Phillpotts, then Mistress of Girton College, Cambridge, a scholar and expert on Icelandic literature and folklore about which she had written articles, asking me to come and live there, not as a student but to write in peaceful surroundings and stay as long as I liked. Father clamoured for me to go, but, grappled to London, and planning to write a novel about it, to his extreme vexation I declined. Looking back, however, I wish I had met Cousin Bertha. Shortly afterwards she married Professor Newell, an astronomer, and eighteen months later died.

I planned to return to London in the autumn of 1924 and devote my time to writing: with Grannie's bequest I could manage without paid work. I wrote to the Minerva Club to ask if they had a vacant room and received the reply: 'Come whenever you like.'

London III. Divided Years

1

In the spring of 1924 I was invited to join a poet and his friends in
Sark, and crossed at midnight from Plymouth Barbican in a little
collier called the *Miranda* whose crew of four offered me a bunk. By
the time I reached Guernsey I was grey with coal-dust and bitten all
over by fleas, but in those days such things did not matter. So magical
was Sark that I abandoned my companions and went off alone to
explore the deep caverns, natural arches, stacks covered with sea-
birds, to watch gannets plunging into the waves, seals playing, and the
waving wild flowers on the cliffs, feeling as wild as they, little guessing
that many years hence I should return to this blessed isle accompanied
by the one person who would share my transports and augment them,
and from whom I should never want to escape to even a moment's
solitude.

After that joyous adventure Mother and I went to Spain, then
almost a feudal country, where we spent hours in the sublime Prado
Gallery, gazing at paintings by Velasquez and Goya. To see El Greco's
Burial of Count Orgaz at Toledo we engaged a car whose driver drove
so frantically through the small villages, raising dust and scaring the
peasants, that they shouted curses and threw stones. Having often
read *Don Quixote* I felt at home in that austere countryside as if I had
been there before. In Burgos Cathedral we paused at the entrance to a
side chapel where a family party was gathered round the font for a
baby's baptism, and Mother, deeply moved, whispered: 'I wonder
what will become of that infant?' I began to feel unaccountably
depressed as if trouble hung over us, and it did. We had reached
Seville, the Guadalquivir flowing past, when Mother collapsed with a
severe gastric attack caused we thought, mistakenly, by the oily dishes
served at every meal. I was about to summon a doctor when she
recovered sufficiently for us to continue to Granada, where we came
upon three little barefoot brothers carrying a baby's coffin to be
buried in the cemetery's public trench. A fat old priest smoking a
cigarette mumbled over the box and told the children to drop it into
the ditch and shovel on the earth. When they had done so the smallest
planted a home-made wooden cross on the mound. Again much
moved, Mother asked who they had lost—their only sister.

2

I had planned to spend half every year in London, half at home, so that I could join Father on the Moor, Mother abroad, and sit in her workroom with Nan. She had been stone deaf in one ear since a girlhood attack of typhoid fever, and now her other ear was failing and she used an ear trumpet. An aurist warned her that she would soon be quite deaf, so to save her strain I wrote to her on letter-pads. Her sight, too, was deteriorating and stronger glasses could no longer improve her vision. As usual she came to see me off to London. My room at the Minerva Club overlooked a house on the corner of Brunswick Square—the very house, as I discovered long afterwards, where eight years later a young man from Massachusetts who had left home because he disliked the American way of life would, after a stormy voyage in an old trader, find an attic lodging—the man I was going to marry. It was strange how from this time onward our paths kept as it were crossing, before we coincided in the same place at the same moment. But now someone quite different awaited me.

In the Club restaurant the attractive young woman I had seen serving two years earlier brought me a menu. Small and plump, with wide-apart blue eyes, long hair coiled in thick braids over her ears, and clear pink cheeks, her personality, gentle and firm, humorous and tender, kind yet determined, appealed to me. After the meal she knocked on my door and asked: 'Would you like a cup of coffee?' 'If you will have one with me, yes.' She was Gertrude Stewart, aged thirty-six, and many years earlier had worked for Annie Kenny, the Oldham cotton-mill girl who played a dashing part in the suffragette movement. The only dashing thing Miss Stewart had done, obeying orders, was to hurl a brick through the Home Office window and await arrest. Later she became the devoted companion of a man much older than herself who could not marry her because he had an invalid wife. Her relationship with him had been over for some time. Her widowed mother and a married sister and brother lived in Bristol, another sister and family in Florida, to all of whom she was devoted. I called her Jan. Before a week passed she and I had become friends, and after Christmas, which I spent at home, decided to share a flat. At last, I thought, my father need not dread a marriage.

Meanwhile I made other new friends and was induced to join the Pen Club, but not being gregarious or intellectual, after the first Club dinner I resigned. I began work on a light novel called *Lodgers in London*, published in 1925 by Thornton Butterworth. I had almost given up the theatre, but did go with Arnold Bennett to the Court Theatre for the first night of Father's bucolic comedy, *The Farmer's Wife*, which Barry Jackson hoped would succeed in London—a hundred to one chance. Arnold clapped gallantly, and sent Father an encouraging telegram; but for three weeks the play languished, and had not Barry Jackson kept it going at his own expense, with cunning advertisements on buses, Underground trains and in the Press, it would have failed. Gradually it picked up and became a stunning success which ran for 1,329 performances. As my father wrote to our Uncle Arthur, Mother's brother: 'It is amusing to have succeeded in the theatre at the thirteenth attempt. I have had twelve London productions—all failures before this play was produced. So much for No 13!'

Now Father suggested that I should collaborate with him, in another country comedy, whose plot he had invented, and though I felt incompetent I agreed to try. Writing to and fro, Father did all the vital work while I contributed two characters, some construction, action and dialogue. I would write a scene and send it to him, and he would greatly improve it and send it back for revision; but my father's work needed no revision. Thus we composed *Yellow Sands*, which Barry Jackson accepted.

3

My parents were glad that I had found a comrade, and in the summer of 1925 invited Jan to spend part of her holiday at Eltham, followed by a week with me at Two Bridges on Dartmoor, where I had stayed with friends two or three times before. They admired her strength of character and sense of humour, and hoped our friendship would thrive. Jan loved the Moor as I did and we tramped to Wistman's Wood, and Crow Tor on whose summit still flourished a clump of bluebells which feature in Father's book *The River*. (How should I guess in what strange circumstances this excursion would be repeated?)

I spent part of the summer writing *Akhnaton*, published in 1926 by Thornton Butterworth, and planned a third novel, about a Bohemian peasant boy, suggested by the life, which Father had given me, of the Jugoslav sculptor, Ivan Mestrovic. When Mother told me that she and I were going to Austria, Hungary and Czechoslovakia I decided to collect local colour for my tale. Ethel Herdman gave me an introduction to two Czech students living in Prague, who took me into the beautiful Bohemian countryside, where we visited castles, hills and vales, and at my wish entered a peasant's cottage, which I described as the birthplace of my hero, Tomek the Sculptor.

In Vienna I noticed that Mother was unusually quiet and disinclined for sightseeing. She explained her tiredness by ageing—she was sixty—but my forebodings grew. Knowing that I was amassing material for a book she insisted on my going out while she rested. So I tramped hither and thither, filling notebooks, but felt guilty about leaving her, and when we reached the glowing double city of Budapest I left her no more. In Salzburg she enjoyed a Mozart concert—he was

Father's favourite composer—but soon after we reached Munich she collapsed with high fever, with the same symptoms but far worse which laid her low in Spain, and had to stay in bed. I was going to ask the manager of the hotel to send for a doctor when she *implored* me to wait, insisting that it was only a bad bilious attack, to which she was subject, and would pass; but the manager, fearing that she might be infectious, told me she must see a physician or leave—a threat which effected a temporary improvement. She asked me to pack and arrange to catch the first express to Paris. Somehow I got her to the station and into the train, where I had engaged a single compartment, and procured champagne, the only thing she fancied or could keep down. We reached Paris, Calais, crossed the Channel, arrived in London, and at last home. Trying to remember that hideous journey, its details are lost and I have only a blurred recollection of terror that she would die.

Dr Lacey, our local medical man, was sent for and it seemed an age before he finished his examination and took our father into the study to report. Our mother had long-standing cancer of the uterus. She must have radium treatment, which might or might not cure. If not, an operation would be necessary. 'We must hope,' Father said. 'We must hope.' Mother was cheerful and smiling: she was not told that she had a malignant tumour. 'Don't worry,' she said. 'I'm going to be all right.' I made myself believe it. Mr Black, a specialist, came from London to consult with our doctor, and the radium treatment began. To our joy Mother revived. Her appetite returned and she gained weight. She had a strong will to get well which, Dr Lacey said, was the best way to do so.

I had given up the idea of going back to London, where Jan had taken a furnished flat in an apartment block near Sloane Square. Through Barry Jackson she had obtained a well-paid post as secretary to Golding Bright, a theatrical agent, with offices in Leicester Square. I knew that if Mother died I should look after Father and Henry. However, they all convinced me that she was going to recover, and Mother herself urged me to go. Believing them I went, half-heartedly, ready at any moment to return.

Holbein House was a dreary old pile behind a thicket of more modern buildings. Our flat, with small living-room, a bedroom each, and kitchenette, was approached up several flights of broad concrete steps. A friend described it as 'something out of Dostoevsky', and dimlit by night it looked as if from the menacing shadows might at any moment materialise Raskolnikov or the ghost of Alyona Ivanovna, the murdered pawnbroker. While Jan was at the office I wrote *Tomek the Sculptor*, which was published in 1927 by Thornton Butterworth. It was my best work, most deeply felt, and I excelled it only a few times afterwards. I still hoped eventually to write poetry. In December I

caught influenza and had a rough ride. Lying awake at night watching
the shadow of an oil heater thrown on the ceiling, I confused it with
the fireguard's shadow in our Eltham nursery, Nan coming in with a
drink. Now from next door came Jan, who helped me to recover
sufficiently to go home for Christmas.

I found Mother fairly well, but sensed that something besides her
illness was troubling her and soon discovered what it was.

4

As child and girl I had been deeply distressed by strife in our family,
usually caused by rivalry and jealousy between Mother and Grannie
Adelaide over Father, and Father's infidelities. Father himself was
never jealous and only wanted peace to get on with his work. When I
was older Mother explained that he had always needed other women
in his life—he was very attractive to women—and he himself told
me that all artists, especially writers of fiction and drama, must gather
as much knowledge as possible about the other sex. I accepted this,
unwillingly, because I wanted my parents to love only each other. But
now that I was mature I realised that nothing was more natural than
that at this time of anguish over Mother's illness, and uncertainty
about the future, he should fall passionately in love with his young
cousin, Lucy Robina, not only because she had been kind to his
mother on her deathbed, but because he desperately needed a
respite—to be able to get away sometimes from the agony at home. To
understand all, however, is not to forgive all, but I tried, and never
ceased to love and pity my father, as well as my mother. Her fortitude
in the face of what might be mortal illness, though the doctor kept up
our hopes, and her courage in accepting this personal anguish, was
truly stoical. But she knew as I did how Father was suffering on her
account, and that he needed an outlet, and deserved compassion. She
must also have known that she meant more to him than anyone else.

About this time Father saved her from what might have been a
terrible accident. She was standing beside an unguarded radiator
when her dressing-gown brushed against it and caught fire. She called
out and Father from his room next door rushed in and put out the
flames. Neither was hurt.

5

That summer my parents arranged for Jan and me to spend her
fortnight's holiday in Cornwall and we went to Porthleven, between
the Lizard and Penzance, to lodge in a fisherman's cottage on the
western cliff with Mrs Broad and her daughter Bessie, who became
lifelong friends. Below towered rocks immersed at high tide so that
from the windows one seemed to be in a ship. Our rooms were filled
with the music of the waters and at night one could tell the position of

the tide. Porthleven was a centre of the pilchard fishery, with a shipyard where luggers were built, their nets and sails made in lofts on the village's eastern wing. Every weekday evening except Saturday twenty or more drifters left the harbour for grounds in and beyond Mounts Bay. Every dawn they chugged back in the foreglow, if lucky holds spilling with pilchards, which were carted to cellars to be cured and eventually packed in hogsheads and exported to Naples, where the toast was: 'Long life to the Pope and death to thousands!' By day crabbers and lobster-boats fished the nearer seas. Every afternoon Bessie Broad fried pilchards or dressed a crab for our tea.

One side of the clifftop cottages spread towards the Lizard, the other towards Newlyn and Penzance. Western cliffs were built of granite, eastern cliffs of limestone, and those at Kynance near Mullion of that purple, green and crimson marble called serpentine, whereof the steps in Rabelais' delectable Thélème Abbey, designed by Gargantua, were constructed, its galleries 'painted with ancient histories and descriptions of the world', its only rule *Fay ce que Voudras*: Do as thou wilt. We did as we willed.

At low tide we climbed over the rocks to peer into pools left by receding waves, homes of blennies, opaline sea-anemones, red and green weeds, and one fluorescent weed which, colonised by bryozoa floating their tentacles to catch plankton, ignited with cold blue fire. Along the horizon passed ships bound for world ports; among them once a full-rigged vessel which Henry, who was staying with us, identified as the *Archibald Russell*, last of the four-masted sailing ships used for deep water trading to South America and Australia.

One morning the aviator Alan Cobham, who had flown from Cairo to the Cape, arrived in a small Avro plane, advertising five-minute joy-rides over the sea, and as nobody else would venture we volunteered to make the first flight. The open plane rose and dived and rocked over the waves, and so windy was it in the cockpit that one's head felt as if it would be blown off. Many an afternoon we ran down the hill to board a charabanc bound for coastal trips, including one round Land's End to St Ives. The drive I preferred ascended Tregonning Hill from whose summit appeared the whole of South Cornwall's wild interior, the Channel, and on clear days the Scilly Isles. We often followed a coastal footpath to Kynance and the Lizard, passing Looe Pool, or another track beyond the Wrestling Field to Rinsey Head with its ruined mine chimney beside a grotesque granite pile resembling a camel turned to stone.

This timeless time ended though its lustre abides till today; and had not Mother been ill, that fortnight would have been incomparably happy; but though I suspected it not, for me cloudless joy was never to recur.

6

On November 3rd, the day before Father's sixty-fourth birthday, our play *Yellow Sands* was produced at London's Haymarket Theatre. I spent the first night in Torquay but Jan attended and telegraphed that it was a success. It ran for a year. Father generously invested half the proceeds in War Loan for me, which provided a small income, and to avoid tax a part of the rest in my name, asking me to send him the dividends for his lifetime, which I did, but to consider the capital my own. (I mention this for a purpose later to be disclosed.)

I had decided not to return to London, but Mother implored me to go, and the doctor said: 'If you go it will be a sign she is better. If you don't she will think she is worse, which is not true. She is holding her own.' He promised to send for me if she did relapse, so I went, unwillingly. For our second home Jan had rented four rooms on the top floors of a house in Gloucester Street, Victoria, which she furnished with odds and ends from street markets. Each of us had an attic room above a general living-room and kitchen, with a bathroom shared with other tenants on the floor beneath—there were several other tenants, some very strange, among them nudists.

The casts of *Yellow Sands* and *The Farmer's Wife* often came to see us, including Cedric Hardwicke and Ralph Richardson whose careers were founded on Father's plays. Jan left Golding Bright to work for Barry Jackson, and I began a new novel, *A Marriage*, published in 1928 by Thornton Butterworth. A publication called *John O' London's Weekly* was running a series of articles about young authors, with reproductions of their portraits in charcoal by Kathleen Shackleton, sister of Ernest, who had died in 1922 on the threshold of Antarctica. When *Tomek the Sculptor* was published I was chosen as a subject and told to go to Miss Shackleton's studio. I remember a tall, dark woman wearing a long tunic and beads, who spoke of her adored brother as if he were still alive, and I realised that she could not accept his death and thought he would come home.

Before I returned to Torquay, Nan came to stay. She had been ill, and as the doctor could find nothing organically wrong he enquired if she had had a shock. She had, but did not divulge it until I insisted that she tell me. Her devotion to our father had endured for over thirty years, but what he felt for her I do not know and never asked. At some time, I now learned, he had promised that should he ever be left a widower he would marry her, and her present illness originated in the shock of realising that it was Robina he would be marrying. She was too good-hearted to blame our father, and she certainly never wanted our mother to die. This revelation quite amazed me. I tried to console her and restore her to health; and with her usual resilience and absence of self-pity she recovered, so buoyant was she, so ready to laugh, not least at herself. She liked to hear the muffin man ringing his bell and would lean out of the window and call 'Don't go away! I'm coming down!' and would fly downstairs to buy a pile of crumpets which she toasted and spread thickly for tea. And she would throw down money to the organ-grinder who still played in London streets.

Twice at this period I visited Arnold Bennett at his magnificent house, decorated in the Victorian style. The first time, he had invited to lunch a young man called Albert Rutherston, and after the meal showed us his manuscript of *The Old Wives' Tale*, printed in his delicate caligraphy without one alteration or erasure. The second time, Dorothy came in carrying their baby daughter Virginia whom she placed on a rug, where she howled with woe. I longed to pick her up and cuddle her but the stupid policy then was to leave infants to cry uncomforted. Again I experienced a strong portent, augmented by the wailing child, that some doom hung over him. Father had sent him *Akhnaton*, and of it wrote: 'It has that fundamental nobility which I found in the previous play of yours I read . . . I like the verse less than the play itself . . . I would sooner have had it all in prose . . . Well, no! I think the last scene and the epilogue are better as they are . . . You previously had the gift of great ideas for drama. Then you acquired technique in construction. What I now desire in you, sweet niece, is a more distinguished style. Yes. I do. Damn it, you have the decency to tell me what you really think of my work; so why shouldn't I have the decency to tell you what I really think of yours?' With his usual kindness he encouraged and wished me well and I felt a warm gratitude.

7

For our last London home Jan took an unfurnished self-contained flat at the top of Elm Park Mansions in Park Walk, the link between Fulham Road and King's Road, Chelsea, then a quiet alley containing coach-builders' and organ-builders' yards. The block had no lifts so when I came to stay I unpacked at the bottom and carried everything up eighty-one steps. Coal-fires had not yet been banned, and how the weekly coal-heaver managed uncomplainingly to haul our hundredweight to the summit, and the postman and milkman to call every day, I do not know. The sitting-room and bedrooms overlooked Chelsea to the north and east; the spare room, dining-room and kitchen faced south-west, from whose windows we watched smoky sunsets glorifying the London skies. To this home I came for short periods throughout the winter, prepared at any moment to leave for good. Mother had given us surplus silver spoons and forks, and a cat's-whisker and crystal radio set. A young woman in the neighbourhood had offered to 'do' for us, and it was not long before she stole the silver. Then, while I was at Torquay and Jan at work, the flat was burgled and she lost the radio set, her sewing-machine, a pearl and turquoise necklace, electric iron and other objects; so we decided to get insured and 'do' for ourselves. I wrote *The Atoning Years*, about Italy, to be dedicated to Mother, who so loved that land; and at Father's wish I turned *Yellow Sands* into a novel, and started another dramatic collaboration with him called *The Good Old Days*. Sometimes I wearied of writing and ran down to the Thames or explored the northern neighbourhood, and one afternoon in the maze of roads beyond Fulham I found myself in a quiet little village street with cottages, a dogcart, a girl on horseback and a bicyclist, cats strolling, and glimpses of comfortable people beside lace curtains, leaning on geranium windowsills. Could this be London? I lingered, to convince myself that it was not a fantasy. But when, some days later, I took Jan to see it, the place had vanished, and I never found it again.

Home for Christmas, I found Mother changed and felt a dreadful certainty that, whatever the doctor said, she was not going to recover. That year of 1927 Father had been revising his Dartmoor novels, shortening descriptive passages, which had been criticised for protraction, prior to Macmillans' publication of the Widecombe Edition, in twenty volumes, beginning with *Children of the Mist* and concluding with *Children of Men*. Each book was bound in pale green and cream, with a frontispiece by Father's friend, Cecil Hunt R.W.S., and there was a Preface by Arnold Bennett to volume 1.

8

Nineteen hundred and twenty-eight was one of those years which stand out in memory and never fade. The previous autumn Florence Hardy, knowing that Mother's life was uncertain, had wanted to visit her for a day, yet, according to what she told Mother, Thomas said they could not afford a car to take her. I assume he did not want to be left alone; but Father was very upset and Mother sad. I knew that great people are often not balanced like the rest of us and must not be judged like ourselves. In youth, however, at one's most idealistic—and what a chasm exists between the ideal and the real—one may believe as I once did that sublime art is created by noble individuals with exalted characters, until, disillusioned, one realises that while some great artists are paragons of excellence, many are petty, envious, arrogant, even criminal. Yet one also perceived that most of these exceptionally gifted people are fundamentally as human and humane as those without towering talents. And even if some do appear to be monsters, their shortcomings should be forgiven, for without them and their works the world would be a more arid place; and their flaws bring them closer to those who, lacking achievements, are also flawed.

Hardy, who died in January, had willed to be buried in Stinsford Churchyard; but Florence was bulldozed into agreeing that his body should be mutilated, the heart extracted and buried in Stinsford, the rest cremated and immured in Westminster Abbey. She feebly protested but was overruled by James Barrie, Bernard Shaw and others who declared that the 'world' expected at least part of him to be enshrined at Westminster. The fact that he was not a Christian and had left other directions did not matter to these heartless people, who professed to revere him. My father, with many others, was horrified at this sacrilege and protested, but went unheeded. Hardy, whose pallbearers were Kipling and Galsworthy, Housman and Shaw, Barrie and Edmund Gosse, had often disavowed being labelled a pessimist and considered it unfair, because, while pitying man's plight, he believed in man's spirit and dignity, and that the world is capable of improvement: 'If way to the Better there be, it exacts a full look at the Worst.'

Father and Hardy were surface friendly but inwardly incompatible; and Father loathed being called his disciple, and used to say that while he said 'Yea' to life, Hardy said 'Nay' and thought it was better not to be born than born. But he acknowledged Hardy's genius. One likes to dwell on a person's good qualities after he dies; and I recall his fondness for animals, and how he wrote of himself in the poem *Afterwards*: 'One may say, "He strove that such innocent creatures should come to no harm, / But he could do little for them: and now he is gone"'.

9

My mother grew suddenly worse, so Mr Black decided that there must be a surgical examination and engaged a room in a London nursing home, to which I brought her. On the night after the operation he told me that he had done his best but the disease was too widespread for the growth to be removed. 'Take her home,' he said. 'She may live for some weeks, even months, her heart is so strong. Make her life as happy as possible. She herself does not know.' But she did know, though for our sakes she pretended that all was going well. One day I saw her looking in the mirror at the ruins of her beauty, so forlorn, though her pride was not broken, and I realised how wonderfully brave she had always been. Father was dreadfully upset, and meaning well, fretted her with feverish attention, and bought her a long opal necklace, though she was long past wanting gems. That she might be able to see the doctor night or day, he gave Dr Lacey two thousand pounds towards the cost of an empty villa opposite Eltham. And no doctor could have been more devoted.

I nursed my mother, but she soon needed professional care, and every day Sister Violet came to give her treatment, a gentle, sympathetic woman to whom she was affectionately grateful. To simplify the nurse's duties, Mother asked Nan to give up her small bedroom and live in a local boarding-house.

The rest of my mother's life was a long-drawn-out tragedy, which she faced with extraordinary nobility. Fortunately, she had no physical pain, though increasing weakness, which is almost as bad; but her mental suffering was cruel. A time came when she could no longer go downstairs and kept to her bedroom. She did not see Father again—they must have already said their farewells. In the last week of her life, to my infinite thankfulness, she attained a sublime serenity, freeing herself from and renouncing her excruciating earthly sorrows, to face death with peace. Henry, who would miss her most, sat in the room for hours, gazing out of the window from which as a child he watched the Brixham trawlers, I the little gazebo on the cliff. Mother had made us all promise not to be with her when she was dying or to see her after she was dead: she wanted us to remember her as she was in life. So we respected her wish.

It was July 28th. I woke suddenly at 3 a.m. as if summoned and went to Mother's room. Sister Violet, who was sitting up with her, whispered, 'It won't be long' and left us. Mother was awake and to my astonishment her cheeks were full and rosy, her eyes smiling and clear. She looked like a beautiful young woman. She took my hand and said: 'I'm so glad you were a girl! It's snowing, isn't it?' It was a warm summery night but her hand was cold. She closed her eyes and imperceptibly the look of youth and health faded. I kissed her and left. Soon afterwards the Sister told me that her death had been 'like peace'.

I wanted to accompany her to the Crematorium at Woking, but Father said he needed me. When the urn came back he planned for Henry and me to drive with it to Dartmoor and lay her dust on Pew Tor. The car stopped about a mile from the tor and we carried the urn to a grassy spot beneath the boulders and spread the ashes there. Little I knew that I should not stand there again for twenty-three years, and then with my husband.

Father was disturbed and sad, but his advice and practice were not to dwell on the death of a beloved or on happy times never to return. 'To feel regret and remorse is futile.' He had no fear of death or belief in an afterlife. Immediately after Mother's death, however, he composed a series of sonnets called *For Remembrance* twenty-five copies of which were privately printed, to express his devotion and admiration and commemorate the joys of their union. He gave the first three copies to Henry, Jan and me, others to Nan, Arnold Bennett, Mother's family and friends. He did not want Robina to know about them, so entrusted to me the copies that were not given away; and as no one is now left to be hurt I print them here. Of all his loves, and he had many and was loved by many, though Mother and he suffered troubles and sorrows, she was his dearest and closest love.

EMILY PHILLPOTTS
1864–1928

"A silent and loving woman is a gift of the Lord; and there is
nothing so much worth as a mind well instructed.

"A shame-faced and faithful woman is a double grace and her
continent mind cannot be valued.

"As the sun when it ariseth in the high heaven; so is the beauty of a good
wife in the ordering of her house."

Ecclesiasticus

I

When lovers part 'tis not the dead who know
The pang of death in their undreaming sleep,
But they who wake and wake and wake and keep
Account with memory; they who still must go
On the old road bereft, and delve and sow,
Fend for the harvest, bend the back and reap,
With second self afar and lying low,
While still they plod familiar path and steep;
   Where beacons fade and ancient watch-fires pale
   To pallor dim that cannot show the way
   Till heart of man doth either fight or fail
   For breath of hope, while steadfast truth says 'Nay'.
   Pity all spirits called to countervail
   The heavy-laden morn of such a day.

II

The little things are agony; the great
Stun and destroy all present power to feel;
But trifles stab the touch, the sight, and steal
To the live quick of Love. Such is our strait
That loss throws open many a guarded gate
Into the heart; remembrance knows to deal
Small stroke on stroke till, torn and violate,
We cry the tented wounds can never heal.
   Such precious thorns will pierce in sudden wise
   And prick our poor pretences, bid to cease
   The mastery and calm, where they surprise
   Our fancied strength; the sealed-up tear release;
   Torture our thoughts and dreams, our hands and eyes—
   Their rack half joy, half woe, all death to peace.

III

And tidings, nought to solitary soul,
Will make the salt of two; but when there's none
To share the little interests daily won,
Their savour perishes; they lack a goal;
Significance and poignancy are stole;
The deed that's done, the deed that's left undone,

Alike fall short of any perfect whole.
Who tends a garden banished from the sun?
   For sense of time we may not share again
   As it was shared, can never fade and die,
   But leaves its own eternal, wistful pain;
   Though mightier grief and suffering pass by,
   A gleam of yore shall lingering remain
   To shadow life and breed the secret sigh.

IV

Yet never can be love annihilate
Where living auræ of the love remain
And still remembrance sings her steadfast strain,
Linking the later to the olden state
With dear tradition; for a vanished mate
May light the ancient home and haply reign,
A part of destiny and future fate,
To the last hope and fear and loss and gain.
   By love they live; upon that bond they bide
   Immortal till their need of love is dead.
   Not lost their heart-room, spent their flowing tide
   Before the last who love them too are sped,
   Leaving no life in love with them allied,
   No love to cherish the unbroken thread.

V

Even so, in many passing thought and deed,
You still are one with me, your ægis mine.
Though other scenes I play, you interline
Your quality; good measure yet you knead
Into my final act; it is your rede
When courage, perseverance and design
Steady my step, for still old counsels plead,
Old inspirations animate and shine.
   No twain close wrought as we through noon of day,
   To share the best and worst of all that fell,
   Can part and leave their little citadel
   A ruin; stable yet they stand and stay,
   Irrevocably one in fate and spell
   Until forgot and vanished both away.

VI

Ere time shall dim the mirror of my mind
And spread his slow, inevitable mould
To cloud the unshadowed memories of old,
I tell, what all who sought would surely find:
That she was beautiful beyond her kind,
Rich with a twinkling magic manifold,
And rare, unconscious gift to win and bind;
As true as steel as generous as gold.

Tender to every living hope and lure,
Herself no superstition held in train—
Her all-embracing will in life mature
To be a link upon our human chain,
Faithful and staunch, still striving to be pure
From rust till she should yield it up again.

VII

Delight she won of life, and gladly took
The signal pleasures it had power to bring
Her ardent spirit; well she loved to wing
And on great scenes and ancient cities look,
Where bygone thunders of dead history shook
Man's fate; she often saw the mountains fling
Their snow to heaven, and from a lakeland nook
Won joys and beauties for remembering.
    And music was her sunshine, for it wrought
    Abundance of well-being, to unite
    Content with peace; great blessing music brought,
    Lifting her heart to many a noble height
    Of reverent devotion and pure thought
    In worship of its glory and its might.

VIII

They who illuminate life's mysteries:
The paramount creators men revere,
Gave added light to her from year to year,
And, by an instinct ever apt to rise,
From less to greater, she would lift her eyes
Seeking supremacy, august, austere,
From art of mastership in highest guise
That wearied never, but grew near and dear.
    For understanding and the deeper lore
    Of deeds consummate to perfection wrought,
    She strove, still gleaning for her precious store,
    With native gift of intuition taught;
    And culture sharpened taste until it bore
    Rare beauty in the garden of her thought.

IX

The brave and comely were her rightful hue,
And radiant health the constant of her mind;
Yet unto sufferers none so swiftly kind;
The stricken pity woke, long ere she knew
What any sickness meant, and they were few
Within her ken who ever failed to find
The ready ruth that, when herself declined,
For tenderness willed none should bid adieu.
    Now 'brave' and 'comely' in my heart remain
    For cardinal essence of her own degree—

The wondrous spirit that could conquer pain
And make of death another dignity,
Declared her as a rainbow lights the rain,
Adorned her as the moon adorns the sea.

X

Who know not superstition know not fear,
And nought availed her courage to abate,
For, at the shadow of unkindly fate,
She watched the peril rise, the cloud draw near,
With sense alert and stable vision clear
To aid and fortify our little state;
Nor would she waste a sigh or shed a tear
To see hope dead and chance unfortunate.
　　Calm before ill, unshaken by success,
　　She walked upon her steadfast way, to move
　　By light of an inveterate fearlessness
　　Through storm below, or sunshine from above;
　　Her joys all shared, where others they might bless,
　　Her cares close hid from every eye but love.

XI

On us her failing thought she would bestow,
Eager to see us yet, ere we should fade,
Still close united, hopefully arrayed
Upon the road that all were wont to go;
And when Death came she met him not as foe,
Nor trembled at the deepening of his shade,
But homage offered, passing unafraid
On Live's sure ebb to Death's eternal flow.
　　'Oh, Eden, Death is a grand thing,' she said
　　Two days before she died: to her surcease
　　Was never threat to fear, or doom to dread,
　　But the day ended, sundown and release;
　　For Death is very loyal to his dead,
　　And holds the promise of eternal peace.

XII

No elegy shall she, or suffer wrong
From muted music of unfruitful sighs;
The light still shines I worshipped in her eyes;
The vanished years they brightened still belong
My own for ever, wing again and throng
To bid me calendar and solemnise
Past happiness in many a secret song
Of gratitude for all I had to prize.
　　I am content, and none shall hear me grieve.
　　Through twilight time, subduing present care,
　　More tender than the after-glow of eve,

Her goodness broods upon me, passing fair,
To knit us, quick and dead, as sunsets weave
A weary earth into the radiant air.

XIII

And while in consciousness I yet delay,
The waking thought shall often, often turn
Where granite sparkles and the furzes burn
Even now as when, upon that far-off day
Together through the mist of moorland grey,
We wandered down the aisles of eagle fern,
Lovers at last on one united way,
Not dreaming that we trod our open urn.
    Later the hour we willed at last to make
    Our sleep, where first we woke and surely found
    Each meant the other, until Death should break
    Our little pact; and then on this good ground
    Dismissal, nullity, oblivion take
    Unshadowed by a hope, or care, or mound.

XIV

Where spreads the ancient pillow of our rest
And I had thought to bide for many a year,
You slumber first, my own, my starry dear,
And in the Mother's everlasting breast
Your silver dust is lying, hid and blest
To make the unseen violet's blue more clear
And bright the heath about a skylark's nest,
Waiting the day again shall draw us near.
    We glowed together as the twin stars glow;
    Said 'Yea' to life, with kindred end and aim;
    Saw our close interwoven story grow
    And finish at the darkening of your flame.
    A moment more, together still, we go
    Back to the mystery from which we came.

And here I will copy two more sonnets, written shortly before
Mother died, from Father to me and, as dedication to a novel, from
me to Father.

Adelaide

Your greatness is to stem life's daily stress
And find a margin of vitality
For all who lack your virgin strength and sigh
Under the common load of helplessness.
Goodwill you bring, an ear for every cry,
The patient care to minister and bless,
Befriend and succour, comfort and redress:
Such spirit sanctifies your energy.

O ye whose feet are firm and hearts are brave,
Reverence the pow'r that your endowments hold:
The might to aid; the potency to save;
The strength to shield the young and serve the old;
So it be said, 'On life's highway they fare
Lightening each load their love encounters there'.

Father

Now memory back to haunting childhood flies
And I behold you like the daystar there,
Who made me beauty love, be truth-aware,
And man's supreme creations recognise;
Then my first labours conned and, generous-wise,
Ignored not, but with kind, large-hearted care
Amended, taught, and from doubt and despair
Released, and roused to nobler enterprise.
My veneration and my love I bring,
Honour and gratitude on you bestow,
From whom innumerable beauties flow,
Enchantment, wisdom, wit and humour spring,
Your lofty task the whole of being to scan
And read with ruthful eyes the soul of man.

10

After Mother's funeral Father decreed that I should return to
London, Nan should stop in the boarding-house, and Robina, of
whom he had been seeing a great deal and exchanging visits, should
come to live with him until, in a year's time, he married her. At
Christmas she returned from Eltham to her family, and Henry and I
spent it with Father—the saddest Christmas we had known. Mother
left a thousand pounds with which Father endowed a bed in her
memory at Torbay Hospital. The staff had asked him if he were going
to continue her practice—unknown to any of us—of giving the
hospital its Christmas turkeys, but Father preferred the idea of an
Emily Phillpotts bed. A day before Robina came back he announced
his arrangements. Henry was to live with them until Father remarried
and left Torquay. Then, at Robina's wish, Henry would have a room
in the boarding-house where Nan lodged. Jan and I were to find a site
near London on which to build a cottage, for which he gave us a
thousand pounds.

Meanwhile, Robina and I went house-hunting and visited dozens of
'desirable residences' round Exeter, where she had decided to live to
be near her mother. She was going to breed cairn terriers and
budgerigars and other creatures, so needed plenty of outbuildings and
space. She eventually chose a large three-storey house near Broadclyst
called Kerswell, with a lodge for Sharland and his wife, and twenty

acres of land. I felt sorriest for Nan, though Father promised she should still work for him and come weekly to see him. However, she was lucky if she saw him twice a year. Eltham was sold to a young doctor and his family.

Father often sent for me, and when Robina was away I helped with the animals. For over twenty years Henry and I spent Christmas at Kerswell, while Jan went to her family or had them to stay with her. Father and Sharland made a new garden, which the poor old gardener—whose heart broke, as Father's nearly did, to leave the Eltham paradise, but they had no choice—said was a 'rubitch patch' compared to Eltham; but it, too, was beautiful.

One autumn Robina's oldest sister, Alice, a pathetic widow of sixty who had been a companion, developed cancer and came to end her days in rooms near Kerswell. I happened to be staying there when her end approached and sat up with her on her last night. For hours her breathing laboured, then she lost consciousness and at dawn died. The vicar's wife and I laid her out. I have never forgotten the moment when her pained features, drawn with suffering, softened and smiled in the repose of death.

11

Back in London I completed *The Atoning Years*, published in 1929, the novel founded on *Yellow Sands*, published in 1930 by Chapman and Hall, and, in collaboration with Father, *The Good Old Days*. Every Sunday Jan and I explored Surrey for a building-site and chose a quarter acre on an estate called Givons Grove, near Boxhill, over-looking the valley of the River Mole and the village of Mickleham. Our plot formed the summit of a chalk hill, sloping to the country between Leith Hill and Leatherhead. We engaged a Sussex firm of architects and builders to design a thatched, stone-built cottage, and building began at once, to be finished in March. We had picked on the windiest, most exposed spot in the neighbourhood, but the views were superb.

Meanwhile during my last London year I accepted an invitation from Barry Jackson to stop with him at Malvern for the Shaw Festival, at which Cedric Hardwicke played King Magnus in *The Apple Cart* with Edith Evans as Orinthia. Shaw was there, and his friends Edward Elgar and Granville Bantock, whose hobby was gambling: they spent much time huddled together over betting news. To Shaw's credit he wrote to Elgar afterwards: 'Although I am rather a conceited man I am quite sincerely and genuinely humble in the presence of Sir Edward Elgar. I recognise a greater art than my own and a greater man than I can ever hope to be.'

Another member of the house-party was a Belgian poet called Pierre. We were attracted and spent time together. He gave me a volume of poetry: I gave him *Savitri the Faithful*, and we vowed eternal friendship and promised to keep in touch. But neither ever wrote to the other and we never met again—such is the outcome of many a salute between 'passing ships', by night and by day. I did not care for *The Apple Cart*, compared to the beginning and end of *Back to Methuselah*, which I also saw at Malvern, the most charming, imaginative and poetical work by Bernard Shaw.

During the same period I was invited to be one of two guests of honour at a 'Women of the Year' dinner and accepted, against my will, stipulating that I should not be asked to speak, and assuming that my wish would be heeded. I arrived feeling unlike myself, in a long black silk taffeta dress and a pink rose. Two large women introduced me to the other guest of honour, a bonny young woman called Stella Gibbons whose *Cold Comfort Farm* was being acclaimed. 'What is your greatest treasure?' she asked me, but I could not think, and she went on: 'Mine is my baby daughter!' and I wished that I, too, had a daughter to be my greatest treasure, and pictured myself making and ironing her dress for a first ball. Recalled to the moment, I was settled at a long table between the two massive women, feeling like the dormouse at the Mad Hatter's tea-party and wishing there had been a teapot large enough to be popped into and forgotten. After the meal one of my neighbours bent over and said: 'Now I'm going to introduce you as our first speaker so that you can tell us all about *Yellow Sands*,' and rose to address the assembly. 'No, *no*,' I cried. 'I told you I couldn't speak,' and I tried to pull her down; but so well try to pull down Mount Everest. The vast one paid no heed and announced me. I stood in a daze, tried to think of something to say. Nothing came, so I remained silent while hundreds of faces faced me. Some kind person prompted me by referring to my father, and I stammered that he had done all the work and all the credit was his. Then I sat down. The huge woman hurriedly introduced Stella Gibbons, who gave an excellent and witty talk. Strangely, I did not feel embarrassed by my failure, or humiliated by my inadequacy: I felt nothing—or, perhaps, as if the real me was not there at all. As soon as we left the table a well-meaning stranger took me by the arm to restore my self-confidence, but thanking him I disengaged myself and slipped away.

To help Florence Hardy through the difficult months after her husband's death, James Barrie had invited her to spend some weeks in the Adelphi, and while there she invited me to have tea with her and the Bernard Shaws, and also to lunch with James Barrie and the playwright Arthur Pinero, at a restaurant called Boulestin. I arrived early and was watching arrivals and departures when I saw Florence approaching, a pathetic little woman, escorted by those ageing men. Barrie seemed unknowable, but Pinero's genial phiz inspired liking and gaiety. Unlike Barrie but like Shaw he had been influenced by

Ibsen, whose work had not only improved his conception of play-writing, but opened his eyes to the follies, injustices and inequalities of Society, its ridiculous values, and sickening class prejudice. Between the two men Florence looked woebegone, as if always on the verge of tears. Like her, Barrie was shawled in melancholy, but Pinero, stone deaf, kept laughing and asking questions, though he could hear nothing we said. Florence tried to blend us into a harmonious quartet, but Barrie sank into silence, and though Pinero babbled away no one could penetrate his deafness. I cannot recall what we ate or drank, only that in my nervousness I choked, and a waiter came running with a glass of water while Pinero thumped me on the back, Florence cried 'O dear, O dear!', and Barrie stared at his plate and frowned.

The happiest event of these last London days was a visit from Henry, who took us to the Docks to see ships from all over the world, and the beautiful barges sailing up and down the estuary—as Ruskin wrote of them: 'By Thames' shore with its glidings of red sail'. Alongside the George V Dock one could get close to the water and watch loading and unloading, smell the sea, the tar, the ropes, the cargoes, and hear unfamiliar tongues of sailors and stevedores, which stirred my ancient desire to sail round the world. I cannot describe my joy at sharing my brother's happiness.

Some time earlier I had a comedy called *The Mayor* successfully produced at Birmingham, and now Barry Jackson transferred it to London—I cannot remember which theatre, and did not go to see it, but heard later that a few hours before the curtain went up on the first night the leading actor was taken ill, and there being no understudy Barry decided to send on a substitute *reading the part*. The play failed. Failure in work and bad reviews did not disturb me, for when a work was completed I lost interest and it passed out of mind. Or perhaps I did not care enough about it. But what Arnold Bennett, who saw *The Mayor*, wrote *did* worry me: 'I must tell you your play is in my opinion too subtle for the general understanding; also not dramatic enough . . . And you have a nerve, too, to put three tea-parties into one play! The satire amounts to cruelty, and is, I imagine, a shade over-done . . . Withal, I would only charge you with one *real* fault—lack of drama . . . The thing is full of originality and just observation . . . *The Mayor* is a promise of a better play.'

Before leaving London for Leatherhead I said goodbye to Arnold, who spoke affectionately of Mother and dwelt nostalgically on their friendship, as if he no longer looked towards the future but over his shoulder at the past. And again I felt that presentiment of tragedy.

Surrey

1

Little Silver, as we called the cottage, after a village in my Father's Dartmoor books, overlooked the North Downs. A deep valley separated it from an opposite hill on which stood Norbury Park, associated, like adjacent Juniper Hall, with Talleyrand, Madame de Staël and other *émigrés* escaping from the French Revolution, and linked with Fanny Burney and her husband, Alexandre d'Arblay, whom she met there. Norbury now belonged to Marie Stopes, who had opened a birth control clinic in Holloway. Through the vale meandered the River Mole, above whose silent waters I saw three kingfishers flying in a blue ring of light. The chalk downs bore myriads of wild flowers, among them flax and orchids, scyllas and marjoram—fragrant hillsides of which our future garden formed a segment, including thousands of cowslips—one of several enchanting surprises that greeted our first Surrey year. A nightingale sang nightly in an oak tree outside my bedroom, and the dawn chorus was sweeter and more numerous than any I had heard before. Every spring, families of great tits built in a letter-box attached to the porch, so tame that they let us watch them brooding their eggs and feeding the young with caterpillars picked off an ash tree on the lawn—the tree under which I buried the Zulu girl's skull that used to stand on our nursery mantelpiece after Uncle Cecil died. Round and round its bole I ran unclothed on summer nights, while rabbits nibbled and stars glinted between the boughs of two forest-size beech trees.

Since childhood I had been interested in the rock under my feet but had not yet lived on chalk and flint. It was exciting when our once-a-week gardener, Albert Raseley, dug up fossil echinoderms which had lain there for over a hundred million years. I still have two sea-urchins, *Micraster*, known as Shepherd's Crown or Fairy Loaf, to remind me of those days, when between us all we transformed the plot into an exquisite garden, for which Father supplied hundreds of flowering trees, shrubs, and herbaceous plants, two thousand daffodil bulbs, and dozens of chalk-loving irises, among them a pale yellow one he had created and called after Mother, *Emily*. He also gave us a greenhouse in which Raseley grew chrysanthemums, to be banked every autumn round the living-room.

I worried because Jan had to leave early for London and did not get back until late. Casting round for something she could do at home, for she refused not to contribute to our expenses, I read in an advertisement 'how to make a small fortune' with a Home Knitting Machine and bought one. But neither of us could even put it together, much less operate it, and had to sell it for half its value. Father solved the problem by asking Jan to take over all his typewriting because Nan had become too slow. At first for Nan's sake she refused, but Father told Nan he was handing his work to a London agency, which she believed, and for some years she did not know that Jan was doing it. However, we thought it right to tell her and all she said was: 'I don't mind at all! You wanted to spare my feelings, and I quite understand!'

We kept in touch with old friends, one or other of whom every weekend came to stay, including Susan Stebbing, until she was appointed visiting Professor at Columbia University, New York; and Florence Hardy, looking ill and grey. She had cancer, and wrote in a farewell letter: 'I'm afraid I am one of the world's unfortunates.' The happiest visits were from Nan, and Henry two or three times a year. With him in winter we went to London to see variety shows at the Palladium, walking back from Leatherhead Station after midnight, discussing the astonishing 'turns' we had witnessed. In summer we all rose before six, caught the first train to London Bridge, hurried across the river to Tower Quay and boarded the *Golden Eagle* to steam down the Thames to Southend, Clacton or Margate, while East-enders sang 'The Lambeth Walk' and drank beer and tea. After several hours on the teeming beaches, there came the magical voyage upriver past Dagenham and Silvertown, Woolwich Pier, where the empties were shot off, Limehouse Reach, West India and Surrey Docks, Wapping and Rotherhithe and the Pool, by which time the revellers had grown quiet, babies slept in their mothers' laps, lovers were enlaced, and a russet sunset blazed between the bascules of Tower Bridge.

I had not been long at Little Silver when I had agonising headaches which lasted for two or three days, with dazzling fits. Susan Stebbing arranged for me to see her doctor brother, Superintendent of a South London hospital. It was only a recurrence of the migraine of childhood but much more severe. Omnipon, a form of opium, was prescribed, but I recollected Uncle Mac and took it only once, having discovered that a better though temporary remedy was a very hot sponge pressed to the brow. I endured these headaches for the next twenty-one years, when that happened which ended them.

During our first year Arnold Bennett, who had moved to Chiltern Court to be near his friend H. G. Wells, asked me to visit him: 'Virginia is in the greatest and noisiest form!' he wrote. Alas, I put off going until it was too late. One afternoon I was walking near Baker Street when I noticed that the road had been covered with straw, and someone told me that Arnold Bennett was dangerously ill. A few days later he died. I recalled his own description in *Books and Persons* of Putney High Street on the Good Friday night before Swinburne died (worthy to stand with Walt Whitman's account in *Specimen Days in America* of the starry heavens when Carlyle was passing). 'As says the Indian proverb,' Bennett wrote, 'I met ten thousand men on the Putney High Street, and they were all my brothers. But I alone was aware of it'; and he describes how the upper windows of Swinburne's house were lit up, but 'nobody looked or seemed to care': 'This enormous negligence,' he added, 'appeared to be . . . magnificently human.' And he tells how he once saw Swinburne walking down Putney Hill, his face 'that of a man who had lived with fine, austere, passionate thoughts of his own'—a man like Bennett himself. Arnold had never possessed good health and often suffered acute neuralgia and insomnia. Nor had he freed himself from the effects of his unhappy marriage. His passing deeply saddened me. Though he had often been caricatured, sometimes unkindly, laughed at, envied, called—what he never was—pompous and vain, our family knew him as an endearing, beneficent man, loyal to his friends, always ready to help lesser authors and beginners, never resentful or mean, fundamentally simple. One of his maxims was: 'Never criticise. Never condemn, never judge . . . Seek to comprehend.' After his death my father wrote: 'He had steadfast vision, clean-cut purpose and healthy devotion to literature . . . Fiction was his aim, but he turned to real life with insatiable curiosity, interest and zest, concerned to tell the truth about character as he found it. He had a generous outlook on fellow artists and handsome praise for what he approved. He was a writer of creative insight and a great-hearted and kind-hearted man.'

During those Surrey years Father sent us, often with Henry, on European expeditions—to Menaggio on Lake Como, to Holland and Belgium, and overland to Naples, where Henry was so upset by the beggars that he would seldom go out. Our visit coincided with the celebration of the patron saint, Gennaro, who was martyred during Diocletian's persecution. Two reliquaries of his blood are kept in the Cathedral—blood which, except on rare occasions, liquefies in spring and autumn, when the ampoules are paraded for the populace to venerate. A priest passed us holding one, tipping it from side to side to show that the blood had liquefied.

I could not rest until we had ascended Vesuvius, then erupting on a small scale. Upon the crater's rim, framed in yellow smoke and steam like a sprite of the abyss, danced and sang a beautiful Italian youth, selling sweet green grapes called *Lacrymae Cristi*, the tears of Christ —a strange contrast to the boiling, bubbling mouth of Vesuvius— one whom Michelangelo would have admired and perhaps copied, with the other Ignudi, on the Sistine Chapel roof.

On 6th May, 1935, I was in Fleet Street when orders arrived to close the roadway and distant cheers announced the approach of celebrities. A carriage appeared in which sat Queen Mary and King George V on their way to St Paul's to celebrate their silver jubilee. Many years later I learned that standing in the crowd only a few paces from me was the man destined to be my husband—another pre-crossing of our ways.

Jan and I collaborated in a thriller called *The Wasps' Nest*, produced at the Nottingham Playhouse, but I remember nothing about it. Father and I collaborated again, in *My Lady's Mill*, which I do not think has been acted. *The Good Old Days* was produced and failed.

2

We never felt at home on Givons Grove, fast filling with new houses and families, and one summer decided to lend Little Silver to friends and join Nan and Henry at a Dartmoor cottage in the hamlet of Jordan, near Widecombe. Past the front ran a stream from which we dipped our water. Heat and light were supplied by paraffin and candles, and an open fire on which Nan cooked. We fetched milk and cream, butter and eggs from a hill farm, and never had I felt closer to Dartmoor. Our favourite jaunt was to the River Webburn, at the foot of a heather-covered height called the Ball, beside a rush-rimmed trout pool surrounded by gorse and bracken, and a marsh sprinkled with bog bean and sphagnum moss. Henry, who as a child abjured the moor, now favoured it and loved this special place.

A few steps from the cottage stood a half-ruined, obsolete mill where lived an old crippled man and his middle-aged wife, Liza, with two teen-aged daughters; and since he could no longer work she supported them by running a taxi service with an aged car, and doing odd jobs for farmers and others. This remarkable woman, of fiery disposition and extreme energy, lean, wiry and tough as a man, shocked the local housewives by cutting her hair short and wearing a man's shirts and breeches, which, common now, was then exceedingly unusual. We often spent an evening with them in their one large room next to the disused grindstone chamber, so damp that all their garments were slung on ropes under the rafters. A peat and furze fire smouldered on the hearth night and day, and everything was grimed with smoke. Sacks of vegetables Liza had raised for market were stored in corners with bundles of rabbit and moleskins. George her husband would tell about his younger years spend peat-cutting, stone-breaking, and pig- and poultry-rearing—a wise old rustic like those in my father's novels. His wife's racy conversation in broad dialect larded with folk words was salty, humorous and sage. For me those evenings passed in a sort of magic, while the girls, the elder an ebon beauty, the younger a flaxen doll, sat on the floor, bashful and silent.

Listening one night to those splendid people, the idea for a novel sailed full-rigged into my mind—a story suggested by this family, but not their story—one closer to my heart. I would call it *The Gallant Heart*, and my heroine, modelled on this gallant woman, would be called Leah. When Nan and Henry went back to Torquay, Jan and I, with still a month to fill, moved to a cottage on Exmoor where, at Withypool, I found a setting for my tale. While we scrambled about the coast and roamed the moorland, imagination worked full blast and I filled notebooks with material.

So much had we enjoyed this parting from Givons Grove that we decided to let Little Silver every year, and when the Jordan cot was no longer available, Mrs and Miss Broad of Porthleven invited us to lodge with them for thirty shillings a week all found. How I looked forward to those interludes! Sometimes Henry joined us, and Susan Stebbing came over from Tintagel, where she and her friends spent their summer vacations. Looking back, those Jordan and Porthleven intermezzos in the concert of my days awaken a special rapture; and though the best of life was still to come, I recall them with a poignant nostalgia no other memory stirs.

3

Thus passed the years. I finished *The Gallant Heart*, published in 1939 by Rich and Cowan, then turned it into a play. Meantime Aunt Frances had moved to Eastbourne after Grannie Anne died, to be near her younger brother and his family. Two or three times a year we spent a weekend with her, and noticed that she was ageing fast, going over and over sad tales of the past and dwelling especially on how relatives had wrecked a romance with her first cousin, a solicitor, because they disapproved of cousin marriages. I had often heard this story, and Mother told me that it was a fantasy. However, I thought her cousin, who never married, must have cared because, when she left Ealing, he bought her the Eastbourne house and gave her enough money to keep it going. On one of our visits she had such a bad cough that I suggested a doctor, but she declared she was perfectly well. Not long afterwards I heard that she was seriously ill and would I come? I found her in bed, attended by an elderly doctor and an old nurse who told me that she had cancer of the lungs. It was plain she was dying, but they were determined to keep her alive as long as possible and forced her against her will to eat. When the nurse crammed the spoon into her mouth she shuddered and tried to push it away, clung to me and begged me to stop them tormenting her; but the doctor said: 'She *must* eat. It's my duty to keep her alive, not starve her to death.' And he directed the nurse to open her mouth and insert the spout of a feeding-cup. My protests were silenced.

That evening when she and I were alone together Aunt Frances

whispered to me to go to a drawer in her tallboy and take out a packet
of letters, which she pressed to her lips and said 'My dear cousin's
letters. Don't let anyone see them. Burn them for me.' Without
untying them I burned them in a corner of the garden. Perhaps they
concealed the truth of her romance. She died soon afterwards.

To my co-executor—an older niece—and me she left legacies and
the contents of her home. All I wanted were a few cups and saucers
belonging to Grannie Anne's wedding tea-service; a Staffordshire
Mask jug featuring Pan wreathed with flowers which, when Mother
and Aunt Frances were small, held their porridge treacle; a child's
sampler; and a stuggy little old volume that belonged to their father,
from which she had read to me in Eltham nursery: *The Life and
Adventures of Robinson Crusoe by Himself*, published in 1818, with
steel engravings of Robinson surrounded by his animals, and under a
home-made umbrella reclining in his piragua, making the circuit of
his island—than which I desired no other keepsakes to remind me of a
dear and lamented aunt.

4

Here I will summarise the books I wrote at Little Silver. The first
novel, *The Youth of Jacob Ackner*, published in 1931 by Benn, was a
strange story about a Jewish youth, and one of the settings, which
included Spain, was our flat in Holbein House. Then came *The
Founder of Shandon*, also brought out by Benn, the tale of a
philosopher, set in Norbury Park, where he founds a community.
The next book, *The Growing World*, was the most ambitious, dealing
with universal problems, statesmen and politics, and published by
Hutchinson, who also took *Onward Journey*, suggested by a 'turn' I
saw at the Palladium, about a clown, his friend and his goose, followed
by *Broken Allegiance*, my only historical theme (except *Akhnaton*), the
tragedy of Benedict Arnold and John André during the American War
of Independence. Of *What's Happened to Rankin?*, a psychological
study, I have no recollection; but with *The Gallant Heart* I strove more
than with any other work. Each book was different from the others: I
never traversed the same track twice. Later I dramatised *Broken
Allegiance*, while staying at Porthleven, but never sent it to a manager.

In 1937 an Austrian Jewish couple working in Germany were
driven by Hitler to fly to Britain: Victor Fleischer, author of several
books, one of which was *Rienzo, the Rise and Fall of a Dictator*, and his
wife, the actress and producer Leontine Sagan, who had directed the
German film and play, *Mädchen in Uniform*, and was now producing
Ivor Novello's musical extravaganzas at Drury Lane. The theatrical
agent to whom I sent the play of *The Gallant Heart* had shown it to
Leontine, and its heroine, Leah, so appealed to her that she wrote and
asked me to visit her. Henry was staying with us, and after an hour or

so at the Zoo, while he and Jan awaited me at Victoria I called at the Fleischers' flat. Victor, badly crippled by polio, opened the door, revealing a vase of multi-coloured tulips on a table in the tiny hall. A moment later his wife appeared, and there stood my ideal Leah: slim, tall, graceful and tough, with shining brown eyes, in her forties, brimming with vitality. Next time we met she took me to a Hungarian restaurant and asked 'Do you like paprika?' I had never heard of it, but not wishing to appear ignorant before this sophisticated woman, I said Yes. It turned out to be pepper! Afterwards she drove me to Drury Lane to a rehearsal of *The Dancing Years*, and I was interested to observe how formidable she could be, a relentless perfectionist, yet never scolding or flustering the actors.

Though *The Gallant Heart* was almost, it was not quite, accepted— and there is all the difference in the world between the two! Other actresses, including Marie Ney, tried to secure a production, but the Second World War started and I withdrew the script and never sent it out again.

Early in 1938 Nan sent us particulars of Fernhill, an unfurnished cottage, to let for six shilling a week in the Dartmoor hamlet of Ponsworthy, a mile through the woods from Jordan, thinking that we might like to rent it for holidays. I was dubious, but Jan urged me to accept; and as her previous counsels had turned out well, without seeing Fernhill we telegraphed acceptance. A few weeks later we went down to look at it. Our fate—and what a strange fate—was sealed.

The small granite house stood at the top of a cul-de-sac sloping to a water-splash across a minor lane between Poundsgate and Wide-combe—a quiet and beautiful corner. With two little bedrooms, kitchen-dining-room, and small living-room built on at right angles, it was all we needed. Oil was used for lighting and cooking, and for water a spring bubbled out of a bank a few yards down the hill. After Little Silver nothing could be simpler. Above rose the moor and the tors. Next door lived Mr and Mrs Leaman, in their seventies, and next to them our landlord and his wife, Percy and Edith Prouse, the village carpenter and undertaker. Opposite, with two widowed daughters, dwelt his aged mother who had had ten children: their ten identical mugs bearing their names in gold hung on the dresser. Everyone welcomed us into their fold.

Delighted with the cottage we hurried back to Surrey, let Little Silver until the autumn, shopped in Brixton for furnishings and despatched them to Ponsworthy, to which we happily returned; and were sad when the time came to go back to Surrey.

On September 29th Chamberlain, Daladier, Hitler and Mussolini agreed to shocking terms imposed on Czechoslovakia. Britain's policy of appeasement began, and the Munich Agreement was followed by blackmail of the Czechs. Jan, who was among the more discerning of human kind, while I still believed in its ultimate benevolence, wisdom, and capacity to avert war, now made another of her startling suggestions. Expenses at Givons Grove had doubled since our arrival while our means had diminished; and whether war broke out or not, she thought we should be provident to sell Little Silver and migrate to Ponsworthy. So we accepted the first offer, of three thousand pounds, from the editor of a Sunday newspaper, and I invested it for Jan. For £130 we bought and I learned to drive a Standard 8 motorcar, stored the furniture, said goodbye to everyone, and left Surrey never to return.

My father, who first opposed the plan, ended by approving it, for my propinquity suited him, and he often sent for me. During our hiatus in Surrey, in addition to many serious novels, short stories and essays, he published nine mystery books, six volumes of poetry, five fantasies, and had five plays produced—that marvellous man!

Dartmoor and the Second World War

1

The first summer was halcyon, our existence arcadian. I wrote two light novels: *The Round of Life* (published in 1940), and *Laugh With Me* (published in 1941) which I dramatised for the Birmingham Repertory Theatre, with moderate success. Ponsworthy was surrounded by ancient woods where *Osmunda* ferns grew on the banks of the Webbern, whose boulders supported miniature gardens of rushes, bluebells and foxgloves, a pine or a willow tree, where dragonflies and mayflies hovered over the water and trout leapt in the pools. Nan and Henry stayed with us, and we picnicked on the Ball again, higher up the river, whose music and our laughter reverberate in my memory. (People say: How comforting to be able to forget! But I say it is a thousand times more comforting to be able to remember!)

One day Jan and I drove to see friends in North Devon and on the way home called at Morwenstow, the home of legendary Parson Hawker whose isolated church overlooks the Atlantic. I wandered between the gravestones, reading their epitaphs, some composed by Hawker, and thought what a peaceful place to be buried, little knowing that a few days earlier my future husband had been there and also reflected how good it would be to lie, at the end, in such a remote place near the sea. We had missed by a few years in Bloomsbury, a few yards in Fleet Street, and now by a few days at Morwenstow. Where and when were we going to meet?

Leontine Sagan came to Widecombe Inn and asked my help with her autobiography, so I spent every morning on her book, which told a remarkable story, and after lunch translated a German play she hoped to produce in London. Now and then we tramped over the moor, which she loved and compared to parts of South Africa.

Meanwhile Chamberlain failed to detect that, seething in Hitler, were fierce emotions stirred by the humiliation and despair of total defeat and degradation caused by the vindictive 'peace' treaty imposed on Germany, which he had determined to avenge. 'The force that has launched the most violent revolutions,' he had written in *Mein Kampf*, has been 'a fanaticism that has stimulated' the crowd 'and an actual hysteria which infected it with enthusiasm'; and he whipped up just such a hysteria, or nationalism, providing as scapegoats both Jews and gypsies. His troops overran Poland and invaded Russia, where he liquidated all people 'of defective blood'. Genocide had occurred before: pogroms, attempted and actual extermination of aborigines, slaves, heretics—but Hitler's 'final solution' outdevilled them all. On 3rd September 1939 Britain and France declared war on Germany. Conscription had already been reintroduced and a force of 158,000 men was shipped to France. The American Congress passed the Lend-Lease Act, and the United States was granted ninety-nine year leases on naval bases from Guiana to Newfoundland.

2

The school run by Susan Stebbing's friends was evacuated to Tintagel, and we lent them the contents of Little Silver. I was asked by the Women's Voluntary Service to be Head Housewife for several hamlets and villages, and as this left spare time I joined the staff of Ashburton Cottage Hospital, and also helped at a Home for Service-women's illegitimate babies—(I recall a half-Chinese infant with straight scarlet hair who gazed at me with such a wistful, ageless look that I never forgot him though the rest vanished from memory.) With hundreds of others I regularly supplied blood, and at Nan's request gave talks to the Torquay Townswomen's Guild. Once a week we attended evening lectures on gas warfare by a retired major, and were enrolled by a retired colonel for civil defence exercises as 'Despatch Drivers', which entailed driving in the blackout. In odd moments I wrote four novels: *Our Little Town* (1942), *From Jane to John* (1943), *The Adventurers* (1944), and *The Lodestar* (1945), published by Rich and Cowan.

Neville Chamberlain died—not the weak character sometimes defamed but a tragic figure, a man of peace with high ideals, interested in social reform, whose misfortune was to be Prime Minister at the time of Munich. After Pearl Harbor the United States entered the war, ensuring the defeat of Germany and Japan, but not before the Japanese had overrun the Pacific. Amongst the horrors were German air raids on Coventry, Plymouth and Exeter. I was staying with my father when Exeter was ignited; and from Pons-worthy we saw the reflection of burning Plymouth, during which an escaping German bomber pitched out a landmine only a hundred yards from the hamlet, leaving a heap of green and white silken ropes to which the parachute had been attached. In a random air raid on Torquay the windows of Nan's room were blasted in, projecting millions of glass needles into her bed, while she and Henry sheltered in the basement.

Henry, though beyond call-up age, was deeply disturbed by this second great war; and when staying with us his intense depression and inner rage were so profound, he was so dangerously mentally ill, suffering from what Hermann Hesse—that gifted writer who in his autobiographical writings reveals himself more deeply and clearly than any other I know, even Rousseau—called 'dreadful abysses of self-contempt' and 'ice-cold loneliness', that I persuaded him to see a psychiatrist, who said he was no worse than thousands of others and suggested electric convulsive therapy, which both of us refused to consider. From a totally unexpected quarter relief eventually came.

During the year of Stalingrad and El Alamein, Leontine brought her husband to Widecombe, where they stayed for a long time. In the midst of that terrible war, shocked and stunned by the gassing of relations in concentration camps, our reunion on Dartmoor afforded all of us a tiny measure of consolation.

If we could save enough petrol or be lent some, we occasionally drove over to Tintagel to see Susan Stebbing, and on one trip met her friend Florence Eddy, a South African nursing sister who left Cape Town to nurse at Halton Hospital. I noticed that Susan looked unwell and Miss Eddy told me that she had come to take her to London for a medical examination—cancer was feared. A few days later Susan wrote to say that it had been confirmed. She was sent to a hospital near Macclesfield, and from there wrote asking me to come and see her. Winter had set in, and not knowing how to get there or where to stay I set out, arriving late on a black rainswept evening. I was directed to a hotel but it was full, and so was every other place I tried. Late at night I sat on my suitcase in an empty street in the rain, wondering what to do, and decided to knock on a door at random, hoping someone would respond. I knocked on the nearest door. After a long interval a woman peeped out of a window and asked 'Who's there?' Hearing my plea she came down and unlocked the door, took me in and said: 'You can sleep here.' She lived there alone, and insisted on remaking her bed and sleeping downstairs on a couch. But first she brought food, kindled a fire and took my clothes to dry, lending me hers. Next morning she told me to stop as long as I liked. My benefactor was Mrs Elsie Etchells, a middle-aged widow whose husband had been killed in the war; and of all the homes and inhabitants of Macclesfield I could not have knocked on a more welcome door or met a more angelic being.

Susan, lying in a large ward, was composed, smiling, serene. At first she said little about herself but spoke of the war and declared that Hitler was bound to be overcome: of that she was utterly convinced. In the First World War she had been a pacifist, but, since no other means of overcoming Nazism existed, like many others she believed it was right to fight in this one. She said her favourite of my books was *The Gallant Heart*. Then she told me no more could be done for her and she awaited death without fear, not believing in a future life, her only regret being the sorrow her death would cause friends and family, but this would pass and she hoped no one would mourn for long. A minor disappointment was being unable to write a comprehensive work she had planned on philosophy. 'But,' said she, 'it will be no loss. There are many much better philosophers!'

Before she died she wrote to us, reiterating her faith in a just peace and better future world. Not only was she one of the small band of women philosophers who have contributed to metaphysical speculation, abstract thought and truth, but she was a lovable human being whom to know was to be certain that, however far mankind sinks into evil, it is capable of rising to the heights of wisdom, goodness and nobility.

I attended her cremation at Golders Green, where I met Miss Eddy—Ray as we called her—again, and as she had no other friendly base in England, invited her to make our cottage her home. I spent that evening with Leontine and Victor Fleischer, who had left Widecombe for a small London flat and were preparing to return to relations in South Africa. During the night a V-bomb fell near and we huddled in the passage. This was the last time I saw Victor, who died not long after they settled in Pretoria. Leontine lived on for many years, founded the South African National Theatre Organisation, and directed productions all over the country, trained black students, and did other work for literature, drama and the stage. We were to meet once more.

I took Ray Eddy to Torquay to meet Henry, and to my relief and happiness they were attracted to each other and became close friends. She fathomed his nature, recognised the causes of his illness, and with understanding helped him to recover.

3

On D-Day, June 1944, four thousand ships converged on the Normandy coast where a Mulberry harbour had been established, and where at a cost of 40,000 dead, over three hundred thousand British, Canadian and American troops landed. By the year's end France and Belgium had been liberated; but dreadful suffering persisted in Russia, Leningrad alone losing a million people from starvation and disease; and in the whole country more than twenty millions perished. In July 1945, the first atomic bomb was detonated, in New Mexico, followed in August by two dropped on Hiroshima and Nagasaki, causing 80,000 deaths. Japan surrendered. Thus ended the bloodiest and some say the most necessary war, which involved sixty countries, and killed in battle, bombing raids, concentration camps and other ways at least fifty million people, devastated enormous areas, obliterated cities, and destroyed some of man's supreme creations. I spent the rest of my life hoping there would never be another world war; nor has there been. But there have been innumerable other wars; and it may be stupid to trust that reason and compassion will ever find a way of avoiding Armageddon, and prevent humanity from destroying itself and all other life on Earth.

Aftermath

1

At a Conference of Foreign Ministers in Moscow the foundations of a Charter for a United Nations was laid, and in June, 1945, at a Conference of Allied and Associated States in San Francisco, the Charter of the United Nations was signed by fifty-one states, who called for a United World. In October, when the Charter had been ratified, the United Nations itself was born, 'to save succeeding generations from the scourge of war . . . to reaffirm faith in human rights . . . to practise tolerance and live together in peace with one another as good neighbours', and to ensure that armed force would not be used 'save in the common interest'—since when 24th October has been celebrated as United Nations Day. UNESCO, the United Nations Educational, Scientific and Cultural Organisation, was founded 'to contribute to peace and security, by promoting collaboration among the Nations through education, science and culture, in order to further respect for justice, for the rule of law, and for human rights and fundamental freedom which are affirmed for the people of the world without distinction of race, sex, language or religion, by the Charter of the United Nations'.

In 1946 the United Nations Organisation held its first Session in New York, and the following year the General Assembly proclaimed the Universal Declaration of Human Rights. A Peace Conference in Paris resulted in the signing of Peace Treaties. At the same time the 'cold war' with Russia began. In Britain a Welfare State and National Health Service were launched; while in Asia, Africa, America and Oceania the British Empire continued to disintegrate.

In our tiny hamlet little changed. Old villagers died, young villagers who had grown up during the war married, and new villagers were born. Dissatisfied with my fruitless life, I wished that I resembled them—capable, independent-minded people, the cream of the earth, farmer's wives among them, living in their old granite farmhouses with farmyards where poultry ran free, butter churns and pans of crusty cream stood in slated dairies, and sturdy young families grew. Knowing that I never should be like them I suffered from a sense of inferiority and futility.

Ray Eddy, decorated with the Royal Red Cross, left Queen

Alexandra's Royal Nursing Corps to become Sister Tutor in a Plymouth Hospital, where I visited her to collect copy for a novel about an adopted child orphaned in the Plymouth blitz. I called it *The Fosterling* and it was published in 1946 by Rich and Cowan. Ray's good influence on Henry continued, and for her he made a beautiful little model of a freighter, a Thames barge for me, and for Father a full-rigged sailing-ship.

Reading about the plight of German refugees ousted from East Prussia and Silesia, we adopted two German families, the Wolfs and the Stolles, and sent them food parcels; but they most needed feather beds, which we obtained from neighbours who were discarding theirs for modern mattresses. (Martha Stolle is dead, but after nearly forty years Else Wolf writes and sends me parcels of good things.)

2

I was persuaded to join the West Country Writers' Association and attended a meeting at Bath. To please Jan and Father I entered their Short Story Competition with a Dartmoor tale called *The Story of Alison Cleave*, and signed it with the pseudonym South Pole. To everyone's surprise South Pole won and I received fifty pounds. But that is not why I recall the meeting. Since the war I had been feeling deeply disillusioned—or rather would have felt it had I not been obstinately tenacious of my Utopian convictions in spite of recent world events—all of which fostered a desire for solitude and long solitary walks over the Moor, to think things out. During the meeting I stayed at Bristol with Jan's sister and her family, and while there contrived by white lies to wangle a whole two days to myself, combined with an exploration of new countryside. Instead of staying in Bristol I told my hosts that I was summoned to Kerswell. But instead of going to Father I went to Nether Stowey, booked a room at a guest-house, and made for the Quantocks, where in an ecstasy of freedom I tramped all day.

Since childhood I had been drawn to high places, beginning with the little temple on the cliff, then Dartmoor and scrambling to the tops of tors to see what was on the other side. I had explored the Chilterns and Cotswolds, and was soon to visit the cave-hollowed Mendips, Welsh and Lakeland mountains, and the Hebrides. Yet on none of those heights did I achieve the sheer exaltation, the passionate delirium I experienced during that day on the rolling Quantocks, happier than I had been for years, and utterly free. I pictured Wordsworth and Coleridge roving there together nearly a hundred and fifty years before, when William and Dorothy were staying at Alfoxden and Coleridge at Nether Stowey, meeting every day. Here the poets planned and published the following year their *Lyrical Ballads*, containing the *Rime of the Ancient Mariner*, while Dorothy composed her *Journal*. Suddenly I saw what *I* had to do: in a sunflash appeared a worthwhile theme. I would write a Song of Man, relate mankind's story, beginning with the void, the condensing of the first nebula, the first star, later the Sun, planet Earth, life, and the evolution of humanity. Visualising this theme was as thrilling as that earlier vision, of the Brotherhood of Man, while crossing the Channel to France. Looking back, I realise how moonstruck this project was, for which my minuscule talent proved quite inadequate. Some have vision but lack technique. Others have technique but lack vision. Very few possess both. I had neither. Yet at the time I did not halt to reflect, any more than I halted on my walk to rest. What I had was unlimited energy, ardour, and hope.

At sunset I descended to the village, of which thirty years after Coleridge completed his Rime he wrote: '*Sanctum et amabile nomen*: rich by so many associations and recollections'. The guest house was full of elderly people, trooping into the dining-room for an evening meal. I was escaping to my room afterwards, to make notes for my Song, when several guests invited me to join them for a cup of tea or coffee and a chat in their rooms, so that I did not reach mine until well after midnight, my mind full of their troubles and triumphs which scattered my epic into oblivion. Yet had not that convivial evening been a sort of song of humanity?

3

About this time Kate O'Brien, my romantic ally of the Brunswick Square hostel in 1921, and her beloved friend E. M. Delafield (Mrs Dashwood), to whose Heinemann party I had gone in 1916, spent a day with us. E.M.D., who knew my father, was the popular author of *The Diary of a Provincial Lady*. She had lost her only son in the war, and now she was suffering from incurable cancer. Cheerful though we tried to be, not least her brave self, we knew that she had not long to live; and during this meeting she was taken ill and it was some time before Kate could drive her home. It was a day of shadows.

Plagued by a restlessness I could not overcome, we spent breaks walking round the Cornish coast, a weekend caving at Cheddar Gorge, and a week at Stratford to see *Romeo and Juliet*, *Measure for Measure*, *Twelfth Night*, *Love's Labour's Lost* and *The Tempest*—Shakespeare in many moods, and productions that for excellence did not approach those I remembered at the Old Vic during the first world war. Between whiles I worked feverishly on my *Song of Man*, which so pervaded me that I thought about little else and sometimes sat up writing all night—a Song that has no ending; but at last I ended mine. Then I wrote a novel, *Stubborn Earth*, published in 1951.

In 1949 we visited the Welsh and Cumbrian mountains, clambered up the Pig Track to the top of Snowdon, and slithered round the circuit of Great Gable. One autumn evening we were astonished to behold in the clear empyrean a pale blue moon, blue as a butterfly's wing, a marsh forget-me-not, a sunlighted sea. And not until twenty-five years later did I read in a magazine: 'Owing to sulphur particles from a forest fire covering 250,000 acres in Northern British Columbia, Canada, the moon took on a bluish colour as seen from Great Britain on 26th September 1950. Similar spectacles have happened since'. But seeing a blue moon has happened for me only once in a blue moon; and not even once would we have dreamed that eighteen years afterwards men would be walking there.

We revisited Porthleven, about which I was planning another novel, to be called *The Golden Gull*; but revisiting scenes of former bliss is as risky as meeting friends of long ago. The Broads had died, and our new lodging was on the opposite side of the village, lacking Ocean View's outlook on to reefs and tides. Perhaps it was the intervention of war, or because youth had vanished, and the joys of the past are irrecoverable, though now and then one may catch an echo of its silenced music, but the magic had fled.

The one person to whom my relationship had not altered, who continued to be the same staunch, helpful, loving person, was Nan, who though ageless to me would soon be eighty. And my filiation with my father was nearly as close as before. Now eighty-eight, he continued to summon me to Kerswell and I always went. His hobby was to raise gladiolas, and every morning we strolled round the garden and ended at the potting-shed, to which I carried large pots which he filled with loam and fertiliser, placed one corm in each pot, planted a label, and I took them to the greenhouse. He called one after me. Remembering him in his near youth, he seemed pathetic and vulnerable in his old age; yet he still wrote more than two books every year, and had ten good years ahead. This was the last time I heard him say: 'When I can no longer hold my pen I shall die.'

I recall only vaguely what was going to be my last Kerswell Christmas, and did not know that across the road at Poltimore House Nursing Home, where Father's doctor presided, my future husband was staying. Once more we were close, this time so close that he could hear the cairn terriers barking, while watching at the bedside of an old friend who had been good to him and whom he had promised to stop with until she died. This Victorian lady—one of Lewis Carroll's loves in her childhood—who knew that Father lived at Kerswell, and admired his books, had suggested that he should call with a note asking if he could come in and meet my father. But he was too modest to do so, though as a youth he, too, had read and liked E.P.'s work, especially *The Girl and the Faun*. If they had met, my future and his would have been different, for each would have found in the other a friend after his own heart. But it was not thus we met.

By New Year's Eve, when I returned to Ponsworthy, I had written more than half my Cornish novel and wondered what I should tackle next. But for the first time I saw only blankness ahead—vacancy, emptiness. I tried to break through, back into the mainstream of life, if only to anticipate a serene old age with Jan and Henry, when something extraordinary happened to turn our small world upside down, and a totally new life began.

PART II

PART II

Marriage

1

On 7th February 1951, a supernova—probably the death of a star in glory and birth of a pulsar—blazed out in the spiral galaxy Messier 101, whose radiance after countless millions of light-years had just reached the Earth. And on that date an event of supernoval proportions shone out for me. It began with a letter from Ethel Herdman, postmarked Buckfastleigh, where she was staying with a wartime friend. Would we drive over for tea? For her services during the war she had been awarded the OBE, and was now living in London. I decided not to go, but Jan persuaded me to change my mind and we fixed an afternoon just before she left. It was freezing and I was not sorry when the old car's self-starter refused to function. However, Jan urged me to try the starting handle and it worked. Our destination was a large villa called Cleavehurst, approached by a drive surrounded with overhanging trees and a huddle of neglected outhouses. The domain emanated desuetude.

I pulled the handle of an ancient bell, heard pealing in the distance, expecting Ethel to open the forbidding front door. Instead appeared a tall, dark, middle-aged man accompanied by a handsome Scottish collie. They made such a startling impression that I felt nonplussed, and so did he, for none of us spoke until Ethel arrived and introduced us. He was Richard Ross; the dog was Roy. She led us into a capacious drawing-room with Victorian furniture, settled us round a table on which stood a silver tray and left, saying she was going to make the tea. 'Isn't it thrilling,' was Richard Ross's first remark, 'a supernova has "swum into our ken"?' So he was interested in the heavens—and even more, I learned, in Heaven. Ethel returned with a silver teapot.

During the meal she explained how they had met, in 1940, when both were working at the Prisoners of War Library Depot in St James's Palace, where books for British prisoners-of-war were collected, sorted and despatched. One evening there had been an air raid and they found themselves seated side by side in a shelter, Ethel with her usual little poetry books from which, to keep up his spirits, she read aloud. But, she told us, he by his imperturbability had sustained her.

In those days Richard Ross, of Scottish ancestry and American nationality and birth, had attempted to join the British Forces and become a naturalised Briton, but while the war lasted this was impossible, and not until 1948 had he become naturalised. We admired the beautiful dog, who gazed at him with unutterable devotion, and asked how they had met, and he told us that while staying in Iona, Roy, being trained as a sheepdog, saw him in the distance, deserted both farmer and sheep, rushed up and lay at his feet. In vain his master chastised him and ordered him back to the flock. After that, every time the dog got the chance he dashed off to Richard's cottage and had to be forcibly hauled back to duty. At last the farmer brought him to Richard and said 'That dog's rubbish. You can have him for two quid or he'll be shot.' Now they were inseparable.

As we said goodbye, Richard lifted a bunch of snowdrops from a vase and gave them to me. I did not expect to see him again; but a month later he wrote, inviting us to a belated St Valentine's Day supper, to celebrate his birthday, which occurred in 1906 during the Ides of March. He took us into a large dining-room hung with his paintings, which he dismissed as 'daubs'. They could not be described as 'abstract', 'concrete', 'representative' or 'realistic', but were highly original, some mysterious, some beautiful, and he explained those we could not understand. Several had been exhibited at the Tate Gallery. One depicted a grotesque and melancholy clown, clearly how he saw himself. He laid the table with a white cloth, lighted candles and opened a bottle of Burgundy with which he filled our glasses. While eating minestrone soup he had made with herbs and vegetables he had grown, to my confusion I upset my glass and jumped up to fetch a cloth, when laughing he told me to sit down and watch. The wine soaked into the damask and expanded. 'Look!' he cried, 'A heart!' Sure enough it settled into a symmetrical red Burgundy heart. 'St Valentine jogged your elbow, for a sign,' said he. And for the first time a faint colour tinged his pale face and his blue eyes glittered in the candlelight.

Over coffee he told us that he was executor and residuary legatee of the estate of his old friend, Evelyn Hatch, who had died at Poltimore House last Christmas, and was about to prepare for the sale of everything except some private gifts, and books of which there were thousands in the library. The house lease ran out in August, when he would return to London to look for work. I hoped he would plan another meeting but none was suggested, and there was no further correspondence. We resumed our normal life and Richard receded into the past.

In May, however, he wrote again, inviting us to picnic on the Moor. We chose Wistman's Wood, the dwarf oak-grove above the West Dart, where since early childhood I had so often been. Leaving the car at Two Bridges we walked above the river to the forest, whose grotesquely wizened trees covered with mosses and lichens, ferns and whortleberries enchanted our companion. Climbing into the branches and swinging from bough to bough, I told him that he looked like the faun in Father's fantasy *The Girl and the Faun*, which as a boy he had enjoyed, and he said 'You mean a monkey.'

We rambled on to Crow Tor, where the bluebell was in bloom, and spread lunch on a flat rock covered with seedums. Granite was Richard's favourite stone, and he described outcrops in the garden of a wooden cottage at Quincy, Massachusetts, where he was born. While he and I arranged the food and Jan played with Roy, he touched my hand and gave me such a look that fire ran through me as wild as the fire which had welded into this boulder its amalgam of mica, feldspar and quartz, and I knew, what I had known from the first moment our eyes met, that an arrow from Eros' bow, or as he would have said an angelic Teresian lance, had struck—in short, love at first sight. But reason, to which Father had accustomed me to attach, as he did, so much importance, assured me that such lunacy was ridiculous and impossible and I must be rational. We took snapshots, fondled Roy, gambolled by the river, and my panic terror passed.

Before parting we all exchanged birth dates, and our singular friend, realising that mine was shared with Shakespeare, planned a Shakespeare tea-party. This time he had lighted two red candles, between which stood in a black and gilt frame a reproduction of the copperplate engraving of Shakespeare's portrait known as the Droeshout, frontispiece to the First Folio, which may retain some resemblance about the head and brow to the living man. 'He is presiding,' Richard said. A copper kettle boiled on the hearth, and in the middle of the table stood a pink and white iced cherry cake piped with a birthday greeting. Beside my place he had put a box containing a dark blue enamelled locket set with three pearls, and a gold chain.

After the party I was helping him in the kitchen when he stooped and kissed me. A few moments later Jan came in and he led us into the garden to see a magnificent flowering cherry tree in whose branches before we arrived he had seen his Guardian Angel. I felt no doubt that he *had* seen an angel, as the visionary Blake saw angels on a tree in Peckham Rye. Before we departed he fetched a green glass bowl, filled it with apple blossom and gave it to me to take home, saying: 'I'm a very homespun person.'

Musing that night on this unwonted being, he struck me as an incarnation of that medieval, or perhaps mythological, character, Denys l'Auxerrois, whom Walter Pater described as 'a denizen of old Greece . . . finding his way back again among men'—the organ-builder of St Etienne's Cathedral at Auxerre, who appears in its stained glass and tapestries, a 'flowery figure . . . with the beauty of a

pagan god . . . who suffered like people of larger spiritual capacity . . .
The sight of him' wrote Pater, 'made old people feel young again . . .
It was as if the gay old pagan world had been *blessed* in some way'. He
was also the 'musician to whom the thought occurred of combining in
a fuller tide of music' all the current instruments, to express the
'whole compass of souls now grown to manhood'—the strange
creature terribly destroyed by the thoughtless crowd who feared that
he was a sorcerer.

Richard's unexpected kiss filled me with bewildered delight,
mingled with anxiety. Unalloyed joy I had experienced only once, on
that primrose journey with Grannie Adelaide when I was six. Since
then there was always, and was always going to be, a shadow on my
joys, a tangle in my golden threads, a stain on my sunrise, some regret,
fear, remorse, guilt, or pity, to mar the bliss.

The day following the party I was summoned to Kerswell, while
Robina went into Poltimore Nursing Home for an operation on her
toes. Every day Richard wrote extraordinary letters that we might, as
he expressed it in a favourite quotation, meet 'in the middle regions of
the air', and signed himself Nicholas, his Catholic name bestowed
when he was received into the Church. As I looked into my father's
old humorous face, expressing that affection which had never
wavered, that certainty I must and should never marry but love him
best until the end, I wondered if he could sense in me any difference.
No: I am sure he could not. Gleeful as a trusting child, 'I've got you to
myself at last,' he said with an embrace. On this visit I was moved as
never before by the pathos of his extreme old age, though he told
me he felt no older, inside, than he did at twenty. How could I ever
bear to hurt him? But, of course, there would be no reason to do so.
Nicholas and I could never be more than friends. He would soon be
returning to London.

While at Kerswell he sent me *The Little Book of Childhood*, the
Child Stories of Dr John Brown, with dedicatory lines from Swin-
burne: 'None there might wear about his brows unrolled / A light of
lovelier fame than rings your head, / Whose lovesome love of children
and the dead / All men gave thanks for' — signed A. C. Swinburne.
The first inscription in the book, dated 1916, reads: Howard
Marryat. In memory of 'The Commerce of Thought', under which
Nicholas wrote: 'Adelaide Phillpotts 1951. In memory of "The
Commerce of Feeling". This book, much loved by Nicholas, was
found on an Edinburgh Book Barrow . . .' I loved this touching gift.

Shortly after I returned to Ponsworthy, Nicholas suffered a bad
outbreak of boils and carbuncles and begged me to come and help
him. Jan, uneasy about our friendship, said it was my duty to go, and
though I felt extremely dubious I went.

He had arranged my room with flowers and a basin of water full of

elder blossom in which to cool my face, in the hot June weather, and
had placed beside the bed Gerard Manley Hopkins' poems, new to
me. Outside the window rose the cherry tree, its blossoms shed.
While I was observing these details he entered, followed by the
faithful collie, who licked my hand. 'You don't mind coming, do
you?' he said. 'It doesn't matter what anyone thinks, because one day
we shall be married.' Surprised beyond words I did not answer,
dismissing it as a jest, though not one I should have expected,
humorous as he often was, impish and comical. I stayed until he was
better, washing and ironing, mending, cooking, and tending his
ailments. During this interlude we told our family stories: here is an
outline of his.

2

To Nicholas in his childhood his father, Norman Ross, related how in
the 1830s his great-grandmother, widow of a Skye crofter, with three
young sons, one of whom was Nicholas's grandfather, decided to
emigrate to the New World, crossed in the good ship *Polly*, and
disembarked on Prince Edward Island, where they tramped inland
until they reached a cliff flowing with waterfalls, so cheering a vision
that she struck her staff in the ground and cried: 'Boys, we will settle
here!' Norman Ross, born in 1867, helped in his youth to build the
trans-Canadian coast-to-coast railroad which unified Canada. Still
young, he left for New England to work in a factory at Quincy, near
Boston, where he married Nicholas's mother, Elizabeth Smith, who
with parents and siblings had emigrated in childhood from Aberdeen.
They lived in a small wooden cottage on Granite Street and raised two
sons and two daughters of whom Nicholas was the third child.

When he and I met, his father, eighty-four, was living in the Boston
suburb of Hingham with his elder son, Stanley, who had risen, in the
Pneumatic Scales Corporation Works, from messenger lad to Vice-
President of the Company, a typical all-American, self-made,
successful businessman, of whom his parents were extremely proud.
Nicholas was as different as my father had been in his family—like
him an artist, of whom his relatives disapproved. They loved him, but
scolded because he idled at school, painted pictures and wrote poems,
some of which he sold to the *Daily Patriot Ledger*. This, his family
said, was a waste of time and 'leads nowhere'. Another failing was his
dislike of baseball.

After various vacation tasks, in order to buy painting materials:
bakehouse boy, paper-rounder, groceries deliverer, at sixteen
Nicholas left school with bad reports and no qualifications, and was
placed in a factory, but gave it up to be programme seller at a Boston
music hall. Later, with his father's and brother's help, he rented a
studio on Boston's Beacon Hill and studied librarianship. For some

years he catalogued private libraries, in one of which, belonging to
a rich Bostonian woman who lived in a mansion off Commonwealth
Avenue, he found a first edition of Keats' *Poems, 1817*, into whose
cover was pasted the poet's admission card to Guy's Hospital.

Hoping that he was settling down, his father and brother set him up
in a bookshop on Joy Street, but the venture failed: he gave books
away and reduced prices to students old and young who loved
literature, had little to spend, and were trying to educate themselves.
Threatened with tuberculosis, he was sent to Battlecreek Sanatorium,
where he met musician Percy Grainger, *Tarzan* star Johnny Weiss-
muller, and the actress Marie Dressler, who stimulated his interest in
the theatre and music hall; and when he left, hopefully cured, he
frequented the Boston Metropolitan, vaudeville and burlesque
theatres, and the Old Howard Music Hall, to watch Jenny Lind,
Sarah Bernhardt, and Eleonora Duse, who thrilled and attracted him.
He was persuaded to join an amateur dramatic society affiliated to
the Ford Hall Forum and played the Poet in Strindberg's *Dream Play*,
where he met Eisenstein, and fell in love with Isadora Duncan, who
was scandalising Boston high society.

In March 1930, he went to the Forum to hear a lecture, 'On
Keeping Your Balance in an Unbalanced World', given by the British
writer and University Extension Lecturer John Cowper Powys—the
most important meeting of his life. They became instant friends,
and at parting in the old Touraine Hotel John said to Nicholas:
'Wherever you are, Ross, and wherever I am, look me up! ITE
MISSA EST! Go, and don't look back!' Nine years passed before they
met again. (For Nicholas's description of their meeting see the end of
this chapter.)

In December 1929, Nicholas had married Weinande, a young
woman he had always known, but the union did not prosper. He
wanted children, and did not learn until after their marriage that she
could not have any. However, they tried to make the alliance work. In
the autumn of 1931 he heard from a friend, the poetess Sarah
Teasdale, that she was planning a book about Christina Rossetti,
whom they both admired, and asked if he would help by going to
England to meet the remainder of the Rossetti family, a 'God-sent' as
he believed opportunity to leave for a time the America he disliked
and the failing marriage, and return to his rootland which since
childhood had beckoned. He loved Christina Rossetti's devotional
poetry, and also that of John Keats, and resolved not only to meet the
still living Rossettis, but to repeat Keats' Scottish tour and visit the
Hebridean islands of his ancestors.

In February, 1932, he booked a working passage on the steamship
City of Flint and sailed on a stormy voyage to the Thames. After
visiting the Rossetti graves in Highgate Cemetery he called on Miss

Mary Rossetti, daughter of William and niece of Dante Gabriel and Christina—a hospitable woman who helped him in his researches for Sarah Teasdale. He had completed his work and was about to despatch the information to her when with sorrow he heard that the poetess had committed suicide. As no money was forthcoming his family ordered him home; but feeling more at home in Britain he decided to stop for a few more months.

He rented an attic in that house my room in the Minerva Club had overlooked, failed to find work, and, his means almost exhausted, was often hungry and his health was permanently undermined. But help was literally on his doorstep, as, in less rigorous circumstances, it had often been on mine. A middle-aged single woman called Phyllis Preston, who lived across the passage from his room, perceiving how gaunt her neighbour had grown, overcame her diffidence, knocked on his door and invited him to join her at supper, pretending that she had been given a chicken and wanted someone to help her consume it.

Phyllis Preston worked for Arthur Mee, the journalist who in 1908 founded the *Children's Encyclopedia* and *Children's Newspaper* and set out to educate boys and girls by 'uplifting' them, visualising his young readers as 'knights in shining armour'. 'It is for you, young England,' he wrote, 'to keep the faith that has brought mankind thus far.' Before the chicken was finished Miss Preston promised to introduce Nicholas to Arthur Mee, and assured him that he would be asked to contribute regularly to the newspaper, which for a time he did. They went to Stratford-on-Avon together, and while wandering alone on Avon's bank who should come along but Bernard Shaw, who stopped and spoke. 'During the encounter,' Nicholas wrote in his Journal, 'I gained no really clear picture of the surroundings, because there in the midst of them, knocking everything out of focus, was the Shavian thunderer himself, exactly as the photos and cartoons had led me to expect: the loose tweeds, the brogues and the woollen stockings, the silvery white beard from which issued a voice that was as silvery in its clarity, eyes as bright as diamond, and a complexion that did credit to his vegetarianism.' Nicholas asked for his autograph and Shaw asked for a pen, but as Nicholas proffered one it fell into the Avon and sank. Shaw, who had elicited that his admirer hoped to become a writer too, smiled and said: 'It is a good omen to drop one's pen into Shakespeare's river!'

Inspired by Arthur Mee's desire to help young people, Nicholas spent some months working at a Boys' Club in Bethnal Green run by a remarkable woman, Comrade Mary Hughes, daughter of Thomas Hughes, who wrote *Tom Brown's School Days*. A Franciscan by nature, she had bought the notorious Earl Grey public house in Whitechapel and called it the Dewdrop Inn, 'for Education and Joy', and made it the centre of her charitable work for the poor, in which

Nicholas helped. But drawn back to the sea, for which he felt a passion not less than mine, he joined the Iceland fishing-fleet and sailed in the SS *Rudolph* from Hartlepool.

He had always been in a mystical sense religious, and though baptised and married in the Anglican Communion, he veered towards Roman Catholicism. While trekking among Iceland's mountains he saw in a vision the Virgin Mary, and later during Mass experienced Transportation to the Holy Trinity, which provoked a powerfully renewed will to become a Catholic. The following year he set out from Liverpool on his Keats Walk, which led across Mull to Iona, an island that meant so much to him, and later to me, returning via his mother's birthplace, Aberdeen. In Iona Abbey, then in ruins, he felt both good and evil Presences. In November 1935, he sailed in the SS *Capulan* from Liverpool for Boston to rejoin his wife, hoping to begin a happier life together, but that proved impossible, and in 1937 they parted and were divorced.

After some despairing months Nicholas heard a Voice calling him to become a Catholic, and this time he surrendered, took instruction, and at Boston's Holy Cross Cathedral was received into the Church by Monsignor, later Cardinal Spellman. His father and brother strongly opposed and condemned this step; but his loving mother and older sister, and his beloved Aunt Olive, his mother's sister, approved. His new life, as he believed supernaturally directed, brought him in touch with a Jesuit priest, Father Terence Connolly, Chairman of the English Department at Boston College Graduate School and Curator of a fine Collection of Francis Thompson's Manuscripts, who had undertaken to write a Life of Thompson and was planning a pilgrimage to Britain to visit the places with Thompson associations. This learned man suggested that Nicholas should act as his amanuensis, go back to England, visit Wilfred Meynell, who with Alice had befriended the poet, arrange for the Jesuit to follow, and then make the pilgrimage together. Here was Nicholas's chance to leave America and become a British subject. He believed strongly in Thoreau's advice: 'If a man does not keep pace with his companions, perhaps it is because he hears a different drummer. Let him step to the music he hears, however measured and far away.'

Six years after his first journey he sailed for London again, and took a lodging in Regent Square, where he renewed his friendship with Phyllis Preston. In April 1938 he stayed at Storrington with Wilfred Meynell, who gave him a few threads of Mary Shelley's hair, a carved wooden Byzantine hand-cross which had belonged to Elizabeth Browning, and a life mask of Keats, that Nicholas passed on to the National Portrait Gallery. Father Connolly arrived in June and they travelled in the footprints of Francis Thompson. While returning from a journey to a Cornish monastery they paused at Morwenstow, where the priest mounted the Reverend Hawker's pulpit, mocked him and the Anglican Church, which he regarded as invalid, and so disgusted Nicholas that he left the Father to finish his journey alone.

Some months later he called on John Cowper Powys, and thenceforth, until 1963, when John died, they frequently corresponded and met at intervals.

Nicholas was in Scotland when the Second World War began. His mother died, and ever afterwards he regretted that the war had prevented him from returning to see her during her illness. His name, his father wrote, was the last word on her lips. In January 1940 he signed on as a farm labourer at Law Farm, near Kilmarnock, but by October the hard life had knocked him out and he returned to London, which was nightly being blitzed. It was then that he got work at the Prisoners-of-War Library Depot, where he met Ethel Herdman, forging a link in the chain that was to bind us. Every night he firewatched at Keats House, and during one raid, bomb metal was blasted into his ears which had to be extracted by magnet.

At St James's Palace he also met an elderly woman called Evelyn Hatch, a scholar and translator, whose father had been a friend of Lewis Carroll and several Oxford divines. At a time when the bombing was at its height Miss Hatch asked him if he would lodge in her house near Kensington Gardens because she was afraid of being alone, and though about to decline, for of all things he most valued independence, he felt sorry for this ageing woman and agreed to stay while the danger lasted. Through her influence he later obtained work at Bumpus's bookshop, where he became friendly with Richard Hilary. Every weekend he wheeled Phyllis Preston, who had been attacked by a wasting malady causing blindness and paralysis, in the Gardens. Though he never could repay her benevolence he did what he could to alleviate her sad lot until she died.

After the war, Miss Hatch, old and failing, begged him to leave London and join her in Devonshire, where he could concentrate on painting and writing, and help her. For years he had been working on an anthology of Mary, Queen of Scots and here, she pointed out, was a chance to complete it and get it published. He agreed to her plan, and they rented Cleavehurst for three years. He was naturalised in 1948 and became 'the King's Bondman'. In their second year Miss Evelyn fell ill with cancer and he nursed her until she died at Poltimore. Looking back over life in the United States, Nicholas told me that the sole spells of unalloyed bliss were boyhood holidays with his family at Lake Pearl, close to nature at its wildest and most beautiful. I have a snapshot of him in a canoe and have often pictured him on the lake, with wildfowl above and moccasin snakes below; and there in his joy I still see him, as if those few benign week are embalmed in the amber of eternity.

3

Near the end of May 1951, I was looking out of the drawing-room window at Cleavehurst at a massive copper beach in full leaf, when Nicholas asked me to marry him. Immediately three overpowering objections confronted me and I set them before him: one, how could I leave Jan who had been so good to me? Two—the most serious— Nicholas being a Catholic and divorced, we could not without dispensation be married in Church, and if married elsewhere he would be forbidden to receive the Eucharist; three, he had wanted a child, and though still possible, it was unlikely we should have one —at least a healthy one. He brushed aside all these obstacles as if they did not exist, and said he no longer wanted children. Nevertheless, unwilling to deny him both the possibility of fatherhood and the blessed Sacrament, I declined to marry him, and returned to Jan. He kept imploring me to change my mind, and Jan implored me not to do so. Never before had I been pitched into such a moral, spiritual, and physical dilemma, from which there could be no escape without someone being hurt. The religious problem most worried me, and that brought Buckfast Abbey into my life.

For two years Nicholas had worshipped there and had friends in the Community, for one of whom, an artist, he had designed a stained glass window featuring St Rose of Lima. He consulted this man, who referred him to the monk in charge of matrimonial affairs, who sent particulars to the Vatican Official appointed to deal with them. Nicholas's marriage was examined and the question of his wife's baptism arose. Had she not been baptised his marriage would not have been valid; but as she had been, no loophole could be found that would enable us to be married in a Catholic church. This determined me not to marry him, for, whatever he said, the Sacraments *must* be more important than I was, and I did not want him to feel he would be damned because of me—though I was not sure if he believed in damnation. To my relief he did not: his Catholicism was as unique and unorthodox as himself: he assured me that God and His holy Mother were on our side—he had been in touch with them—and after that he felt no difficulty in reconciling his conscience to our union taking place in a register office. He hung a little ornamental pendant compass round my neck saying: 'Now you are going in my direction'; and he truly believed that Miss Evelyn had planned our union from Heaven, and said: 'I never thought she'd be able to work so fast!' But if his conscience was clear, mine was not, and it was long before I was utterly convinced that he no longer wanted a family, and would not miss the Eucharist.

If only poor Jan could have accepted the situation, but she could not—she blamed Nicholas, not me, assuming that I was the victim of momentary infatuation which I should bitterly regret. Therefore

Adelaide Eden Phillpotts in youth

Nicholas Ross and Roy at Swanage, 1951

Adelaide Ross and Roy at Swanage, 1951

she did everything to prevent our union, secretly consulting nuns to find out if Nicholas's sin could have terrible consequences on Judgment Day. The sad irony was that had she not insisted on going to Ponsworthy, and out of kindness insisted on our going to see Ethel Herdman at Cleavehurst, this calamity would have been avoided. So my joy was shot through with sorrow, and my pain in wounding Jan was extreme. Henry, too, begged me not to marry. Only Nan stood with us and approved.

Now I must tell my father. I wrote carefully, not to shock him, yet such tidings were bound to shock. No less did his reply shock me. He belittled my information, did not take it seriously, laughed at me, bade me put the whole 'daft notion' out of my head. What on earth was I dreaming of? When Nicholas read this letter he was disbelieving. He had been looking forward to meeting my father and assured me that 'Everyone loves a lover. When he sees us he'll be glad.' He wrote to Father, a firm but kind announcement of our betrothal. He could always write the appropriate thing. Not this time! Father did not reply. I wrote again, telling him more about Nicholas and his family and mentioned that his father lived in Quincy, Massachusetts, forgetting that he now lived with his other son in Hingham—a mistake which saved the Ross family and me some woe. For instead of answering my letter, Father, without telling us, wrote to Nicholas's father, directing the letter, insufficiently, to Quincy, so that it was returned to him 'Not known here'. Then, for some inexplicable reason, he sent his returned letter to me. In it he urged Mr Norman Ross to forbid his son to marry me, adding that neither he nor his daughter was in a position to 'keep' Nicholas. I had to show my betrothed this fatal letter. It was too much. He wrote a stinging reply, showed it to me and asked if I passed it. I did. Afterwards we regretted it and he wrote again, apologising, and asking when we might come to see him, that everything might be explained. Father answered, to me, that, deeply underlined, he would *never meet Mr Ross*. I might come if I wished. But I refused to go without him. Nicholas urged me to go, and perhaps it would have been better if I had gone, but I would not. He telephoned to Kerswell and begged Robina, who replied, to plead with Father to let us come. She rang off without answering; and we discovered later that she never reported this call to my father, and when challenged said she had not received it. Nicholas obtained a form from the telephone service to prove that he had rung up, but Father chose to believe Robina, not him. Thenceforth she did everything to turn him against us, and Jan rushed to Kerswell to implore them to stop our marriage. Nan went there too, with a good account of Nicholas, whom she liked, to change my parent's mind, in vain. If he would meet Nicholas only once it would, I thought, be enough. Or would it? I am not sure. 'You must

never marry' came echoing down the years. But I know that had
my mother lived everything would have been different.

One day we set out for her grave on Pew Tor. Tramping across the
wilderness we passed a bog shining with golden asphodels and
Nicholas picked two bunches, one to send to John Powys who, like
Nicholas's family, including his first wife, had welcomed our union,
one for Mother's resting-place. Sprinkling them there he said: 'Never
mind if your mother is dead and your father resents me. They made
you. I shall always be grateful.'

He gave me a star-sapphire betrothal ring, fixed the wedding for
25th August at Newton Abbot Registry Office, and arranged to spend
our first months in a small furnished house at Swanage. On a drive to
inspect it before we were married we passed Max Gate, and I recalled
my visit thirty years earlier. Having looked over Hebroyd, as the
house was called, we walked along the Dorset cliffs and watched
the setting sun illuminate Corfe Castle until it resembled the fabric
of a fairy tale. Nicholas took a room in a hotel and went out alone,
returning with a little china ornament he found in a local curiosity
shop: a diminutive blue and white couple seated in the corner of a
high-backed couch, he wearing a tall cone-shaped hat, she a sun-
bonnet, and said: 'That's you and me when we grow old and sit
together in the evening.'

On the wedding morning he gave me an old ivory brooch carved to
represent Raphael's *Madonna of the Chair*, and an Iona silver crucifix
—Christ's birth and death. Neither Jan nor Henry would come to
the ceremony but Nan, who was staying with us, was a witness, and
that remarkable dog Roy was also present. Strictly a one-person
animal, unlike so many humans he wholeheartedly accepted me.

At midnight we were walking with him along a dark country lane
when ahead glimmered a green spot, which grew brighter and
brighter until it shone with a halo's mysterious lustre. 'A fairy citadel!'
my husband cried, but when I touched the cool green rays my fingers
sank into a crumbling log—a mass of luminous wood. ('Say to the
Court it glows, and shines like rotten wood', Sir Walter Raleigh
scolded the Elizabethan Establishment.) We kept a few fragments but
their luminescence, caused by the Honey Fungus, sweet by name but
sour by nature, soon disappeared.

Before leaving for Swanage we spent a few days at Ponsworthy with
Jan, hoping she might eventually remain our close friend. Nicholas
asked her to stay with us whenever she wanted to; but she was so
convinced that I was going to perdition, and made the parting so
harrowing, that my hope died. I urged her to stay with her family in
Bristol for a time and often invite them to the cottage, also to visit her
sister in Florida—all of which she did, but with us she would not be
reconciled.

I cannot end this chapter without a word about my Father, lest he be misunderstood. He was an epitome of human kind, a multifarious, compound being, capable of heights and depths, combining instinct and intellect, often at war with himself—a fusion of moral, immoral, and amoral tendencies—a comprehensive, universal man, and a great artist, a genius. He would have told this story quite differently, from his point of view. As to him and us: had only physical passion, strong and even temporarily irresistible, been in question, he might have had power over us to part us. But he had no power over love.

[Copied from *Letters to Nicholas Ross* from John Cowper Powys, published in 1971 by Bertram Rota Ltd]

J.C.P. and J.R.N.R.

I first met JOHN COWPER POWYS on the evening of March 16th, 1930 at the Ford Hall Forum in Boston (Massachusetts) after he had delivered a lecture on 'Keeping Your Balance in an Unbalanced World'—his fourth lecturing visit to the 'hub of the universe'.

We clicked at once because of my friendship with his cousin Fr Hamilton Johnson, a Cowley priest who lived nearby, and because of our mutual admiration of the dancer Isadora Duncan—'she who sprang full-fledged from the head of Zeus'. He took a lively interest in the Dramatic Society affiliated with the Ford Hall of which I was a member, and glowed to hear about our production—the first in Boston—of Strindberg's *Dream Play* in which I played the major role of the sunflowery poet who fell so hopelessly in love with the Goddess-Daughter of Indra-the-Mighty.

The following morning with his permission I visited him at his hotel in Boylston Street with a copy of his 'Suspended Judgements' under my arm to be inscribed for me. The Touraine was Mr Powys favourite hotel in Boston and mine also, for the reasons he sets forth in his autobiography '. . . except at Ford Hall Forum, or when encouraged by such a kindly radical as Longfellow's grandson, Dr Dana, I have seemed fated to get into violent rows in Boston . . . I have come up against sheer hostility, hostility as bitter as my own diatribes. This atmospheric and I might almost say Astrological Clash between myself and the Bostonians was modified for me by the fact that I so greatly enjoyed staying at the Touraine Hotel, the only hotel I have ever known that possessed a comfortable library. This amazing library always had a glowing fire, and contained on its shelves all the works of Henry James. I was also mollified during my Boston visits by the pleasure I derived, which was a very intense one, from visiting my first cousin, John Hamilton Cowper Johnson, among his "Cowley Fathers" at the monastic church of St John in Bowdoin Street.'

These two meetings with Mr Powys I shall never forget. He seemed like one of the gods returned to earth from Olympus or Valhalla, or a Flaming Montezuma, not in spangled loincloths and beaten discs of thin gold, but in modern dress. I praised his books and praised his lecture of the night before, seeming to realise the words he was later to write in his autobiography: 'My lecturing was a sort of focusing, through one single, twisting, leaping, shuffling, skipping, bowing and scraping human figure, or some special comic-tragic vein in the planetary consciousness . . . I often found it impossible to stop. That was my worst fault as a lecturer. I used to try to STOP; and even begin my peroration; but something, some delicate nuance, some metaphysical nicety, would come sliding into my brain, and I would go whirling on again in my spiral dance, like that mad war god in *Hiawatha*. There were even times when I would lecture without a pause and in a mounting crescendo for no less than three hours! Cagliostro as I was, it seemed beyond my juggler's art to bowl Hegel out in the wretched sixty minutes usually allotted to lecturers. My attitude to my audience was the attitude of Catholic priests, not that of Protestant ministers. I rebuked the mighty and exalted the leper . . .'

When in 1938 I sailed to England for the second time Mr Powys had by then given up his American lecture-tours and returned to North Wales to write more books. To me the time seemed propitious to make contact with him again. Were we not together on an island instead of a continent? Friendships are best cultivated in narrow places. Moreover it was the time of the 'Ides of March' again, another March 16th, the day and month of our first encounter in Boston. It was also the especial date he had chosen for his Glastonbury Epic for the flooding of the Abbey ruins and the inspired suicide of Mr Geard: 'The great waves of the far Atlantic, rising from the surface of unusual spring tides, were drawn, during the first two weeks of that particular March, by a Moon more magnetic and potent as she approached her luminous rondure than any moon that had been seen on that coast for many a year . . . It is a recurrent phenomenon in the affairs of men that certain emotional conflicts, which no normal events can effect nor any spontaneous efforts alter, are brought to an end, reconciled, harmonized, blotted out, by some startling elemental catastrophe. It was not until they both had been working desperately for some hours at rescuing marooned people that the father and son met, but when once they had met—without a word having been spoken between them of a personal character—it was taken for granted by both of them that they should remain together'.

So, high up in my little room in Regent's Square in London, I wrote to Mr Powys my first letter and recalled the final words he bellowed at the 'Touraine' as he jogged me through the busy lobby to the front door: 'Wherever you are, Ross, and wherever I am, look me up! ITE MISSA EST! Go, and don't look back.'

                                                             Nicholas Ross.

Swanage and Sark

For the next nine months we lived on the Isle of Purbeck, that strange region which had once been inhabited by Brythonic Celts, then Romans, and served as hunting-ground for Saxon and Norman kings. Nicholas was, as he said, a very homespun person, and thankful for a home. At his wish I tried to finish the novel I began before I met him, but the will to write was lost. And though I did complete the book, it was rejected and I did not try to place it again. Many years passed before I reverted to writing.

We spent whole days on the forelands and beaches, often driving westward to walk through Encombe Woods, past a pond on which floated above its reflection a solitary swan, to a semi-circular bay beneath a waterfall near Kimmeridge's sombre cliffs. The shore was scattered with driftwood of which we construct a 'house' and a bonfire on which to cook. Curiosities of flotsam and jetsam littered the windrows and tide-wrack along which we loitered in search of treasures—green glass balls used as floats, wooden 'limbs', 'animals' and goblins, and useful objects: a platter, a rolling-pin, bread board, teapot and flowerpot stands, chopping-block, besides old wooden ships' capstans and other parts which Nicholas turned into candlesticks and fire-iron holders.

Ammonites abounded, buried for millions of years on the seabed, which rose into cliffs and then eroded into terraces, their fossils appearing aeons later to human beings which, when they lived, did not exist, though a 'first pulsation of mammals', as it has been called, was stirring in their Mesozoic world. Mighty headlands rise there rooted in basalt, banded with diagonal cream-coloured rock that forms a serrated parapet jutting into boulders, some of which have crashed on to the strand — Purbeck marble, Britain's best building stone. The cliffs whispered of disintegration, drip-dripping stone-flakes which dribbled down and spurted onto the beach, a never ceasing sussuration, occasionally rising to the roar of a landslide, disclosing skeletons of Jurassic dinosaurs. How beautiful was that ammonite haunted shore!

We pictured the scene millions of years ago when the fossils were alive, swimming in their convoluted shells in warm seas round low peninsulas bearing cycads, ginkgos, tree ferns and lofty horsetails, gambolling with other shelly creatures clinking on the shingle. One little fossil, *Dactyloceris*, was rippled to Nicholas's feet, and he carried the segment of a whopper up St Alban's Head. Where that magnificent promontory thrusts back the Channel and a fierce tide rip runs, we stepped over hundreds of their shining intaglios buried in pavements which at low tide stretch seaward, uncovering miles of pools and weedy ledges sprinkled with bladder-wrack and sea anemones—a platform worn smooth by flowings and fallings of innumerable tides.

Once we dislodged a stone in the shaly band, to expose a perfect fossil ammonite that, while continents rose and sank and rose again, had lain buried in pristine darkness, its faint colours, patina of ages, glistening from flutings on its outer coil which diminished curl by curl, into a spiral so fine the ridges were almost imperceptible. After aeons of night its prismatic form shone in the sunlight—the same Sun it felt in its lifetime, but Earth how changed. In the pools were purple and green seaweeds, and on the foreshore shells—not only the mussels, pearly-tops, periwinkles and whelks of more wave-trampled coasts, but glistening crescents of nacre, lilliputian chalices, cornets, spindles and pyramids, marvellous miniatures which could not survive on fiercer strands. The saddest flotsam was oiled-up birds, whose corpses since those days have tragically multiplied. From these salty rovings Nicholas brought armfuls of tangle and bladder-wrack, oarweed, ribbon and dulse, with which he filled the nightly bathtub where like dolphins we sported together.

Though we had so much in common and were alike in many ways, there were subjects on which we held opposing views. I had always been a 'left-winger', republican and internationalist. Nicholas inclined to the 'right', felt a staunch love of Britain, and was a royalist, a believer in the divine right of kings—a liegeman of our Queen. We learned much about each other not surmised before, and for me there were pleasant surprises. He was more tolerant than I, with a mischievous streak, and could be droll, full of verbal fun, a Merry Andrew, a man of cap and bells, who wrote comical stories and painted humorous pictures, and made just judgments on people at first sight. But perhaps because our union had begun, for me, in anguish over Father's refusal to meet Nicholas, and dolour over wounding Jan, my ineptly concealed suffering provoked misunderstandings, not because we loved too little but because we expected too much. However, we merged closer and closer: he accepted some of my notions, I acceded to some of his. After a few months we never quarrelled or fell out again. One advantage of late marriage is that the couple seldom grow away from each other, but rather towards and into each other, until they amalgamate.

While I called Nicholas my child of God he called me his child of Nature. I knew that he hoped I would become a Catholic, though he never pressed me; and from the start his Christianity and my humanism did not clash. He told me, humorously, that though he would have to linger a long time in Purgatory, I should already be enjoying the Beatific Vision, and because of me he might at last be admitted through the golden gates, and declared that in spirit I was already a Christian, beloved by the Mother of Jesus. Wiser than I, he helped me to become more reasonable and temperate. I knew that there are many kinds of truth, not mutually exclusive, and that people must strive to see other people's points of view and keep open minds. Nevertheless, because it would have given him joy, I regretted that I could not become a Catholic or even a believer in the faith, and that he could not receive the Eucharist. But, he declared, being denied it made no difference to his felicity; and a time came when he decided to receive it again. We went to the local Catholic church together and shared in the services.

We made a few Swanage friends, one of whom was a widow who peopled her garden with tortoises, and commissioned from Nicholas two watercolour paintings, for which she gave him twenty-five pounds. One was *Flower Ghosts*, the other *Perfume Distillery* to illustrate Sir Thomas Browne's words: 'Within the wood was discloseth one distillerie of perfumes. And on every fallen beam did flourish aromatics of light whereby the phosforescence was wondrous to behold', which I assume comes from his treatise *De lucis causà et Origine*, printed at Amsterdam in 1663. Nicholas took the pictures to be framed at Bournemouth, and when he came back looked so disconsolate that I wondered what had happened. He confessed that he had called at a labour exchange to enquire about work, but there was no suitable vacancy, and no hope was held out that for him there ever would be one. He offered to do labouring jobs but the interviewer must have seen that he lacked the stamina. This failure had cast him down. I begged him to do what he could do best, painting and writing, at home; but he was determined to support us both. Neither of us cared about money, except enough to live on, and I pointed out that he had valuable literary collections which if sold would keep us for years, and I had a small income, so why waste our precious months parted by uncongenial work? At our ages who knew how long we might have together? Finally he assented, and how thankful I am that he did.

Now something very unpleasant happened. My father wrote, demanding that I should get in touch with his accountant, a Mr Bishop of Torquay, and ask him to have that part of the *Yellow Sands* money Father had invested for me, but of which he kept the dividends, transferred into his name, for which my signature was necessary. I realised that he could not bear the possibility of Nicholas benefiting from it, though he had assured me he was only borrowing the dividends for his lifetime to evade income tax. I did not want either capital or dividends, but knowing what exaggerated importance my parent attached to money I determined to use it as a bait to force him to meet us. Nicholas disapproved and said: 'Make it over to him and tell him I would never dream of touching it. Get rid of it as quickly as you can.' But I thought that if I could tempt Father to see him, his hatred and jealousy would die; so I wrote and told him that I would do what he ordered *if* he would meet us. He replied with a furious letter calling me a thief, and refused ever to see either of us. Then he wrote again, pleadingly, but still refused a meeting. He could not bear to lose the money, but still more he could not bear to meet my husband. 'For God's sake, do what he wants,' stormed Nicholas, 'and let's forget all about the damned stuff.' But I had hardened. Father's attitude scorched me. Why was it a crime to have married? However, I consulted Mr Bishop, whom I had met and knew was trustworthy, for I did not want to be a thief. I would abide by his advice. He advised me *not* to return the money, so I did not. But I still had qualms, for my *instinct* had been to renounce it. We never touched that money, and I sent Father the dividends until he died. The capital is willed to a good cause. Nicholas said sadly: 'Your father is afraid to come face to face with truth, or even me.'

Henry, now our friend, came to stay and enjoyed beachcombing. He was too loyal to Father to say one word against him or Robina for which I admired him. That he and Nicholas were reconciled was my joy. Another pleasure was a weekend with Nan, now living with an old sister at Hindhead, and still full of mirth. On our way back to Swanage we visited Grassendale, which had become a Jesuit seminary; for though as a schoolgirl I had rebelled against everything it stood for, it was the source of my present gladness.

My father's eighty-ninth birthday came round, the first on which I had not greeted him, which so upset me that Nicholas suggested I should try once more to heal the bleeding wound by visiting him on my own. The day before starting I wrote a loving letter to tell him I was coming, without Nicholas, and implored him to receive me; but as I was setting out a telegram arrived: 'Do not come. E.P.'. That was the end.

In the spring of 1952 I had a serious operation in the local cottage hospital where, in a ward with seven others, I spent nineteen days. One evening Nicholas brought me a cobblestone he picked up on the shore which became my lodestone: a triangular talisman compounded of sandstone, grit and clay, into which had congealed two commingling quartz rings—a criss-cross pebble with interlocking circles symbolising our eternity; its intersections our encounter, its crystal bands our conjoined destinies. To hold it was comforting.

2

The Hebroyd tenancy ran out in July so we had to find another perch, and glancing through the advertisement columns of a magazine we saw, within half a mile of each other, a thatched cottage and a gypsy caravan to let in North Cornwall, and decided to book the caravan for September and the cottage from October to March, after which we would look for a permanent home. Meanwhile we spent August at a farmhouse in Little Sark where, again and again, we visited an isolated inlet Nicholas called Golden House, encrusted with golden lichens, where we bathed in a sunlit pool. In this golden world of the spirit and senses we played the verse game: each wrote a rhyming couplet to which the other added another couplet, and so on until the rigmarole reached a conclusion. If kept in by storms Nicholas wrote stories with randy plots—he had a bawdy sense of humour—and we collaborated in a novel, but got no further than chapter one.

That lyrical month ended and we migrated to a showman's caravan facing the Atlantic above Widemouth Bay in Cornwall, where Nan, jocund as ever, spent a week. When the time came for her to leave I felt inordinately sad, fearing that I should never see her again and haunted by a premonition of disaster. Yet she was in good health and promised to visit us in the new year. As she waved from the train I felt as if my heart would crack.

In October we moved to the cottage we had rented for the winter, which Nicholas dubbed a whitewashed sepulchre, for though charming without, it was repulsive within. The tiny kitchen was encrusted with dirt; the bedroom floorboards were full of holes covered with bits of threadbare carpet; the wind roared in a huge chimney with the wail of doom. How could we spend a whole winter here? But we had paid in advance and would have to stop. The only water-supply was pumped by hand from a well in the garden into a filthy sink, and this proved our means of escape, for we had not been there a week when the local Medical Officer of Health called to say that the water was contaminated and not fit to use. Nicholas wrote to the owner, cancelling the tenancy and asking her to reimburse the rent. Two days later a truculent woman arrived and refused to do so. But a tussle between her and Nicholas ended by her giving in.

To find a new home Nicholas visited two Bude house agents, in vain, while Roy and I sat in the little grassy triangle I remembered as it looked in 1909, when it was inaugurated, its fountain playing surrounded by flowers. Now the fountain was dry, the flowerbed full of weeds. There was only one agent left, and I was wondering what to do if that failed when Nicholas came running, waving a large key and a piece of paper describing two freehold cottages for sale or to let,

built of cob and stone, in the village of Kilkhampton six miles north of
Bude. One, rented at six pounds a year, had a sitting tenant; the other,
Cobblestones, ready for occupation, had been 'discreetly modern-
ised', and could be rented at three pounds a week or bought.

In five minutes a bus left the Strand for Kilkhampton. In half an
hour we were there, crossing the churchyard to West Street near the
end of which, flanked by other old cottages, stood Cobblestones. A
herd of cows was strolling to meadows in the valley, above which
shone a blue wedge of sea. Nicholas unlocked an ancient door and we
stepped into a low-ceilinged, crooked-beamed little room. He looked
round and said 'We're here until the end.'

Cobblestones

1

Cobblestones comprised a living-room, opening into a kitchen converted from a wash-house, and up little steep stairs a bedroom,
partitioned into two. Over the kitchen had been added a bathroom
with hand-pumped water from a well. There was no drainage, but the
house was electrified. An earthen path led from the kitchen door to a
linhay, once a donkey shed, now used for coal, against whose outer
wall leaned an earth privy, and beyond spread a wild patch bounded
on the south by the village graveyard, and on the west by narrow fields
sloping down a coombe to cliffs against which pounded the Atlantic.
Nicholas immediately saw the possibilities of this small domain.

In the adjoining cottage lived a widow, Mrs Annie Burrows, who
had brought up a large family there, and with her visiting sons and
their families became our good friends. West Street was a friendly
place; and though we were 'foreigners', we were accepted as neighbours. When a neighbour in the street died everyone subscribed for a
wreath; and when a new baby was born everyone brought a gift.

We rented Cobblestones for two months, then bought the two
cottages and much of the furniture for £1,358 12s. 9d. After two years
main water and drains reached the village. Nicholas became gardener, carpenter, mason and decorator, as well as writer and artist. He
made a beautiful garden, handling every loose rock until he got it
where he wanted. One, discovered at the bottom of a rubbish dump,
was a monolith of local carboniferous limestone, which he set up on
the grass and called Carn Gloose, Celtic for Old Grey Stone, where it
resembled one of the Merry Maidens from a Megalithic Circle of
ancient days, and became a favourite bird perch—'A new personality
in our garden' as he described it.

Every summer we sent for new plants and spent autumn afternoons
unpacking and tilling them; but we left one corner wild for a 'pixy
plot'—that coign in old English gardens traditionally dedicated to the
fairies, where groundlings can come and go and must not be rooted
out, a corner like the 'little wilderness' beloved by Andrew Marvell's
fawn. Into ours the wild flowers crowded.

Fortunate in snapping up 'unconsidered trifles', from an old house
being demolished in the village Nicholas obtained dozens of heavy

blue Delabole slates of which he made a path from house to garden
—a heavy job, but in those euphoric days not the most sisyphean task
seemed onerous, and neighbours were always anxious to help. A
massive beech, its bole over five yards in circumference, grew beside
this path on a mound of ferns and bluebells, its boughs slanted by
westerly winds, the whole tree manifesting in every branch its
struggle with at least two hundred years of salt-laden storms. Each
spring it shimmered with tender fimbriated leaves fringed with silky
white hairs, every two or three years dangling with soft golden
flowers, pouring a vernal rain of tassels, and in autumn a spate of
brown nuts and voluminous cloak of russet foliage.

Sometimes a mysterious sound pervaded the garden, like swirling
wind, a distant drumroll, or the throbbing of a gigantic pulse, systole
and diastole, now swelling, now diminishing, sound of neither earth
nor air—the swell, the pulse of the sea. At equinoctial periods of
exceptionally high spring tides, when pulls of sun and moon are
rectilinear and night and day of equal length, mighty torrents rush
towards the shore and crash against precipices, foam into caverns,
recede and drain away; and it was the noise of this tidal motion dying
into distant thrumming that filled the air. People said: 'When the sea
roars it's going to rain.'

We had sold our car and were driven by Mr Frank Gist, a neighbour
and friend, to isolated coves at the feet of cliffs, where he left us to
spend days of sublime solitude, and met us in the evening. Piles of
driftwood came in on every tide, including boards suitable for collages
which Nicholas made in spare moments. Ah, the bliss of those 'days of
joy' as he called them, watching the rollers crash, hearing the pebbles
scuttering—stones of many colours which betokened the poignancy of
passing time. We visualised the gradual transfiguration of the cliffs—
how their filigrees of crystalline veins had fused into the matrix and
hardened into multiform designs, how the promontories had dis-
integrated into boulders, boulders into cobblestones, crunched under
millions of tides into pebbles and finally ground into sand and silt.

How superb are those north Cornish cliffs, twisted and buckled
into fantastic arches, synclines and anticlines, to form one of Earth's
most storm-battered seaboards, round whose bases countless years
of thundering cataracts have scooped caves that run back into the
land, caverns that swill the sea. Spiny reefs rising to pinnacles jut out
at right angles. One resembles an abbess surrounded by kneeling
nuns. After thousands of wave-beating years a nun begins to
crumble, but another will take her place, until the abbess herself
dwindles and vanishes beneath the surge. Streams threading valleys
end in waterfalls, leaping the brinks of glissading down slopes on to
the shingle, so that in one ear tinkles a trickle of fresh water, in the
other the hiss of billows shattering on the strand.

Sometimes we went to Morwenstow, and my husband grew more
and more interested in the poet, priest and mystic, Robert Stephen
Hawker, still like a living presence there. After sauntering through
the churchyard and greeting the figurehead of the brig *Caledonia*,
wrecked in 1842 on the rocks below—a weird white wooden lady
wearing a Scottish bonnet who presides over drowned mariners—we
would linger in the church, with its Saxon font and Norman pillars,
and then cross the fields to Hawker's wreckwood Hut, sit there and
picture him, a big, vigorous man wearing seaboots and jersey, lugging
up the escarpment fragments of wooden ships with which he constructed his eyrie, or collecting the parts of sea-battered corpses to
inter in his graveyard. In this Hut he wrote his masterpiece, *The Quest
of the Sangraal*, and entertained Tennyson, whose *Idylls* are far
transcended by Hawker's unfinished poem.

How often, on our way to Morwenstow cliffs, we paused among the
tombs, the oldest standing beneath a sprawling oak, wind-twisted into
the shape of someone stooping over the mounds of the dead—a region
that breathes a spirit of peace akin to the Protestant Cemetery in
Rome, of which Shelley, whose ashes lie there, wrote: 'It might make
one in love with death to think that one should lie buried in so sweet
a place.' So sweet is *this* place that we resolved to be buried there.

2

My brother's welfare constantly concerned me and I visited him as
often as possible, sometimes with Nicholas. Before our marriage
Henry and Nan had been obliged to move to another, inferior
boarding-house where each had a small bedsitting-room, and when
she left to look after her sister, and Ray Eddy could seldom leave her
work to come to him, he was lonely. Father had bought him an
annuity of £324 a year, on which with other help he lived until he
received the old age pension. One day he and I met at the deathbed of
Aubrey Sharland, Father's old gardener, who when he retired came
with his second wife—our former cook, Blanche—to live at their
Torquay cottage, where she had begged us to see him before he died.
He knew us, and from murmured words seemed to be wandering
again in that beautiful Garden of Eden he and our father created fifty
years before. Blanche told us that Eltham was going to be pulled down
and the garden swept away to make room for the South Western
Technical College. Shortly after our visit, Sharland died. So did
Nan's sister; and I was relieved to hear that Nan was coming back to
live with Henry, and would stay with us in the New Year.

Nicholas loved Christmas as heartily as any child, and brought
home a tree to spangle, decorated the rooms and made a Crèche. The
religious and worldly significance of the festival to him were one.
Shortly before Christmas Eve, when Mr Gist was going to drive us to

Midnight Mass at Bude, a letter came from Henry to say that Nan was
ill and would I come at once? Mr Gist drove me to Torquay. Nan had
had a stroke and was paralysed. I had her moved to a nursing home;
and for the first time I learned from Henry, who had promised her
not to tell me before, that after her Widemouth visit, on the way back
to Hindhead, she was walking along the platform at Paddington,
when an impatient young mother pushing a baby in a perambulator
shouted at her to get out of the way. Being stone deaf she did not
hear, and the girl shoved her aside with the pram, knocked her over
and rushed on. She struck her head on the platform. Someone helped
her up and carried her suitcase to a waiting-room, where she was left
until she felt able to continue the journey. Somehow she got to
Hindhead, but refused to see a doctor, and her sister did not think
it necessary to call one, or to tell me about the accident.

The matron of the nursing home said the fall, the delayed shock,
and Nan's worry about her sister, whom she nursed until death, had
probably caused the stroke. At first, her condition improved and we
thought she might recover. She insisted on me going home for
Christmas Day, and the matron promised to summon me if she grew
worse before my return. I was getting ready to go back to her on
Boxing Day when Mr Gist hurried over to say he had had a telephone
message that Nan was sinking. I got into his car and left. The matron
met me and said: 'She's waiting for you. She can't die until you come.'
I took her in my arms and she opened her eyes, smiled and died.

Henry and I accompanied her body to the Plymouth Crematorium,
where Jan Stewart and Ray Eddy joined us. I hoped that for the sake
of Nan, who had tried to reconcile us, Jan and I might resume our
friendship; but realising that I was not going to leave Nicholas, Jan
would not be reconciled and all we could do was to part in sorrow,
though I continued to hope that some distant day we might meet
again.

Nan, a compulsive hoarder—'It will come in handy some day'
—had accumulated a huge assortment of oddments which had
been crammed into an attic at their previous boarding-house. When
they moved, she carted it 'lock, stock and barrel', as she put it,
into a cellar at Torre Vicarage where the vicar and his wife offered at
an exorbitant price to store it, and where like a bower bird she
frequently visited the hoard to add fresh trifles; for even when she
realised that she would never have a home of her own she could not
stop collecting. On our move to Cobblestones she had dipped into her
treasures and given us a heap of useful things. Now we had to sort
through the remaining pile, which included scores of cardboard boxes,
some dating from Ealing days of the 1890s, full of 'remnants' she had
bought at sales, packets of pins and needles, thimbles, yard measures,
at least a hundred boxes of matches, cartons of soap powder and bars

of Sunlight soap, besides every kind of kitchen utensil, and quires of typing paper, with other stores stocked during the two world wars but never needed, even our long-discarded toys, to remind her of her happiest days. The cellar, which was icy cold, bulged with her collection. Among it I found a little box containing the glass, limpet shell and stone I had turned with the magic wand of imagination into my 'family': without knowing their meaning, but knowing I loved them, she had kept them. Though we worked all day, the parson and his wife never offered us a cup of tea, let alone a word of sympathy. I caught a horrible microbe which ended in severe tonsillitis and fever; but we had to finish the task.

Nan's death, and this illness, so affected me that for weeks after we got home I succumbed to crying fits and could not stop grieving for one who had been my second mother. At last Nicholas could stand it no longer and implored me to overcome this hopeless sorrow, so I pulled myself together and vowed I would never weep again.

Nan continued to be as vivid to me as she was in life, and often reappears in my dreams, laughing and young. To her I owe more than I can describe; and though hers was an obscure, unknown life, like countless others it was worth a thousand times more than lives of many who are seldom out of the news and are perpetuated in history. But thus she would have wanted it to be; and had she read these words she would have told me not to write such 'arrant nonsense', and would say 'I'm nobody!'

The Wagon

It was February 1955. Nan had left Henry and me legacies, and I decided to spend mine on a gypsy wagon, or *varda*, to stand in a corner of the garden overlooking the sea and the sunset. We advertised and received several answers, to two of which we responded. While I tracked down one on Dartmoor, Nicholas traced one to a small-holding at Abbotskerswell, and we met at nightfall to compare notes. My quest led to a farm under Pew Tor, but that caravan was too big and cumbersome. Nicholas's belonged to Mr Davis, a farmer, who bought it from a gypsy family in Glastonbury, who had owned it for nearly a hundred years. We bought it in memory of Nan. Mr Davis removed the shafts, hitched it to his car and towed it to Cobblestones; but as it was too wide to enter the garden path, he anchored it on a site belonging to our neighbour, Mr Arthur Jeffrey, who built a ramp several feet below the garden, over our field hedge, up which he sloped planks to grip its iron-shod wheels, and planned to haul it in with a tractor—the only way to reach our lawn. It was Good Friday when he clamped his tractor to the caravan and drew it to the ramp, up which inch by inch, he manoeuvred the tractor until it tipped on to the grass, dragging behind it at an angle of forty-five degrees the great wooden *varda*. I could hardly bear to watch lest it topple over and smash, for it swayed sickeningly, its tyres so near the planks' edges that a quarter of an inch further and they would have slid off. But thanks to Mr Jeffrey's skill it landed safely, and Nicholas with three stout neighbours pulled and pushed it into the corner he had prepared.

How my husband delighted in that little fancy home! He repainted it outside and in, regretfully covering part of the original Romany colours, maroon and yellow, in order to preserve the wood, chiefly ash, as our friend Mr William Kinsman—local craftsman whose forebears made farm-wagons of exceptional beauty—told us, and admited its wholly hand-made workmanship. His father-in-law, Mr Prouse, who lived over the fence from us, called it the Crystal Palace because, after Nicholas had ornamented it with miniature mirrors off an old Chinese robe, it glittered in the moonlight, and inside on winter evenings reflected candlelight in two large mirrors he procured, cut to his design of water flowers by the fairground supplier, Glamorglass.

Nicholas Ross at Istanbul

Adelaide Ross at Istanbul

Henry Eden Phillpotts

Nicholas and Adelaide on the shore

Out of the *varda*'s double bunk he constructed a table flanked by benches, polished brass handles, wheel hubs and mantel rail until they shone like gold, renovated the roof whose chimney was topped by a cowl he painted scarlet, and fixed to its apex a cut-glass crystal from a chandelier scattered in the London blitz. But it was not long before a tempest blew the crystal into the cemetery and smote down the chimney-pot. Its double-door and eastern windows overlooked the garden; through its western lights we watched the sun go down into the sea or behind the cliffs; and the small southern window framed the graveyard. On the lower half of the door, which Nicholas painted dark blue to represent Space, he pinned circular maps of the oceans and hemispheres, with smaller globes of Sun and planets, and called it the Door to the Universe—to let us out or to shut us in. I sewed curtains, and a flag which on special occasions we flew from the roof, and he made a windbell to ring in the breeze. Roy loved the wagon as much as we did and would sit on the footboard, or lean against a wheel in the shade below. Children loved it and played there before they grew up.

On Shakespeare's birthday Nicholas planned a grand 'christening' for our caravan. As the moon rose, with a red campion dipped in wine he sprinkled the wheels and consecrated them to Fire, Earth, Water and Air, and all of them to Time, likening them to the burning wheels of the Throne in Daniel's description of the Ancient of Days; and to Ezekiel's vision of fiery rolling wheels circled with eyes 'like the crysolite stone' which accompanied the Cherubim, 'for the spirit of life was in them . . . and the glory of God was over them'. And he named the wagon Crystals.

What joyous times we spent there—Donne's 'One little room, an everywhere'—and how hard Nicholas worked there on his books and pictures, and correspondence. On stormy nights we sat opposite one another, playing writing games, reading—he his beloved Plotinus who chimed with his own spirit—storytelling, talking, or silent, thinking of the gypsy families who had lived there, and picturing its history from the time its walls were alive in the forest, waving with branches, bending to the wind, putting forth leaves and flowers. Sometimes it still seemed alive. But no longer could it wander along the lanes, halting in fields and quarries, alongside verges, groves and ponds, while the Travellers unpacked its kettle-box, kindled sticks and hung the fire-kettle and stewing-pot over the flames on cooking irons, while the young people danced and sang. Now it was settled in our garden until, some day when we were dead, it would be blown down in one of those terrible gales from north, south, east or west that, as Nicholas said, 'ripped out one's nerves'. Even now on rough days it rocked enough to rattle the ornaments. But the only part which travelled was its shadow on the ground.

Every day Nicholas spent hours in the caravan writing about his *alter ego*, Hawker of Morwenstow; but one day we went to Plymouth, to put flowers on Hawker's grave, and visit the remains of Charles Church where his grandfather had been vicar, and in 1803 Robert Stephen was born. Only the shell remained, round which half buried lay fragments of stained glass destroyed in the 1941 blitz. We grubbed up a bagful that when washed, revealed multi-coloured patterns of fruits, leaves and flowers, and one an angel's head, which with other pieces he incorporated into a covering for the wagon's southern window.

In Crystals he wrote a short story, *The Sequin Factory*, for a competition, and began a play about Hawker in which Frank Pettingell, an actor friend who singularly resembled the vicar, hoped to appear on the London stage. Sadly the story did not win a prize or the play acceptance; but no setback wounded Nicholas for long, and in the midst of crushing disappointments he would begin a new work. Though he valued and rejoiced in other people's triumphs he never anticipated any of his own. Now he contacted all the people associated with the Hawker family, several of whom lived near. In the vicar's old self-designed rectory lodged Miss Amy Tape, in her eighties, whose parents had worked for Hawker and his wife during the last century. And at Widemouth another old lady connected with the family, Miss Pitman, pressed on him Hawker's hand-written sermons, Bible, and other books, letters and photographs. 'Take them! Take them!' she begged. From his great-granddaughter, whom we ran to earth in Highgate, Nicholas bought Hawker's seals, the log reckoners, or sandglasses, discovered in the pockets of the drowned captain of the *Caledonia*, and other treasures, of which the greatest were two manuscripts of *The Quest of the Sangraal*. A collateral descendant, Mrs Molly Gibson, gave Nicholas Hawker's Jacobean chair, featured in a Hawker photograph; and others who helped were Father Kingdon, the aged Vicar of Bridgerule, Mr and Mrs Michael Kelly of Lifton, and members of the Tape family at Coombe Mill.

Slowly Nicholas built up a comprehensive Hawker Collection, which he catalogued, and studied in depth *The Quest of the Sangraal*, compiling notes and references for a line-by-line Commentary, to be incorporated into a general work he planned about the Vicar of Morwenstow. We explored the whole Hawker country, from Hartland and Exeter to Plymouth, including Welcombe, Tintagel, Bodmin Moor and our own village. Among the people with whom my husband became acquainted during this project was Colonel Charles Wilkinson, Vice-Provost of Worcester College, Oxford, who had also amassed a Hawker Collection: they exchanged Hawker gifts and became regular correspondents; but when he invited Nicholas to stay he would not leave home.

The most remarkable and sympathetic of his new friends was Father Anthony Bloom, now Metropolitan of Sourozk and Head of the Russian Orthodox Patriarchal Church in Britain—a Church to which Nicholas had always been drawn—whose television talks and appearances he greatly admired. The man's mysticism and noble personality appealed to him. They exchanged letters, in one of which the Bishop suggested a meeting in London. But when the time came he was called away and they never met. In his book, *Living Prayer*, Father Bloom wrote: 'The world shall never know peace while one man will look at another and pass judgment on him, for this is the seed of war. But I say to you; when a man can look at another and understand why he is so, and being totally unaffected by what he sees can guide his need, then self will be overcome and peace on earth shall be fulfilled . . .'

As that year subsided into winter, so did our poor dog Roy, who was suffering from incurable old age. No longer willing to eat, he still padded beside us down the lane, but spent most of his time leaning against Nicholas, looking patiently into his eyes. One evening he gazed for the last time, licked his hand, subsided at his feet, on which he laid his head, and died. Nicholas buried him beside the wagon step. Though profoundly sad and missing his devoted creature, his sorrow was mitigated by his belief that animals, too, have an everlasting existence, and he hoped to be with Roy again.

First Journeys

1

Many friends stayed at Cobblestones, among them Leontine Sagan, whose husband had died; Barry Jackson, who was ill and came to say goodbye; and Ethel Herdman, also ill, though she would not admit it. But shortly after her visit her brother wrote to ask me to come and see her: she was in a nursing home dying of cancer. I found her calm and reconciled, without regret or fear; and in that spirit she died. A humble woman, she would not have claimed a place in the long story of women's emancipation and education, world disarmament, peace, and the fundamental freedoms of mankind; but in all these fields she laboured and achieved a little. Above everything else she was a faithful friend.

Henry came two or three times a year, and I went to him when I could. After Nan died his landlady moved to a smaller house at the top of which he had a large room, where he resumed the painting of greeting cards, for which we obtained orders, and lived for the next seven years.

Meanwhile John Powys and Phyllis Playter moved from Corwen to a cottage in Blaenau Ffestiniog, from which, short of space, John returned Nicholas's letters, suggesting that he should keep them with J.C.P.'s own. However, on one of my fraternal expeditions, Nicholas burnt his half of their correspondence, destroying a unique collection which I hoped would be preserved. Disposing of treasures, John sent him a weird, hedge-begotten being he called Arthog, which began life as a bramble-root, described in his Welsh masterpiece, *Porius*; and a horn cup resembling a chalice associated, John thought, with Celtic rites in ancient Wales.

Another exceptional cup now crossed our way. Two elderly friends of the past who lived in a caravan invited us to tea, and while Muriel twanged a guitar, Mabel set the table, on which she placed a large pinkish cup and recounted its history. In the late 1860s her Austrian grandmother, who lived in Vienna, met Goethe's widowed daughter-in-law, Ottilie; and when Ottilie returned with her sons to the Goethehaus in Weimar, Mabel's grandmother and her small daughter, subsequently Mabel's mother, visited her. The old woman took to the child and before they left gave her that large pink cup, now on the caravan tea-table, from which in Goethe's old age he drank his hot chocolate every morning. The small child grew up, married and bore Mabel, to whom she bequeathed the Goethe cup. Nicholas and I shared it filled with tea, and I imagined Goethe in the 1820s and 1830s, until he died, during his meetings with Eckermann, recorded so spell-bindingly in the *Conversations*, sipping from its lip, and wondered if it were this very cup of which he was thinking when, in *Wilhelm Meister's Apprenticeship*, he mentions a 'cup of chocolate' that the Baroness at the Count's castle hands to Wilhelm for breakfast, while the Countess, to whom he is hoping to read his play, greets him, in the hands of her hairdresser who is completing her 'tower of curls'. Enter not only the Count, but officer, gentleman, a footman, and a milliner who opens his bandboxes for her delectation, so that Wilhelm never gets a chance to read her his manuscript—an amusing little scene.

Goethe's cup prompted me to reread his *Italian Journey*, in which he skilfully combines what he calls 'the sun of sublimest art and simple humanity', and blames Michelangelo for causing him to lose his 'taste for nature, since I cannot see her as he did with the eye of genius'. And so strangely does one thing lead to another that this book inspired a sudden desire to make an Italian journey with Nicholas, who would see everything with *his* own eyes. So when I read an advertisement of 'The Catholic Association's St Ignatius Fourth Centenary Pilgrimage to Rome, under the leadership of Archbishop Roberts, SJ' I showed it to him, knowing that he would say 'Let's go!'

On our way to Rome with seventy other pilgrims we broke the journey at Turin, to be shown a copy of the Sudario, believed by many to be the shroud in which Joseph of Arimathea wrapped Christ's body after the Crucifixion. In Rome we stayed at a hotel on the Via della Quattro Fontane, next to the Piazza Barberini in whose centre rises the stupendous torso of Bernini's Triton, more reminiscent of antiquity than of the seventeenth century, recalling Wordsworth's 'I'd rather be / A pagan suckled in a creed outworn, / So I might . . . Have sight of Proteus rising from the sea; / And hear old Triton blow his wreathèd horn.' While in Italy it was this beautiful creature's wreathèd horn, rather than the message of St Ignatius, which I heard.

In St Peter's Basilica, where a vast audience was blessed by Pope Pius XII, we were profoundly moved by Michelangelo's noble *Pieta*, and with our group we mingled in the Sunday crowd to welcome the Holy Father as he stood on the Vatican balcony. But it was not long before Nicholas decided to forsake our fellow palmers and go our own way—first to the Protestant Cemetery to lay flowers on the graves of Shelley, Goethe's son, and Keats from whose violet coverlet we nipped a sucker to preserve until we got home, where he planted it on Roy's grave, whence it spread over the garden and scented our vernal evenings. From Keats' resting-place we walked to the house where he died, to see, among its many remembrances of writers who loved Italy, locks of Keats' and Shelley's hair, and innumerable editions of their works.

After spending hours with sublime pictures and sculptures, we met two Cornish youths training to be Canons Regular of the Lateran, who arranged a private Mass at the high altar of Santa Croce, for Nicholas's Hawker Intentions, where my supplications to all the gods who may or may not be were for the success of his projects. Thence we made our way to the Baths of Caracalla where Shelley wrote part of *Prometheus Unbound* by which in youth I had been so passionately bound to him.

Of all these glories Nicholas was most thrilled by Michelangelo's frescoes on the Sistine Chapel roof; and after our return to Cobblestones, inspired by the cracks in those frescoes he conceived and created a picture called *First Invention of Physical Man*, with his description of which I conclude this glimpse of our Roman journey: 'The first vibration in the mind of the Supra-conscious Spirit of the Universe (God) preceding the creation of Man—As Goethe maintains the colour of Eternity to be GREY, the principle theme of the work is of that colour in its varying shades. Arising from the left bottom corner is the spectrum, the lights of which constitute Man. Above the violet bars, the first and lowest, is represented an aboriginal form symbolic of the black races; opposite in the top corner right, in the higher and more spiritual bars of blue and violet, is a form symbolic of Evolutionary Man in an attitude of conjuration. Man is beheld coming together, assembling, forming; made of eternity, and the chemical and metal components of the cosmos. He weeps, as at his birth and death. He is suspended in a reclining attitude upon a disc of light of which Angels are made, Angels having been created of a substance before the Fiat. Man's unformed arm reaches for a companion who will bear his children. This female element, as well as himself, occurs in the green bar of the spectrum. The legend of Genesis is suggested by the streak of silver lightning in the right ribs, the side of the highest spectrum. The phallos is suggested by precosmic lightning, having no straight lines or right angles, rounded electricity of another sphere. To this grows a suggestion of Yggdrasil, the Tree of Life. Bars throughout the design suggest the imprisonment of Man's Soul, so long as he is resident upon the planet.

N.R.'

2

Fired by our first pilgrimage, we booked for a second, to Fatima, and with thirty others travelled by train to Bayonne, where we changed into a coach for Spain and Portugal. Just before it left we watched a diminutive donkey, ridden by a huge man wobbling with fat, wilt under his weight, give at the knees, and sink slowly to the ground. Next moment the coach started and we lost sight of them, but that collapsing *burro* haunts me still. At Loyola we saw the birthplace of Inigo Lopez de Recaldo, the soldier who, recovering from a wound received defending Pamplona against the French, planned the Order of Jesuits and ultimately became St Ignatius. Green heights rolled all round, cleft by deep valleys through which we drove to Miranda and on to Burgos Cathedral, burial-place of El Seid, as the Moors called him, eleventh-century freebooter and warrier who fought under banners Moorish and Christian. But stalwart as he was, the real Rodrigo Diaz de Vivar had little in common with the heroic Cid of literature and art as, mounted on his charger Bavieca, he appears on his monument. His iron-bound coffer is suspended from a wall of the Corpus Christi Chapel, which also contains a leather figure of Christ crucified, with human hair and a cloth skirt, said to have performed many miracles, which Nicholas revered and loved.

We rattled on to Salamanca and into Portugal, passing Coimbra where we sat among beggars beside the river, with a stop at Batalha with its magnificent southern-gothic abbey—one of those splendid surprises yielded by many journeys. Founded in 1388 by King John the First, this extraordinary ornate and unfinished edifice contains the grave of Portugal's Unknown Soldier, and in the Founder's Chapel the sarcophagi of King John, his English Queen, and their son Henry the Navigator, who established the Foundation for Mariners and Explorers at Sagres, where he died—promoter of seaborne expeditions and inspiration of discoverers like Bartholomew Diaz and Vasco da Gama, who, without him and his caravels, might never have doubled the Cape of Good Hope or reached India.

A thunderstorm broke and rain pouring through the abbey's roof shone on the pavement. We could have lingered, but were summoned to Fatima, overtaking pilgrims in all kinds of vehicles, on horseback and on foot, bound for that once humble village, now one of Christendom's most venerated shrines, where in May 1917, ten-year-old Lucia and her cousins Francisco, nine, and Jacinta, seven, while herding sheep in a limestone declivity called the Cova da Iria saw the vision of a beautiful young woman, who promised to return on the thirteenth of every month until October, when there would be a sign that she came from Heaven. Meanwhile they must make sacrifices and recite the Rosary every day. Accompanied by more and more people they returned every month to greet the Lady, until officials locked them up among criminals to prevent them from keeping their tryst. However, they were released in time for the last visitation when, with fifty thousand others, they awaited the Apparition, while rain descended from a stormy sky. Suddenly Lucia cried: 'Here she comes!' She asked the Lady who she was and what she desired of them, to which the Vision replied: 'I am the Lady of the Rosary. Build a Chapel here in my honour. Men must do penance and ask pardon for their sins and not offend Our Lord.' The rain stopped and Lucia called out: 'Look at the sun!' which appeared to be whirling in the sky and spinning towards the Earth . . . Two years later Francisco and Jacinta died of influenza, and when she was nineteen Lucia became a lay sister and afterwards a nun at the Carmel Convent in Coimbra.

We arrived in the evening during another thunderstorm, which flooded an area round the hospice where our party was expected, so we stopped in the coach until the water receded. The vivid lightning recalled to Nicholas El Greco's eerily illumed landscapes, suggested, he thought, by displays like the one we were witnessing. (Many years previously he had painted *Christ Dying on the Cross*, lit by a lightning flash, which of all his works I most admire.)

We waded to the darkened hospice, its lights doused by the storm, where someone handed us a lighted candle and we groped our way to a whitewashed cell with a bed, two chairs, a basin and cold-water tap. By this time my husband had developed virulent influenza, caught from another pilgrim. But so exultant was he at being in Fatima that he made light of it and refused to miss one moment of the festival. It was late as we mingled with the crowds—pilgrim groups from all over the world, and thousands of fisherfolk and other peasants, their mules and donkeys tethered beside them. Some were camping under the steps rising to the basilica, others in the open who had kindled small fires that lit their ardent faces, mothers suckling babies, children sleeping in each other's arms. Nicholas spoke to them and they understood one another.

At ten o'clock we joined a candlelit procession walking slowly round the Cova singing Mary's song, while an all-night vigil began outside the main church where the exposed Sacrament awaited the first Mass. Nicholas wanted to stop up, but, feverish as he was, I persuaded him to return to the hospice. Meanwhile we visited the Capelhina—little Chapel of the Apparitions—a rustic building, to which pilgrims advanced on their knees, erected over the spot where the children first saw the Lady, a simple shrine where Nicholas said he felt more humbled and more exalted than in any other place. While he knelt an aged peasant woman shuffled up and stroked the scarlet poncho he was wearing to keep out the cold on this chilly night—a moving gesture. By the time we reached the hospice he was shivering and coughing, and as most people were in bed or keeping vigil I had difficulty in persuading a nun to get him a hot drink. I tried to keep him warm but neither of us could sleep. 'What does a germ matter compared to being *here*?' said he.

After Mass next morning we joined thousands of other suppliants at the Capelhina whence the Statue of Our Lady was brought for the

Mass of the Sick. Along a line of stretchers walked the presiding bishop, blessing the sufferers and offering the Sacrament, and the radiance of those faces, transfused with devotion and worship, was marvellous to behold. The Procession followed, a million people accompanying the Statue round the Cova, singing her refrain, and as it returned to the Chapel the multitude fluttered their handkerchiefs, looking like breakers on a choppy sea.

When we left Fatima, Nicholas was nearly well, but I had caught the virus and recall little of the journey home except a night in Valladolid, where Cervantes had lived and Columbus died. That pilgrimage had an overwhelming effect on my husband, though the exhausting travelling and his illness, coupled with the emotional strain, left him weak. Every day he spent in the wagon, composing an account which I hoped would be published if only privately, that others who will never go there might enjoy it. But after his previous rejections he decided never to send out scripts again or exhibit pictures. He had no ambition for acclaim, only for recognition by friends, like John Cowper Powys, who called his short story *The Sequin Factory* 'a little work of genius'. And though at the time I regretted this, looking back I am sure his later years gained serenity by avoiding the mart. He had already commissioned several pictures from Henry, including one of the wagon, one from an old engraving of Well Walk, Hampstead, associated with Keats, and now he asked him to paint one of Batalha Abbey, which he treasured. He told me that he received from Fatima 'for the first time a true shaft of absolute pure happiness', and declared that 1956 had been his life's peak year.

3

Early in 1957 I heard that Alice, an old friend of ninety living at Eastbourne who went to school with my mother, and befriended me in London, was in failing health and wanted to see me, so I went to her. Unlike most of my women friends she had approved of our marriage. On my last morning she gave me a cheque for a hundred pounds to be shared with Nicholas, and told me to spend it on a visit to Paris, which she loved, and another pilgrimage. We decided to go to Paris for a few days and on to the Provençal Gypsy Festival in honour of their Patron Saint, Sara, and then to Lourdes. While planning, Arend-Roland's comet arrived from outer space, shining like a golden spear; and later came Mrkos, a foggy-skyball, followed by more of their kind.

In Paris we went first to Père Lachaise to search for the ashes of Nicholas' boyhood love, Isadora Duncan, but when we found them, in a kind of marble chest of drawers, we felt so depressed that we wished we had not come. We visited the cathedral of Chartres, whose blue thirteenth-century windows made my husband feel he was

melting into an illumination; where he said of the Black Madonna
'She is glad we have come'; and where he loved the elongated statues
round the lateral portals.

We reached Arles on a warm summer evening, and finding the gate
to a mysterious region unlocked, entered Les Alyscamps, an ancient
Roman cemetery through which winds an avenue of marble and
granite sarcophagi, leading to a half-ruined church overshadowed by a
beautiful ginkgo tree. Glow-worms gleamed among the hollow
coffins, suggesting to Nicholas the 'corpse-lights' seen in damp
churchyards, which he believed were illuminations from the spirits of
the dead. Nightingales sang in pine and cork trees and dew released
pungent scents from poppy, wild sage and thyme springing in crevices
between flagstones. Bay trees shed fragrance from above, poplars
rustled and cypress plumes waved.

This old pagan necropolis, mentioned by Dante and Ariosto, has a
romantic, half-legendary history: Christ's disciple, St Trophime, who
founded Arles Cathedral, decided to consecrate it for Christian burial,
and before he did so Christ appeared, put forth His hand, knelt and
blessed the ground. Trophime built a chapel over the spot, and was
buried there. Long afterwards Constantine enclosed the chapel in a
church where a hermit monk from Greece, Honorat, who became
Archbishop of Arles, was also laid to rest; and in the Middle Ages so
were the heroes of Roncesvalles. Now only the sanctuary survives, its
pillars supporting a dome and a Byzantine drum pierced by arches,
like a lighthouse watching over the dead.

Next day we bought a brown loaf and cheese, olives and cherries,
with a small bottle of wine and returned to Les Alyscamps for lunch,
while birds sang and lizards scampered, butterflies settled on us and
the place was demi-paradise—that reminded me of Rousseau's meals
with Thérèse, whom he later married, which they took at his window
'opposite to each other upon two little chairs, placed upon a trunk,
which filled the embrasure . . . The window served us as a table, we
breathed the fresh air, enjoyed the prospect and the people who
passed . . . Who can describe, who can feel, the charm of these repasts,
consisting only of a loaf of coarse bread, a few cherries, a morsel of
cheese, and a small bottle of wine which we drank between us? . . . I
have always said and felt that real enjoyment was not to be described'.
Such was our feast at Les Alyscamps. We were told that its gate was
always locked before sunset, so why on our first evening had it been
left open? Nicholas said his Guardian Angel had tampered with the
lock. But that angel evidently thought once was enough, for the
following night it was locked!

Next morning we rumbled in a shabby old bus across the Camargue
to Les Saintes Maries de le Mer, passing gypsy caravans of all
descriptions. The independent Romany race had attracted us since in

childhood Nicholas went to Buffalo Bill's Circuses and Henry and I frequented the painted wagons at West Country Fairs; and we regretted the poor deal to which they are subjected. Why should their chosen way excite prejudice and be discouraged? What harm did it do? If destroyed, a bond with nature and preservation of nomadic freedom would be needlessly sacrificed. Now we were on their pilgrimage in honour of Jesus's aunts, Mary Salome, sister of the Virgin, and Mary Jacoby, mother of James and John, and their gypsy servant Sara, who, according to legend, landed after the Crucifixion at Les Saintes Maries on the Provençal coast, in a vessel miraculously borne from the Holy Land. This small town is to the Romanies what Mecca is to Muslims, Kandy to Buddhists, Ise to Shintoists, Badrinath to Hindus, Jerusalem to Christians, Muslims and Jews. Their spirits, like ours, must have glowed when from far across the rice fields of the flat lands and Rhône delta they spied the fortress church's lofty bell tower, built a thousand years ago to defy the Saracens, from which land and sea are visible for over a hundred miles.

Dumping our bags at the Hotel Bar Restaurant Chez Camille, we watched the Travellers pitching camp under tamarisks on the common, after which we all crowded into church to venerate Saint Sara, first pausing to kiss the painted wooden figures of the two Maries in their boat; while from a spring once dedicated to Artemis, later to Mithras and now to Christ, women filled bottles of holy water, into which a few of them scraped grains from a lump of marble in the north wall said to have pillowed Sara's head—a potion guaranteed to make childless women conceive. But there was little unfruitfulness among these gypsies, surrounded by drifts of children as abundant and beautiful as the wild flowers on the margin of the strand. We trooped down steps grooved by five centuries of feet into a dark hollow under the sanctuary, stepping back nearly two thousand years, where side by side stand pagan and Christian altars and, illuminated by hundreds of candles, Saint Sara's image reigns. Clothed in varicoloured silks and glittering with jewellery given by her votaries, her dusky features, rubbed smooth by Romany lips and fingers, mysteriously smile. Carried away by rapture her lovers were presenting her with photographs, necklaces, charms, 'diclos', and if they had nothing else old clothes. Young mothers lifted infants to press their mouths to her cheeks, men bowed, children reached on tiptoe to stroke her feet, old people drew knotted hands across her robes, and many whispered petitions or like us tendered invocations. The grotto, filled with smoke and the smell of burning tallow, grew hotter and hotter while molten rivulets dripped from collapsing candles and roped to the floor to mingle with a runnel of water. Eyes sparkled in ecstatic faces, and in a climax of devotion one woman tore from her ears a pair of flashing rings to hook on to Sara's cloak.

By dawn the gypsies were replenishing their fires and left dogs to guard the camps while they attended High Mass, presided over by the Archbishop of Aix at an altar in the Square, and afterwards kissed his ring and begged him to bless their children. Effigies of the Saints were taken from the Church, a procession formed, and with Sara swaying on Romany shoulders, and the Marys borne by Camargue horsemen, everyone marched towards the beach for the immersion of the Saints. Behind them the mitred Archbishop waving a silver arm containing the Saints' bones strode, and alongside rode cowboys on white horses descended, according to tradition, from those which drew Poseidon's chariot when Artemis was worshipped here, and escaped to the land— steeds still flecked with foam. The multitude stood in a semi-circle on the sand, while raising the reliquary the Bishop blessed the Saints, the People and the Sea. *'Vivent les Saintes Maries!'* *'Vive Sainte Sara!'*; after which the gypsies dispersed to partake of a traditional feast for which every family had brought a bird prepared the previous night; and the shore was filled with the savour of the sacrifice.

We returned to church for the Descent of the *Châsses*, a double reliquary holding the Marys' bones which is kept in a *Chapelle haute* and let down twice a year. The Archbishop pronounced a Salute, praising tolerance and peace, and while the Magnificat was chanted the congregation of the Romanies, Arlésiens and other devotees and tourists lighted candles and stared upwards, flames illuminating their chins, waiting for the door in the triforium to open and the casket to appear. And again everyone shouted *'Vivent les Saintes Maries!'*, the gypsies hollering *'Vive Sainte Sara!'*. An orchestra of flutes and drums, tambourines, guitars and violins struck up as an enormous coffer, its double cable bedizened with roses, carnations and marigolds, descended, while, believing that the first person who touched it would gain his dearest wish, the younger faithful sprang; and as it came to rest on a stand in front of the altar the ebullient mob cheered and waved, embraced and kissed the *châsses*.

Merrymaking echoed into the night and fires glowed along the dunes. On the Plaza and in each encampment Romanies were dancing and so were we, with each other and with them. Some invited us into their caravans, in one of which belonging to an Armenian family a young woman offered me her newborn son to hold. Spanish and Romanian gypsies sang and played to us. Sometimes a fight broke out and people ran to look on; but in the small hours strife and revelry ceased and there was silence except for the slapping waves.

During the last day those who were not packing for long journeys returned to church for the *Adiaux aux Saintes*, when the Chest soared back to its Chapel of Honour, and old people gazed at it sorrowfully as if bidding a beloved friend farewell, knowing they would never see it again; yet their sadness, which we shared, was tempered with gratitude. And though for them and us this pilgrimage must suffice, most of the Travellers would return. A few lingered with us in the crypt, until a weary sacristan ejected us into the tamarisk scented evening. By dawn every tent, van and Romany had disappeared.

4

We left by train for Lourdes, running between the Cevennes to the north, to the south the foothills of the Pyrenees, and arrived before nightfall—Lourdes—surrounded by heights fledged with wild box, rising to lofty mountains—Lourdes which had lured Nicholas since he first heard the story of Bernadette Soubirous. Here we took part in all the ceremonies, were immersed in the holy spring, knelt in the Chapel of the Apparitions, and rode mules to a magnificent hollow near Mont Perdu called the Cirque de Gavarnie down whose scarps avalanches were foaming. On the last day we picnicked opposite the grotto in a flowering meadow from which, ninety-nine years before, Bernadette, barred by authorities from entering the cave, had seen her last vision of Mary the Mother of God. The river was in spate and myriads of marguerites had sprung among the tall grasses, as we pictured her—itself a vision. I brought home a wild box cutting which has grown into a thriving shrub.

One other pilgrimage of that period was to Dartmoor, where we stayed at Beardown Farm and revisited Wistman's Wood and Crow Tor, Longaford and the Beardown Man, scrambled through the Cowsic Valley, and tramped to Whiteworks and Nun's Cross. Now and then the phantom of my father seemed to join us, notebook in hand, jotting down entries for his moorland books; for sometimes the past is all too present, and I had been wiser to have buried it; but I never could.

The Studio

Our gypsy wagon's roof was leaking, and in spite of tarpaulins, which sooner or later got ripped to pieces by the gales, and other measures to keep out the rain it was damp, which with fumes from the oil heater was affecting Nicholas's health; so we decided to turn the dilapidated donkey shed into a cottage-studio where he could work during autumn and winter, and in spring and summer be let to holiday families. In 1958 this, with a neighbour's help, was his task. When an old cottage in the village was pulled down he secured its bay window to fit into a wall overlooking the garden, where it caught the westering sunlight; an ingenious chimney was constructed, and the interior partioned into a living-room, double bedroom, kitchenette, wash-room, and shed, over which, reached by ladder, were a bedroom and lumber-room. When water, drainage and electricity were run in the linhay became a self-contained home.

To finance the work Nicholas sold his Francis Thompson and Lewis Carroll Collections; I sold Mother's and Nan's autograph albums filled by Father's friends of Eltham days. At sales we picked up furniture, a set of *Household Words* with contributions by Hawker, and thrown in gratis an oblong mahogany box we thought was empty yet when opened disclosed a Victorian glass prism. How long that creature of light had lain in darkness we did not know, but placed in the window a sunbeam transmuted it into a column of opal and it splashed the walls and ceiling with spectrums that glided from one object to another as Earth turned.

Before the reconstruction was finished, every evening we lighted candles in the window; and during the short winter days while returning to the cottage along the garden path, a street light on a telegraph pole suggested to me a lamp illuming the garret of some modern Chatterton—a fantasy which became so real that I looked forward to seeing it and thinking of Milton's lines: 'Or let my lamp, at midnight hour, / Be seen in some high lonely tower . . .'; and when the telegraph pole and its light were moved I missed my ghostly poet in his roost.

I recall a weekend that year at Sennen Cove, with a coastal walk from Land's End to Porthcurno, and a bathe in Nanjizel Bay; and a hunt for dolmens, menhirs and stone circles, crawling through the mysterious holed-stone called Men-an-tol.

One evening at home we were watching television when on to the screen hobbled a little old man bent nearly double, accompanied by the poet John Betjeman in a straw boater and Edwardian suit. They entered a garden and sat on a seat where I had often sat. The ancient man was my ninety-six-year-old father, and the shock of seeing him again, so shrunken, was shattering. They contrasted today's poets with those of earlier generations, and my parent decried the current breed: his mind was still diamond clear. Henry had told me that he recently underwent an operation for cataract and could now see well and read and write as usual. This television meeting made me long to be with him once more. Was it even now possible to heal the wound which could still trickle blood, though I knew that any hurt he suffered would long be cured? At first I thought it might be kinder to leave my poor ancient father in peace, but when my *Song of Man* was published by the Linden Press I decided to send it to him. He did not acknowledge it.

At last the cottage-studio was completed and we had a brochure printed, advertised in the *Observer* and received dozens of enquiries. But before the lettings began we answered an advertisement in the *Catholic Herald*, inserted by Monsignor Coonan, Head of the Catholic Students' International Chaplaincy, with charge of overseas students needing holidays, offering the studio to three of his students and him. One July evening the elderly priest arrived, with Cyril Okose from Nigeria, studying engineering; Ashley Tagoe from Ghana, studying surveying; and Ari Chanmugam from Ceylon, studying science. How delightful and delighted they were! The studio's first guests—Nicholas took them to our favourite beaches where they bathed, climbed rocks and ran races over the sand. Sometimes they spent evenings with us, telling us about their lives in Sri Lanka and Africa. I wonder where they are now.

For five summers the studio was full of parents, children and their pets. A baby was conceived there. An old dog died there and was buried in the garden. But as soon as expenses were recovered we gave up letting and kept it for our friends and ourselves. One autumn the Reverend Stephen Hawker's collateral descendant, Lady Ella Whitaker, came to see Nicholas and gave him a rare first edition of the Vicar's earliest printed poems, *Tendrils*; and she was followed by Hawkers from Tasmania, Mrs Allport and her brother, who told him that the remains of Joseph Conrad's sole command, the iron barque *Otago* described in *The Shadow Line* and *The Mirror of the Sea*, had laid, before being fired, with her bows in an apple-orchard on the Derwent River near Mrs Allport's home. Nicholas, who greatly admired Conrad's work, begged her to send him some fragment

which had survived the flames, and a few months later she sent a
rusted iron bolt, which inspired him to compile a 'Conrad scrap-
book', containing pictures of other ships associated with Conrad, and
the copy of an article written by his friend G. F. W. Hope, related
by marriage to a friend of ours who lent us the article, which describes
how the two men sailed on the Thames. Conrad corresponded with
my father, so we felt that in a roundabout way he, like Hawker, was
our friend.

Now began years of more extended travelling, beginning in 1960
with a visit to the Holy Land.

Pilgrimage to the Holy Land

1

We had been considering how money for a journey to Palestine could be raised, when Henry and I each received a legacy of six hundred pounds from an American millionaire who, when we were children, had met Father and admired his books; so part of it went on tickets for a pilgrimage led by Miss Mildred Whibley, of Our Lady's Pilgrims, accompanied by Monsignor Victor Guazzelli of Westminster Cathedral. Three weeks were to be spent in Old Jerusalem, then part of Jordan, and two in Israel, with visits to all the great Shrines, and to the Qumran caves where the Dead Sea Scrolls had recently been discovered, calling at various ports and cities, including Athens and Rhodes. (Before starting, Burnham's Comet arrived in the region of Ursa Major. Hail and Farewell!)

At Victoria Station we met fellow pilgrims from several different countries, among whom were four priests, nine middle-aged spinsters, two bachelors and one widow. We were the only married couple. Standing out was a stout, four-square, ageing woman with golden curls under a floppy straw hat who carried a hefty staff, Miss Mildred Whibley herself, leader of the band. She and Nicholas immediately took to each other and became friends: he admired her truly Christian spirit, less evident in several of the others, and esteemed her for making a vow when teaching in the East End during the war, that if her pupils came through unscathed she would found Our Lady's Pilgrims, and for the rest of her life lead annual pilgrimages to Fatima, Lourdes and the Holy Land, assisting poor people to go without payment; which she did for thirty years until she died.

At Turin we left the train for the Basilica of Santa Maria Ausiliatrice, Mother Church of the Salesian Fathers, visited St John Bosco's Shrine and attended Mass, before embarking at Genoa on the motor ship *Esperia* for Naples, Alexandria, and Beirut—five days at sea. Travelling fourth class, Nicholas and I were parted at night, I sharing with four other women, he with two other men. Mass was said every morning in the ship's cinema, and he, anxious to take his turn at serving, in his eagerness to do everything right sometimes got the priest's vestments mixed up, and the one he was vesting became hopelessly entangled. None of the pilgrims could make him out, except Miss Whibley: they were in perfect accord.

The ship was packed with not only palmers—New World Franciscans in flowered shirts and Old World Benedictines in threadbare habits—but with Alexandrian merchants and Arabian sheikhs, Cypriot emigrants and German tourists, Egyptian soldiers and American commercial travellers, British families joining servicemen, cheerful nuns, and one sad nun who leaned over the taffrail weeping into the sea. Amidst the throng was a very old man, so fragile that the strong wind could have wafted him overboard like a silvery sapless leaf. One morning we sat near him and wished each other good-day, whereupon he told us that he was a Muslim missionary from Hoogly in West Bengal bound for Mecca. Sheikh Munsi Masur Ahmed had been there before, and described the Kaaba—the stone building in the centre of the Great Mosque—whose original, legend records, was a Tabernacle of radiant clouds that descended into Paradise, where Adam worshipped and saw Angels dancing. When Adam died it returned to Heaven; but Seth copied it, and after Seth's Tabernacle disappeared in the Deluge, Abraham built the present one, to which the Angel Gabriel brought a Stone to be set in its south-eastern wall. Many people believe this dusky stone was originally white, until the sins of kissing pilgrims turned it black. One of the kissers was Sir Richard Burton, who thought it was an aerolite of crystal-sprinkled basalt. Some experts suppose it to have been a pagan idol long before Muhammad lived, when the Kaaba was a temple to Saturn.

This gentle old man, dedicated to the brotherhood of humanity, left the ship at Alexandria and we missed him; but we had promised to think of one another on our pilgrimages: were they not fundamentally the same?

Whether it was the food, eaten at a long crowded and dirty table, or I had caught a chill, I had a nasty intestinal attack and felt feverish and shaky when we reached Alexandria, but insisted on going ashore. I wanted to stand on Africa. We were amazed by the swarming millions, the beautiful children, the heat of the sun. Next day we disembarked at Beirut and waited for a plane to Jerusalem. Nicholas hated flying and felt apprehensive when he saw the little tinpot contraption into which Miss Whibley led us. Flying at ten thousand feet we looked down upon a golden desert, here and there a settlement, or refugee camp for Palestinians dispossessed by the Jewish state. Yet one sympathised also with the Jews, six million of whom had been murdered in concentration camps. If only the two sides could have co-operated and become reconciled, brothers as they were. It was not to be.

We descended into Jerusalem and were driven to a Franciscan

Pilgrim House in the Christian quarter of the Old City, not far from the Jaffa Gate. Here we had the good fortune to be allotted the best room, with a balcony overlooking small dome-roofed dwellings and tiny gardens where near twilight a breeze sprang up, which set cypress trees nodding like worshippers bowing to a divinity, while laundry which had hung limp all day filled and swayed. From minarets came the call *'La iliha ill'Allah, Muhammadan rasulu Allah'*, and from a campanile rang Christian bells. Nicholas bought a large water-melon whose pink flesh we sucked in the fragrant nights as we sat on our balcony.

Through the narrow *souks* we walked to the Basilica of the Holy Sepulchre, damaged by earthquake and eroded by age, its façade shored up by massive iron beams and girders, its interior of chapels, convents, choirs and shrines divided into six different areas, each belonging to one of the religious communities who control the fane: Roman Catholic, Greek Orthodox, Syrian and Armenian, Coptic and Abyssinian. The holiest shrine, belonging to all, is the diminutive marble chamber of Christ's tomb, where Nicholas served Father Guazzelli's Mass, and had a vision of the Crusaders who in the twelfth century had helped to build this amazing church.

A large party of German pilgrims sat opposite us at meals; and our lot and their lot were incompatible. The climax came for us when Nicholas developed a bad sore throat and fever, and Miss Whibley insisted that he must see a doctor, the only one available being a loud-mouthed masculine Fräulein attached to the German group. When she and Miss Whibley appeared in our room and she commanded him like a sergeant-major to open his mouth, he refused to do so. A painful scene ensued. Miss Whibley looked pleadingly at me, but what could I do? Outraged, and saying something dire in German, the doctor retreated and slammed the door.

As usual, Nicholas's spirit surmounted his physical ills, and during the following days we spent most of the time on our own. Every evening we walked in the Old City's lanes, along which plodded loaded camels and donkeys, and Nicholas would suddenly dart into some booth or shop to buy strings of praying-beads and converse with the Arab owners. At a cobbler's workshop he made friends with Abdulla Jolain and his apprentice Ziad Khedar, a lively boy who implored us to take him to England: 'I will do *anything!*' Some shopkeepers asked us to their homes for a meal. One lasting relationship was made with Jasmin Sabat, a pretty little woman in a gift shop—where Nicholas bought me a bedouin skirt and blouse embroidered by Palestinian refugees—who described families crammed into squalid camps of sickness and heartbreak, so that one marvelled how for minute reward they could produce such exquisite work.

We followed the Via Dolorosa, which starts at the Praetorium and ends on Calvary, and spent hours in the vast Haram-an-Sherif with its minarets and domes, arcades and fountains, and tombs of Kings, Counsellors and Benefactors of Islam. How beautiful is the At-Aqsa Mosque, to which Saladin brought mosaics from Constantinople, from Aleppo a *mihrab*, and carved cedar wood *minbar* inlaid with mother-of-pearl and ivory. But we were most powerfully affected by the octagonal Dome of the Rock. Damaged by the war of 1948, renovations were still in hand and over the golden dome towered a giant crane. Inside, half hidden by dust, beneath the cupola sat workmen to whom were hoisted buckets of cement; and far below, illuminated by glorious windows, lay the sacred Rock which, though it is the summit of a hill, suggests suspension. Called Mount Moriah in memory of Abraham's sacrifice, Muslims believe it to be the place from which Muhammad, mounted on Al-Bürak, ascended to Heaven. It was covered by grey tarpaulins to protect it from cement spatterings but, as Nicholas said, one could 'feel its Presence'.

Another moving region is the site of the Fortress Antonio, where the public part of Jesus' trial was held, into whose original flagstones, fluted to keep horses from slipping, Roman soldiers had cut rough sword and crown designs for their game of *Basilikos*, recalling the scene when they left their game to play an all too real and terrible one with Jesus, shouting 'Hail, King of the Jews!'

We joined an expedition to the River Jordan, and another to Hebron with its cenotaphs covering the traditional tombs of Abraham, Isaac and Jacob, Sarah, Rebecca and Leah. Passing a pottery workshop a potter gave us miniature terracotta pots resembling the large ones whose forms have for thousands of years remained unchanged.

One day we crossed Mount Scopus to Emmaus, where Jesus spoke to Simon and Cleophas, 'whose eyes were opened and they knew him. And he vanished'; and on to Jacob's Well, near Joseph's Tomb; and to Nablus, chief city of Samaria, not far from a dolorous camp of six hundred thousand Palestinians, where to greet us came a majestic and aged Samaritan, a poignant figure, leader of two hundred and fifty people who possess an ancient manuscript, which he showed us, of the Pentateuch, the only part of the Hebrew Scriptures they recognise, and cling to a religion that nobody else accepts.

Other visits were to Bethany, the Tomb of Lazarus, and Bethlehem, scene of both Jesus' birth and the idyll of Ruth and Boaz, passing the domed Tomb of Rachel: 'So Rachel died, and was buried in the highway that led to Ephrata which is Bethlehem.' Long before reaching it we saw the white hillside town. Franciscans guided us down narrow steps to the Grotto of the Nativity, with Constantine's original mosaic floor, where a Syrian priest polished a silver star let into a marble slab above the traditional birthplace. Nearby stands the cell where St Jerome composed the Vulgate version of the Bible.

A memorable drive was to Jericho, down, down, through the glowing desert of Judah, pausing at the Good Samaritan Inn, traditional site of our favourite parable. But the most exciting expedition was to Khirbet Qumrän, and the Dead Sea, in which, as I discovered during a bathe, one cannot sink, while out of a white-hot sky the sun blazed over the mountains of Moab. Here we explored caves where the Dead Sea Scrolls were found, and the ruined monastery to which the Essenes, disapproving of the ostentatious magnificence of Herod's Temple, withdrew to lead a simple life of prayer and study. Here was their scriptorium, with stone writing-table and inkpots of bronze and clay, probably where they kept those copies of the Old Testament, including Isaiah, a thousand years earlier than the earliest known Hebrew copy, and hitherto unknown works—a possible link between the Old Testament and the rise of Christianity. Broken pottery lay about and we kept a shard to add to stones we had picked up at every holy place. We pictured the frightened Brothers when the Roman Tenth Legion arrived to sack the monastery, hiding their treasures, hoping some day to reclaim them, in vain—for it is thought they perished with the Zealots at Masada.

Our last Jordan journeys were to the Mount of Olives and Garden of Gethsemane, its air scented with aromatic shrubs and trees, and to the Pool of Siloam, from which we climbed an ancient street trodden perhaps by Jesus on Holy Thursday to the High Priest's palace, where Peter denied him. A church raised in memory of Peter's repentance encloses a shrine served by Augustinian Fathers, one of whom descended with us to the dungeon where he believed Jesus was imprisoned, and pointed out crosses carved by early Christians in the walls. A man of sublime faith, tending this holy place gave him joys as lofty as man can know.

2

During the night before we left for Israel we walked halfway round the outside of the Old City walls, on which starlight cast a silver sheen. Next morning we crossed at the Mandelbaum Gate, to be met by our guide, Isaac Rosenberg, a Jew from Czechoslovakia who with his family had escaped from Nazi murderers. An excellent cicerone, Nicholas and he became lasting friends. Through the following days 'Rosie', as the pilgrims called him, took us on coach tours to the Grotto of St John the Baptist's nativity, the Shrine of the Visitation, a Carmelite monastery, and Nazareth, built on a ridge north of the Plain of Esdraelon—planted with corn and maize, millet, cotton and sesame—out of which rises Mount Tabor.

From Nazareth we drove to the Franciscan Church at Cana, built

over the remains of Nathaniel's House, when at the marriage feast
Jesus turned water into wine, onward to Magdala and Tiberias, and
Capernaum on the Galilean shore, to see the ruins of a synagogue built
some think by the centurion whose servant Jesus healed. Amidst its
sculptured fragments was a stone block carved to represent the
wheeled Ark of the Covenant, which almost exactly resembled our
gypsy *varda*. One night, on the banks of the Galilean lake, in which we
waded to cool our roasting feet, near the Mount of Beatitudes, where
Jesus preached the Sermon whose advice so few people have ever
followed, we watched fishing-craft with brilliant lights signalling to
Peter's fish to come into the nets and be caught; and next morning we
crossed the lake to lunch at a *kibbutz* beneath the Golam Heights,
where we ate ripe figs and some of those delicious fish fried. To the
north rose Mount Hermon's snowy crown.

Nicholas was entranced by these places where Jesus walked, most
by Mount Tabor, scene of the Transfiguration, where in the vast
summit church he served a priest at Mass. Far across the plain
glistened the white buildings of Nain, where a chapel has been built to
commemorate the raising to life of the widow's son, and where in a
vision Nicholas saw Jesus, half running in his eagerness to restore the
dead, whose bier he touched, saying, 'Young man, arise,' and to the
mother, 'Weep not,' and her son sat up and spoke.

Rosie guided us to the Horns of Hattin, expressing his horror at
Saladin's victory, and to the ancient fortress of Megiddo commanding
the road from Egypt to Mesopotamia and Syria, where contests had
raged from 1468 BC, when Pharaoh Thut-Mose III defeated the King
of Kadesh, to AD 1918, when the Allied armies under Allenby drove
out the Turks—the symbolical Armageddon of the Book of Revelation where the 'final struggle between Good and Evil shall be fought'.

On our way to Haifa, from which we were to sail, we stopped at
Acre, where a tiny Arab girl offered us a bunch of wild flowers but
refused to accept anything in return, pushing our coins and sweets
aside—the flowers were a *gift*.

So the longest of our pilgrimages ended, and the person we most
regretted leaving was Isaac Rosenberg, with whom we parted at the
foot of a gangway leading to the deck of the MS *Messapia*; but he and
Nicholas promised to write to each other, which they often did, and
every spring he sent oranges and grapefruit from the land to which
may peace come. Shalom, Rosie, shalom!

At 11 p.m. we sailed, mauve and golden lights gleaming from the
shore until they diminished and vanished. The *Messapia* put in at
Rhodes, which Meleager called the 'home of sweet lads', and spent
some hours ashore among wild flowers and windmills; and after
another night aboard saw day break over the Cyclades, Mount
Hymettus and the distant Parthenon floating out of a haze, which

melted to reveal Piraeus, where we disembarked, bought sponges in the crowded Athenian streets, padded up the burning Pentelic marbles of the sun-drenched Acropolis, and set foot in the realm of my age-long dreams.

The dwarf tug *Titan* drew the *Messapia* through the Corinth Canal at the foot of lofty perpendicular walls, like a beetle crawling in the bottom of a well, brown jellyfish floating past on the swift current. With Delphi near and Mount Parnassus to the north, we reached the gulf, and sailed across the Ionian Sea to Naples, to entrain for Rome.

Compared to our other pilgrimages this one, so far as the pilgrims went, had not been very harmonious, and at the rundown Rome hotel several long-festering quarrels came to a head and burst. Most of the company were tired, including poor Miss Whibley, who, having made various miscalculations and mistakes, became the butt of the troublemakers, who one evening attacked her in the hotel lounge, until Nicholas, furious with them for blaming his friend who, whatever her failings, had done her best, suddenly rounded on them and shouted '*Shut up!*' which, astonished and shocked, they did. Everyone had been very kind to me, especially Father Guazzelli who, knowing as they all did that I was neither Christian nor Catholic, invited me if I wished to partake of the Sacrament, which I thought was truly Christlike. After my husband's outburst things went better for a while.

He and I shared the overwhelming wonder of that journey and he called it a test of faith: it strengthened his. And it increased my compassion for Jesus, the pathos and poignancy of His life and death, the sublimity yet simplicity of His teaching. I recall Miss Whibley with affection and gratitude, who patiently bore abuse for the least mishap, bobbed up smiling again and again, her marvellous vitality and faith intact. She kept in touch and sent us long records of her pilgrimages and American journeys until she died.

For some weeks Nicholas was spent; but as usual he soon began to write about our adventures, until he reached the Church of the Holy Sepulchre and his vision of the Crusaders, when he became so agitated that he suffered severe headaches and was obliged to break off. Our doctor could find no physical cause except emotional strain and prescribed tranquillisers. Every time he resumed his account the pain recurred: with him, physical, mental and emotional stress acted together as one. I begged him not to worry if he could not complete his work but failure to do so saddened him.

3

On 29 December, 1960, we were watching television when on to the screen was flashed my father's face and the news: Eden Phillpotts, the well-known author, died today. I felt grieved for Henry's sake, grieved that Father had never met Nicholas, grieved that every effort to secure a meeting had failed, and that I had lost ten years of his companionship. I remembered how once we had loved each other, and in childhood he had encouraged me to admire all manifestations of beauty, from flowers to forms of the noblest art, for which I felt grateful still—but, above all, grateful for life. I thought of his compact made with Mother on Pew Tor, that their ashes should mingle there, and pictured Henry fulfilling it. Some days later he wrote to tell me what happened.

Our stepmother, whom Father had trusted to carry out his wish, decreed that his ashes should lie not on Pew Tor but several miles away near Crockern Tor, where he had courted her. She did not accompany my brother but told the car driver where to stop, and Henry where to deposit Father's dust. On a cold January day with snow threatening, Henry and my stepmother's niece Mary set off to fulfil her orders, but long before they reached the chosen spot snow began to fall, thicker and thicker, until the driver said he could go no further or they would be snowed up. Henry quickly carried the ashes a few yards off the road, laid them on the heath and hastened back to the car, to be driven back as fast as possible—a touch of irony our father with his sense of humour might or might not have appreciated. Perhaps his true spouse, his everlasting beloved, was Dartmoor itself, to whom he had always been faithful, and so long as he lay in her generous bosom he would be satisfied, and Mother would have understood.

Thus Grannie Adelaide's immediate family, so tragically lopped when her husband died, came to an end. Or did it? What happened to Uncle Cecil's love-child in Australia? May she not have continued that branch of the family? I shall never know.

As to Father, he should be judged, as he wished, and it must be favourably, by his works. He believed in the sovereignty of reason and on that he set his hope for humanity. Probably he would have echoed Jefferson's words as he proclaimed the Gospel of Liberty, won by the American War of Independence: 'All eyes are opened, or opening to the rights of man', to be attained—and I quote the American scholar and historian H. S. Commager's *The Revolution as a World Ideal*—'by those laws which reason could command and in the ability to achieve those ends which reason dictated as just and sound.' But I am afraid my father, like many others of his generation, was unwise to trust in such a rickety ladder to the stars. As Goethe said to Eckermann: 'It is not to be imagined that reason can ever be popular. Passions and feelings may become popular; but reason always remains the sole property of a few eminent individuals.' Father was one. From his rationalist philosophy, which has been called 'genial and manly', and his deep love of nature he never deviated. To his noble ideals he was true. Only a small part of his nearly three hundred published books is still in print, though I hope many more will be reissued. I believe that his achievement is crowned by his Dartmoor books, notably his own favourite, *The Thief of Virtue*, his tragic dramas, and his poetry. He himself might also have chosen his *Comedy Royal*, from the novel *Eudocia*, and the 'Fairy stories' or fantasies, which he greatly enjoyed writing and are so characteristic of the writer. His sense of humour is Shakespearean, his sense of tragedy Greek. His many-faceted spirit was dressed in motley, like the Joseph's Coat Caterpillar he drew for me as a child on Dartmoor. He has not yet received the recognition he deserves.

I like to remember the young father who told me stories about the Zagabog, at seven encouraged me to write, and on the pianola played the music he knew I loved; the father who enjoyed picnicking on the moor, the good son, artist and friend, who wrote so many beautiful things. I am proud of him, and grateful for existence.

Henry missed him most, yet concealed his sorrow, as when Mother lived and died he hid his love. So much of Henry was hidden from us all. When someone said to him after Father's death: 'But you didn't see him often, did you?' he answered: 'I know. But he was *there*.'

Iona and Skye

1

Not long after my father's death Henry wrote to say that his landlady was leaving and had told him to get another lodging as soon as possible. So I went over to find one. He did not want to leave Torquay, which had always been home, with the harbour and library he daily visited. I called on the few people who might help but none could. At my wit's end and Henry growing more and more frantic, I telephoned to a widowed friend of Nan, Mrs Maude Briault, recently remarried to a widower, both of whom knew Henry and might suggest someone who could look after him; and to my relief and amazement I heard her say, 'Would he like to come and live with us? He could come in two days' time.' It seemed impossibly good! Henry and I walked to Babbacombe Downs and sat there, too moved to speak: certain moments of tragedy or joy can be endured only in silence. So he went to live with Mr and Mrs Briault, not as a lodger but a friend.

Meanwhile Nicholas and I planned a journey of the heart, beginning with a visit to John Cowper Powys, then to Iona, and on to Skye to trace his paternal ancestors and their graves. Before leaving, we heard that Major Yuri Gagarin in Vostok 1 had orbited the Earth; and when he appeared on television my husband said it was overwhelming to look into eyes—very beautiful eyes—which had seen our planet from space.

John Powys and Phyllis Playter lived in a cottage overlooking the Moelwyn Mountains, near a quarry and a waterfall. Phyllis opened the door and led us into a small room where lay John, frail, welcoming, humorous and charming, who drew Nicholas to his breast. He had the unearthly look of one living partly in another sphere. Sometimes his mind wandered and he said strange things and saw strange visions; but for the most part he spoke the language of here and now—a great man, simple, profound, and wise—who throughout life had explored regions where ordinary people cannot follow; but nature and the solid earth were equally familiar. From his upper window he liked to watch the sun set behind the mountains. On every place and person he cared for he shed his own intrinsic radiance. After three intimate days it was hard to leave those friends:

we knew we should not see John again.

By way of Oban, Mull, and in a boat across the mile-wide Sound, we reached Iona, where in 563 St Columba landed with twelve companions to make it a centre of Celtic Christianity. Geologically one of the world's older islands, with miniature tors and plains, it is formed of Archaen rock. On clear days northward are visible Canna, Rum, Eigg and the mountains of Skye, eastward Ben More and Staffa, westward the Dutchman's Cap, Coll and Tiree, and southward the Paps of Jura, Colonsay and Islay, besides innumerable rocks and islets.

We stayed in a farm on the west coast, and after friendly greetings from the farm folk ran down to the sea where seals were swimming, gannets plunging, curlews and larks flying, and the fair rock dove, *Columba livia*. Before sundown Nicholas took me to the north coast where thick veins of basalt, spurted from ancient volcanos, have filled cracks in the granite-like black serpents, to show me where long ago Roy had found a dead German sailor washed off a torpedoed ship.

Next morning we climbed to an inlet called Sloc nam Boll, Gully of the Tangles, a hollow once filled with sea, but now high tide turned some yards from its entrance which forms a natural arch leading to rufous pre-Cambrian rocks, veined in pink and green, preceding life by two thousand million years. Into a chasm below pounded the rollers, polishing its walls marble smooth, where at low tide we stood on multi-coloured stones, from basalt to crystal—like the 'inestimable stones' of Clarence's dream—and wondered if it was here that Keats collected for his sister those 'pebbles blue'.

Another day Nicholas brought me to St Martin's Caves, heaped with washed-up seaweed torn from its rock hold by storms, where a square, porphyry-hued window overlooks the northern Atlantic, and a rock-face, down which we slithered, to a crack at whose head, in a cave, we found a bottle, launched five years earlier in mid-ocean on 23 July 1956 from the French liner *Liberté*, that must have drifted here on the North Atlantic current. Inside was the message: 'If found please send picture postcard of place found. Put number 2 on card somewhere', followed by the ship's name, date, and an address indecipherable except for 'Char . . . ville, USA', presumably Charlottesville, Virginia. Nicholas wrote to the French Line, which confirmed that there had been an eastbound sailing at that time, but they had no list of passengers and crew.

One rainy morning we waded through bogs to the Bay of the Coracle to hunt for Iona greenstones, fragments of semi-transparent serpentine shattered from a reef running under the ocean, smoothed by surges and cast up on the southern shore—marble, quarried only in Iona, which embellishes the Scottish Chapel in Westminster Cathedral. We had unshingled some pale green pebbles, but none of that special colour and degree of translucency we were seeking, when into my hand rolled a circular, olive-green stone, in which a minute flaw resembled a full-rigged sailing-ship, or a seagull, or a cloud, or a speck of spindrift; and Nicholas found two smaller ones like dark green jade. In such a region, I told him, we might meet Ariel and Caliban, and he said 'We have met them. You're Ariel, I'm Caliban!' Then along came an ancient woman who invited us to her croft to show us a fine oval greenstone set in a silver ring. 'My friend and I were picnicking at Coracle Bay where the Saint landed,' she said, 'when this stone was washed up at his feet. He gave it to me and asked me to marry him. I doubt he'd have had the temerity otherwise, because he couldn't afford an engagement ring.' 'Perhaps the Saint had something to do with it?' suggested Nicholas. 'My fingers are too swollen to get it on now,' she went on, 'but sometimes I take it out and think of my man.' Her man, dead these twenty years, lay alongside Macbeth, Duncan, and other Scottish and Scandinavian kings in a small God's Acre opposite the red granite Ross of Mull where, soon afterwards, in death she joined him.

Of Iona, Nicholas wrote: 'The Isle has a way, very mysterious, of transfiguring one's thoughts. All here is clean and tends to edify. Nothing can be base or suspect or unseemly. The most elemental feelings—infant or adult—give innocent happiness and joy, and one lives in an atmosphere of continual thankfulness. Have the oldest rocks in the world something to do with it? It certainly is bedrock of existence.'

2

In Skye we stayed at a Portree boarding-house kept by two industrious sisters, one of whom was an exceptional cook. Our room overlooked the bay and Nicholas would stand at the window visualising the 'good ship *Polly*' anchored below, while his great-grandmother and her sons forsook their croft for an unknown continent. He imagined them embarking and sailing to the New World to start new lives, much as a hundred years afterwards he had sailed back to the Old World to start his life anew. And he wondered if they surmised that a descendant like himself would ever return to Skye.

Far off rose the Black Cuillins; but before our wanderings began in this island of giants and fairies, witches and ghosts, hermits, warriors and saints, we attended a ceilidh where one song, *The Rowan Tree*, deeply moved us. Then, assisted by helpful people, we began the quest of forebears, walked in all directions, and lingered in ruined crofts not inhabited since the Clearances—'It could have been here,' Nicholas would say—and frequented long unused burial grounds surrounded by tumbling walls and chapels fallen in. We scanned

tombstones and sometimes found the name Ross, without being able
to associate it with Nicholas's family—until a shepherd directed us to
a deserted cemetery with a small, broken obelisk commemorating
John Ross of Scalpy, who might have been connected to his pre-
decessors. On one side of the memorial was inscribed: 'I love them
that love me: and they that in the morning early watch for me shall
find me' Proverbs VIII, 16. 'Lovely,' said my husband, 'and suitable
for me when my turn comes.'

On the penultimate day we sought the mountains, passing the
majestic cone of lone Glemaig which rises between the Red and Black
Cuillins, crossing Lake Scavaig and climbing over glacier-burnished
rocks to sombre Loch Coruisk, where Nicholas pictured rugged old
Turner painting this rugged scene, and where, surrounded by singing
thrushes, we sat on a knoll watching gulls and cuckoos flying far
beneath the pinnacles.

On the homeward journey we shared a railway carriage with a
drunken man, and a blind man who told us he used to tour the music-
halls impersonating birds, whose songs and other animal noises he
imitated with remarkable verisimilitude.

Home again, Skye seemed remoter than any other place we had
been to, more of a planetoid than an island, somewhat austere and sad;
but Nicholas was pleased to have stood on the ground of his ancestors.

Byzantium and Italy

1

Our fever for pilgrimages still burned and in 1962 we decided to go to Byzantium of the Crusaders, alone. Before starting we revisited London scenes and Nicholas said: 'How close you and I came to each other more than once in gone time!' Preparing for the 1,900-mile journey of three and a half days in the Orient Express to Istanbul, we bought a small cold roast chicken and a carton of Ritz biscuits, assuming there would be a restaurant car and set off. At 11 p.m. we found the famous train in the Gare de Lyons, where a conductor showed us into a little two-berth compartment whose bunks, made up for the night, would form a settee by day. Above the inner door shone a round purple light shedding a mysterious glow: Nicholas called it the tiger's eye. At a few minutes to midnight we glided away, almost imperceptibly, and he climbed into the upper bunk and fell asleep. I lay awake listening to a repetitive tune the wheels played as the train tore along the track. When it halted, the Westinghouse brakes sighed. Before sunrise I discerned by streaking waterfalls that we were in Switzerland, and an hour or two later, parched for a drink, we left our roost in search of breakfast, to hear that there was no restaurant, no breakfast, no tea, no coffee, nothing to eat or drink on the celebrated Orient Express. However, during a wait at Domodossola, Nicholas procured coffee, rolls and oranges, and thenceforth, after our chicken and biscuits were consumed, he foraged successfully.

Long before Trieste the Express began to dawdle like a tired old provincial train, often stopping at nowhere, and after ambling across the great plains of Yugoslavia and Bulgaria, pumpkins shining among the corn, scarlet pimentos hanging from cottage rafters, and miles of sunflowers turning myriad faces to the sun, we crossed the Greek frontier at Pithion, and at last sidled into Turkey, to halt for several hours at Edirne, which enabled us to stroll in the town and buy a melon, fresh baked brown loaf, chocolate and wine to enjoy in our nest. Nicholas signalled to a peasant child sitting on the track and gave her the biscuit carton filled with sweets, which she clutched with joy —one more of many boys and girls we met on our travels, and whom I still remember as children though they have grown up long ago.

Nearing Istanbul, Nicholas conceived a picture, to be created out of paper mosaic when he got home, symbolising, as he noted, 'Our entrance into Byzantium: train whistling arrows and fireworks. Bronze Moon cut by a bar of blackest cloud. Jupiter, and the reflection in the window of the violet pilot light in our compartment, while the coast in semi-light shimmers past.' We were running through the precincts of Constantinople, 'the Crusader Moon shining like an orange dome over Justinian's dome of St Sophia'.

Twelve hours late, we reached the terminus, after midnight, and a youth grabbed our bags and hurried us to a shabby old hotel where a sleepy porter showed us to a fourth-floor room. All through the night ships hooted on the Golden Horn, motors revved, voices shouted, cartwheels ground on cobblestones beneath the window and a plane tree rustled, until at dawn street sellers started crying their wares, transistors blared—and a caged bird sang. From the misty water rose vague Levantine odours. I could see the Galata Tower. We were in Byzantium!

We made for one of Europe and Asia's great thoroughfares, the Galata Bridge across the Golden Horn, dense with people from all over the world. Warped to the framework rocked varicoloured fishing-boats from which men were unloading catches, others angling in the estuary where larger boats were moored. Midway, on a steel drum beside a dwarf in a conical hat, stood a giant pelican—one of a score of astonishing scenes—and beyond rose the tawny city topped by Suleymaniye's mosque.

Our first cynosure was *Hagia Sophia*, now a museum, whose dome, as many have noted, appears to float on light. Beneath it the effect is less of an interior than of space, and everything in every religion that is sublime. The multifarious colours recall the reflecting sea.

On the site of the old Hippodrome, where military Triumphs used to be celebrated, criminals executed and martyrs burned, rose an Egyptian obelisk brought from Heliopolis in AD 390, its pedestal carved with bas reliefs of Emperor, Empress and their sons presiding at ceremonies and games; and a triple intertwined Serpent column filched from Apollo's Temple at Delphi, where it was set up in 479 BC to commemorate the victory at Platae. Nicholas, a wall-lover, was impressed by the renowned city walls, built between 600 BC and AD 450, that defied assault for a thousand years until breached by the Turks. Footsore, we shipped for a voyage on the Bosporus, its waters stirred by a weird wind blowing through the narrow Black Sea strait.

We spent the last day in the northern suburbs guided by a young taxi-driver, Seyfik Aybar, who, like Ziad of Jerusalem, begged us to take him to England. He drove us to the Church of St Saviour in Chora, its dazzling mosaics shining as if they had just been finished, but were less moving than those in neglected St Saviour Pantocrator,

now a mosque, where pigeons fluttered under the roof and a feather
dropped at our feet. (Many years later I found an envelope on which
my husband had written 'From Christos Pantocrator', containing that
feather, and it exemplified what he felt, and was, in Byzantium—
a winged being floating in delight above this tragic world.)

Sorrowful to leave Istanbul we embarked on the *San Giorgio* for
Venice. Traversing the Dardanelles at sundown my reveries were
of the First World War; and as we glided into the Aegean, stars that
looked only mast high were blinding bright. Dawn found us passing
Mitylene before reaching Izmir, site of Smyrna, where we disembarked in the sunrise for Ephesus. Through the hot, flat countryside, surrounded by cotton and tobacco plantations, and orchards of
figs and sultana grapes, plodded strings of dusty dromedaries led
by donkeys in charge of little girls. While we explored Ephesus, the
San Giorgio's hold was packed with crates and bales of local com-
modities, before reclaiming her passengers and sailing between
Andros and Euboea, while a scorching sun sank behind the Cyclades.

2

The best way to approach Venice is from the sea, and to watch its
campaniles materialise on the horizon. After many hours visiting and
revisiting Venetian treasures, we dallied an afternoon away on the
Rialto, and in the cool evening returned to St Mark's where Nicholas
had fallen in love with the bronze horses; and sat on the Sciavoni to
watch worldwide shipping come and go: from the distant past my
brother's image lingered there. On the last morning but one we
crossed the lagoon to Torcello—once a prosperous city, now a village
approached by a flower-girt stream, where we entered a columned
basilica, founded in 864, with mosaics more appealing in their
simplicity than all the gilded glories of St Mark's, including a
Madonna as refulgent as if the workmen had just laid aside their tools,
a lifelike frieze of Apostles, and a stupendous Last Judgment which
my husband found 'so overwhelming, so striking, so blinding, so
visionary—affecting and terribly disturbing', that it 'made me see our
present humanity in an entirely new aspect'. Perhaps the remoteness
of this island's history endows it, like other numinous places, with, for
this age, its uncommon serenity.

Nicholas bade Venice and its Quadriga farewell—'Goodbye,
Venice, let me ride your horses some day with whatever I deserve
of Eternity'—as a gondolier oared us to the coach for Padua. Here
Galileo taught, and St Antony is buried in the enormous *duomo*,
where we attended Mass. I thought the most beautiful object there
was Donatello's *Crucifix*, which hangs over the high altar he designed.
Giotto's frescoes in the Scrovegni Chapel were being restored and
hidden with scaffolding; but Nicholas, for whom scaffolding held a

mystical significance, seemed more pleased by it than he might have been by the frescoes. I wished Giotto could have been buried here instead of in Florence, where his tomb is surmounted by the epitaph *'Denique sum Jottus . . . Hoc nomen longicarminis instar erit'*—In short I am Giotto . . . This name shall tell you more than a lengthy song.

We had been looking forward to the Botanical Gardens, of which Goethe wrote: 'Here, where I am confronted with a great variety of plants, my hypothesis that it might be possible to derive all plant forms from one original plant becomes clearer to me and more exciting.' Alas, the Gardens were locked, and all we saw between the railings was a cat pouncing on a lizard.

It was time to start for Ravenna, where we sought the tomb of Dante, who spent his last years there. I recalled how in childhood I had disliked him, because he sent people of whom he disapproved to Hell and gloated over their torments, though in marvellous poetry; and I thought he should go there too. But even then I enjoyed his poems, which assured him of immortality, not Heaven's or Hell's, but on this world's scroll of remembrance where the names of all sublime creators are inscribed; and I never really wanted him or anyone else to be committed to his Inferno. Strange it was to stand within a few inches of his dust.

Ravenna is a noisy city of commerce and industry but its ancient glories have been preserved. On our way to the Basilica of St Apollinaire in Classe we rested in pine woods that Dante immortalised in his *Purgatorio*, comparing the 'heavenly forest dense and green' of Eden, the Earthly Paradise, to this forest of trembling leaves and singing birds, and the sweet fragrant wind which 'through the pinewood runs each hour, / From branch to branch, upon Chiassi's shore, / When Aeolus lets loose Sirocco's power'. These woods, sung, too, by Dryden, Byron in *Don Juan*, and mentioned in a Boccacio novel, are near a majestic basilica consecrated in 549, whose noble apse is filled by a breathtaking green mosaic landscape, with processions of sheep, to represent the Faithful, and a cheerful St Apollinaire, first Bishop of Ravenna, who died a martyr. Man and flock stand among lilies and daisies surrounded by jewelled rocks, ferns and sprouting trees which greet the Saint as he blesses them— a picture of the true Earthly Paradise, heavenly fair. In Ravenna itself we were dazed by the mosaics of two Baptisteries, Orthodox and Arian, the Basilica of St John the Evangelist and other buildings; but the finest mosaics are in the Byzantine Church of San Vitale and the tomb of Galla Placidie, within a quiet green enclosure impenetrable to city roar. Built about 450, the sarcophagi in the mausoleum are thought to have contained the bodies of Galla Placidie and her son Valentinian. On its night-blue walls float forms like ice crystals or spiral galaxies, with a tendrilled vine and garlands of fruit,

and fountains at which stags and doves are drinking, the loveliest
scene portraying the Good Shepherd of All Souls seated on a grassy
mound in Paradise among affectionate sheep—an idyll so peaceful, so
natural, that for a few happy moments one seems to be sharing it.

A few paces lead to San Vitale, an octagonal marble church
consecrated in 547, home of the mosaics Nicholas most longed to
see—the panels of Emperor Justinian and Empress Theodora at the
Byzantine Court: he, crowned and robed, accompanied by prelates,
nobles and warriors, offering a gold patten to the basilica; and
opposite, she, with pearl diadem and purple raiment, surrounded by
matrons and ministers, bestowing a chalice—a handsome, gifted
woman, who had long cast her spell over my husband, now joyful
to meet her face to face—startlingly lifelike people who transported
him to the true Byzantium.

My favourite Ravenna treasure was the sepulchral monument of the
knight, soldier and scholar, Guidarello Guidarelli, assassinated in 1501
at Imola, represented in armour on his deathbed, surely the most
poignant image of a dying warrior, which manifests a haunting optical
illusion: looked at sideways his beautiful face is serene; but observed
from the front it expresses deep mental anguish and physical pain.
Since childhood, when my father brought a photograph from Italy
and hung it in his study, I had been enchanted by this effigy and
frequently gazed, first at Guidarello's agony, then at his tranquillity,
expressed in two aspects of the same countenance. Did the sculptor
achieve this effect intentionally or by accident?

Nicholas grieved to forsake his precious mosaic people who, he
said, had awaited him for over a thousand years, he them for most of
his lifetime. He would die, but they were immortal.

3

Encircled on three sides by mountains, Perugia stands on a range of
hills east of the Apennines, sloping to the Tiber valley—a panorama
we conned from a terrace, a long, long view into the distance of the
ravishing Umbrian countryside and Tuscan plain, flooded by the
rising sun. On our way to the picture gallery we passed an ancient
fountain whose double circle of columns supported diminutive
carved figures, including a travelling scholar whom Nicholas dubbed
Walter Map—a marvel of symmetry, beloved by Perugian pigeons,
beak-dipping in a ring round the bowl.

In the Gallery are works of earlier centuries, displaying a lost
idealism, which deeply appealed to Nicholas, charmed by the
mystical stars which shine from the blue robes worn by Madonnas of
celestial beauty. Here is the great Perugino by himself; and how
winning and sympathetic is Perugino's Perugino. Nicholas noted a
Fra Angelico *Polyptich*, Pintorrichio's *Child with a Spoon*, and

Agostino di Duccio's young and amused terracotta *Madonna* with her amused and amusing Child. My favourite work, by an unknown sculptor, was a Crucifix expressing with simplicity so sublime a sacrifice that it is the most truthful I have seen.

We were standing on a high place overlooking Assisi, shimmering like a pink star across the Umbrian vale, when along came a Chinese pedlar hawking suitcases, of which Nicholas bought one to hold our accumulating purchases. To meet this aged gentleman in an Italian town with Venetian, Byzantine, and Marco Polo associations delighted us, and we wished him a safe return to China, where he hoped to be buried. Our eyes on St Francis' eyrie in the sunset, we looked forward to being there in the morning.

Assisi, spread under the slopes of Mount Subasio, with buildings hewn from that mountain's apricot-coloured stone, is dominated by two vast churches, founded in 1228 when St Francis was canonised. Before entering, we wandered through the town, surprised to see the Corinthian columns of a Temple to Minerva dating from the time of Augustus, its classicism not blending with the medieval and modern scene, though it filled Goethe with such indescribable sensations that he wrote: 'I know they are going to bear fruit forever.'

In the crypt of the Lower Church the Saint's urn is enclosed in its original iron cage, near four of his disciples, surrounded with murals by Martini, Giotto and their followers, including a portrait of Francis said to be the only genuine likeness. To me the most moving fresco is Pietro Lorenzetti's tender *Sunset Madonna*, where the Child looks lovingly at his Mother, who returns his gaze and with her thumb indicates Francis standing beside them. We were shown his sandals, tunic and hood, a chamois leather which protected his stigmata, and the garment in which he died. Giotto's *Scenes from the Life of St Francis* are in the Upper Church.

Our hotel room, round which bats flew all night, overlooked endless vistas of the Umbrian plain, but before descending we strolled through olive groves to the Church of St Daminano where St Francis, praying beneath a twelfth-century Crucifix heard the Crucified say: 'Go, Francis, and repair my falling house', meaning the city of human souls, but Francis took the command literally, restored the neglected church and prepared a convent for his friend Clare, who, like him, had forsaken her rich family to serve God. We walked in her garden, where he wrote his *Canticle of the Creatures*, then drove to the valley Church of Santa Maria degli Angeli, built round the rustic chapel where Francis and his disciples prayed before their journeys, and where he died. In the shrine, quivering with light and crammed with people at the conclusion of a wedding, a priest was discoursing to the couple about '*Amore—amore—*' the one word we could catch, and a good word here. When the crowd had left and the candles were snuffed we entered the minuscule retreat, of which Nicholas wrote: 'It was a wonderful experience for me, when the entire planet slipped from under me and I found myself cudgelled by a glare of colourless fire, all light . . . *What* exactly happens to the mind on rare occasions like this? I wish I knew. Perhaps Francis himself might make the operation clearer.'

Our last call was at the caves in the forest of holm-oaks where Francis and his friends knelt in penance. '*O beata Solitudo! O sola Beatitudo!*' The sun set behind the violet countryside and twilight shrouded the church where Lorenzetti's *Madonna of the Sunset* faded into darkness, and St Francis reposes in peace.

4

It was October 8th, John Cowper Powys' ninetieth birthday, when we travelled to Siena along the reedy shores of Lake Trasimene. Grapes drooped the vines and olives glistened in the Tuscan autumn. Enclosed in the russet-hued city we went to the home of another Saint my husband loved, Catherine of Siena, Patroness of Italy, whose skull is preserved in the Church of St Dominic. Nicholas saw neither the pathos nor the grimness of the Relic, but a sweet countenance more beautiful than any living or legendary beauty. We found several portraits but only one authentic likeness, by her friend Andrea Vanni, in the Chapel of the Vaults where she prayed in ecstasy—a woman who declared that she was 'drunk with the light of faith'. Beside the tabernacle which holds her head hangs Sodoma's masterpiece, *St Catherine's Swoon*, where her stigmata are visible.

After beholding many other wonders, we explored streets and squares and passages, mingled with the people, and returned to the saintly Head, of which Nicholas wrote: 'A spiritual wonder. Like a locomotive charging into me from the altar. I forgot the entire world—yes, even my Darling who stood at my side. Everything went black and into light; and that mysterious dimension descended from spiritual spheres. When I looked towards the Relic it was as a flame, and I saw clearer than all the light given by the sun, the eyes of the Saint. And I heard words and they said: "I take to her". I followed the direction of her eyes, and lo! there at the altar stood Adelaide. I prayed "Let it be so from this day onward". When this experience closed, Adelaide was at my side; now I am certain that St Catherine has something for her, and it is my joy to nurture it.'

We were tired when we left Siena for Florence, and Nicholas had begun a heavy cold and cough, but ignored it and refused to stop in. So once more we tramped off on the treasure trail. I thought of Mother, whose favourite city this was, and of Father, admiring his endearing Andrea del Sarto pictures, and how in my childhood he showed me their reproductions and told me that del Sarto's wife, so beautiful that he chose her to model his exquisite Madonnas, used in old age to sit beneath the originals, pluck onlookers by the sleeve and say 'Look! That was me!' and I was filled with pity. Sickened by noise and traffic and pining for the country, we fled to Vallombrosa, where Milton and Galileo are believed to have walked together; and then, for the last time, we said farewell to the saints and the villains, the artists and their creations, the little towns, the great cities, and the glorious landscapes of Italy.

5

Before going home Nicholas wanted a few days in Paris, to see the Museum of Man and then go to Rheims Cathedral, so we booked a room at the Brighton Hotel. As we wended through the Museum, passing from pre-hominid to Man, he sighed and said: 'It makes you think!' I was beyond thought, as we dragged ourselves and each other back along the Seine, to make plans for a day at Rheims.

Passing through Champagne, with its forests of congregated vines, I knew that my husband's illness was worsening. But he *would* pray where yet another of his beloved saints, Joan, secured the anointing of the Dauphin; and where his dear Mary, Queen of Scots and her husband were crowned. A spirited equestrian statue of St Joan stands before the towered cathedral, whose stained glass was saved from destruction in the Second World War, but incendiary bombs set fire to the timbers, melted the lead, and caused devastation which had not even then been restored. Nicholas, thrilled by the lofty portals and their statues of saints and prophets, kings and queens and smiling angels, was glad he had come.

This was the swansong of our Byzantine journey, when, as he said, the Heavens were opened and he saw the visions of God. By the time we reached Cobblestones he was seriously ill with virus pneumonia. However, thanks to our good doctor and, said Nicholas, to his darling saints, he recovered; though for me that coda to our travels, which began so melodiously in our little snuggery on the Orient Express, was jangled out of tune. In this chapter I hope it regains an echo of its pristine harmony.

Requiem

Saturated with marvels all close to his heart, my husband started work on the paper-mosaic recording our entrance into Constantinople. Washed up on a beach he found a driftwood board for its foundation, and out of gold, green and purple papers cut out tesserae with which he built up the illustrations as he had described it in Istanbul: 'The entire coastal route was like a coast of illusions. It might have been "imagination", yet the persistence of the mood would seem to have in it "something else". We ceased to be people and became OPTICS. Maybe we were in a little jar being shot beyond the Milky Way! There was magic in the hour and an enormous fret. Were arrows actually butting against our compartment window, banners fluttering and bundles of "Greek Fire"? We were certain of Jupiter, for he was the first heavenly body to shine out from the night sky, like an asterisk-dish used by Greek priests behind the Anastasis. Then came up the Moon, moving faster than the planet and taking up a place to the right of it. All my senses seemed to be gathering into a complete impression: all the various themes resolving themselves into a ONENESS: feelings, realities, sights, sounds, smells and colours. When all this had happened in one timeless moment I saw in the racing airs a design in mosaic I hope some day to make for Adelaide —a true conglomerate of this particular part of our journey with its special luminosity: The Marmara, the Saviour Fish and Chi-ro, a sea-serpent, a spectrum fish, a current of the Dardanelles, two martyr-Saints, a dome, a Greek Cross, holocausts of flame, the broken walls, whistling arrows, Jupiter, the Moon dominated by the Ravenna head of Justinian, the reflection on the window glass of our purple votive light (in the theme of the purple birth-room of the old Palace), chariot wheels, locomotive wheels, a piston, and the title CON-STANTINOPALITANA MCMLXII.' In the centre of his mosaic he painted an image of a loose marble fragment from the pavement of St Sophia.

The winter of 1962–63 was the coldest we had known. Water barrels and the mains under the street froze solid. The ground cracked, and clanging winds glazed walls and blackened plants. Trees crystalled with ice glittered in the sunlight. Birds clustered round chimney-pots and crept under eaves. Then, one glacial morning, Nicholas said: 'How would you like to go round the world—on tramp steamers, buses, old railways, on foot, donkeys, anything?' It began as a fantasy of far-away ports with names of gold: Valparaiso, Buenos Aires, Hong Kong, Rio de Janeiro, Yokohama—Boston, and like a game passed the freezing hours. 'Make up your mind,' he said. 'It's now or never.' My mind was made up when I was nine and Nan gave me my first Atlas. 'We'll decide on April 1st,' said he, and I pointed out it was April Fool's Day. 'I know,' he laughed.

On 16 February, 1963, the carapace of ice into which everything out of doors had been locked began to melt. Trees dripped as if weeping for joy and birds which had not perished piped a few notes. On April the first Nicholas said: 'We're off!' and we began to prepare for a journey of thirty thousand miles. He called it the Magic Carpet and said lift-off would be early in 1964. A travel agent who planned individual journeys to anywhere at any time helped us to draw up a rough itinerary, to end in Massachusetts with the Ross family.

Written on Nicholas's birthday in March came a last letter from John Powys: 'Well, my old friend, we certainly you and I are living just now on the same . . .' further he could not write. Phyllis Playter explained that for ten days he had not been well: 'He is not himself, and very far away,' she wrote; 'Don't be too anxious . . . for whatever is wrong it isn't serious.' Nicholas continued to write but it was beyond John's power to respond. Phyllis, too, was unwell, and when her letters also ceased, we wrote for news to their friends at Blaenau, who reported that they were both in hospital and she was going to have an operation. Phyllis recovered, but on June 7th John Powys died. At his desire his ashes were laid on the Chesil Bank for the tide to carry away. Nicholas remembered that long ago in one of his characteristic letters John had written: 'Oh! how lovely it is to feel like a feather or a bit of straw, or to feel like a bubble on a stream or a wisp of foam on the beach. When you see these things as they really are with your second soul, it is a great satisfaction!' This was a grievous loss; but my husband believed that if he himself attained the Happy Land they would meet again.

'Magic Carpet'

1

We picked February 1964 for the start of our journey, whose story I have told in *Panorama of the World*, published in 1969 by Robert Hale, and will summarise here. Only once before had I experienced the thrill of setting out on that winter morning, and in Liverpool's Canada Dock looking up at the flaring bows of the Pacific Steam Navigation Company's SS *Cuzco*, due to sail for Valparaiso. Of 8,000 gross tonnage, launched in 1951, this was her fortieth voyage. Before embarking we waited in a twilight warehouse, piled with cargoes smelling of unfamiliar substances about to be winched into her holds, until we were summoned to mount the gangway.

During the first cabin night we spoke of John Keats, who stayed in Liverpool with Charles Brown, before their Scottish Tour, to see his brother George and sister-in-law Georgiana off to North America; and of the ghastly slave-ships, whose tragic hulks rose in our imaginations.

Mooring cables splashed into the dirty water sucking *Cuzco*'s hull, as tugs manoeuvred her into St George's Channel, where buoys and inbound ships lighted her passage out to sea, and shoreward dimmed the nocturnal Liverpool glow. At Milford Haven we embarked small arms and dynamite for South America and thenceforth flew the scarlet flag. 'Our cabin's so near this fiery stuff that if we go up in a devilish blast we'll be two flames seen through flames,' said Nicholas. The bosun's mate, an elderly Pole who had served in sailing-ships, invited us into his storeroom and showed us how to splice a steel hawser, tie rose knots and cringles, and make turks heads for handrails; while the carpenter taught us to put model ships into bottles.

Off the Azores *Cuzco* ran into a storm, and hove-to while a wound in her arterial system was patched, then progressed on one engine instead of two. 'Only a minor breakdown,' explained the first Officer. *Sargassum* weed floated past and round us leapt porpoises, and flying-fish whizzed—like seraphs with crossed wings, thought Nicholas. The breakers flashed with rainbows by day and luminescence by night—a shimmering wake of glimmering whirlpools, 'Titania's wedding veil,' said he; while to me the waves echoed that far-off song of my youth 'All men are brothers, every land is home'. Northern constellations dipped beneath the sea and southern ones rose. Scorpio stood over the port beam. Nicholas was joyful when the Southern Cross, his 'lattice of magnificence' with mystical significance, appeared. Every day the sun went down into a purple haze, until one evening when it stood poised on the horizon, sank slowly, and sparked a green ray—the 'green flash'—of which tradition tells that whoever sees this 'living light' will never be deceived in love.

Cuzco sailed between Guadaloupe and Dominica to Curaçao, where we spent a day among its singularly beautiful peoples of blended races, while she refuelled and watered; then onward to Cristobal and a nine-hour transit through the Panama Canal. We remembered the thousands of navvies who died during its construction; and I recalled that the second ship to sail through was the convict hulk, *Success*, which in 1905 had affrighted me. Watching water spirals whirling round the hull, we looked back millions of years, before the land bridge sank, when marsupial mammals crossed this way to South America, and lived in security until placental mammals arrived and exterminated most of their primitive cousins, though sloths and armadillos survive. And we recollected how man himself reached the southern continent and lived safely for millenniums until his white cousins came down from the north.

So we sailed into the Pacific, to realise that our western horizon was no longer bounded by the New World, but beyond sundown lay the old Orient. The nights were so hot that sometimes we stayed on deck, the cross-trees' light swinging from side to side as the ship rolled. In the zenith hung Orion, the red giant Betelguese glittering on his shoulder, the blue giant Rigel in his heel, Sirius and Procyon sparkling underneath. Canopus blazed in the stem of myriad-sunned Argo and Antares flashed on Scorpio's breast. Now the Southern Cross stood well clear of the sealine. How Nicholas loved these 'clusters of golden lustres'.

While *Cuzco* discharged merchandise we explored Guayaquil, followed by serious-faced little mestizo children, whose elders brooded under flowering shrubs in a dusty square, and sat beside a sluggish river with water hyacinths drifting past. Under a carob tree we watched a large green iguana sitting overhead; and in the ancient Church of Santo Domingo, Nicholas, contemplating a crucifix, saw Christ's right shoulder become luminous where the Cross had bruised it, and said it was the Sixth Wound.

In Ecuador we spoke with our first Amerindians, fulfilling my childhood dream. The intense heat abated when we reached the cold Humboldt Current, fished for over five thousand years, whose plants and animals nourish millions of fish which feed millions of birds which produce millions of tons of guano which raise crops to support millions of humans. One evening in a blood red afterglow followed by moonrise, Venus and Jupiter, whose approach had lasted since the voyage began, met and shone side by side where the Milky Way streamed across the sky, and for the first time we saw the Magellanic clouds.

Nicholas was looking up at the mast one night when he said: 'Who's that odd creature in the rigging bawling out names of craft?' I could hear and see no one but to him this spectre was clear. Months later he was reading Commander Woolard's *Twice Round the World in Sail* when he lit on a passage describing a drunken shipmaster in this very spot, suffering from delirium tremens, who stopped on deck all night shouting out the names of imaginary ships.

At Payta, from which in 1595 sailed Alvaroda Mandarna whose pilot was the great and tragic Fernandez de Quiros, last of the Conquistadors, we landed in a lighter, surrounded by pelicans standing on the rails, to walk in the dusty town, watched by melancholy Indians, and tried to converse with them—surprised that strangers from some distant country wanted to be their friends.

In numerous other small ports *Cuzco* landed food, drink, and machinery, while we stood on the grey Pacific sand to watch fishing-fleets setting out, and millions of birds which evening by evening swept in from the fishing-fields looking like skeins of black lace, to roost on the cliffs and islands. Early in March we anchored at Ancon, where semi-circles of topaz lights ringed Lima Bay, and explosives were offloaded to be reshipped to Valparaiso. Round the hull pulsated giant jellyfish scavenging.

After a night in Lima—which suggested to Nicholas a golden skull—we sought the Church of St Rosa, the compassionate woman who in the 1600s cared for the country's old, poor, sick and faithful, in whose convent infirmary nuns still tend the afflicted; and then walked in the cathedral where, wrapped in crystal, marble and bronze, lies Francisco Pizarro, who founded it six years before he was murdered by the half-Inca son of his rival, Almagro.

Our hotel overlooked a square and the statue of a nobler man, Simon Bolivar, endowed with gifts of action, vision, reflection, and leadership, whose revolution embraced the continent, which he visualised as a confederation, eventually to include the world. Roused at 4 a.m. we set off in a small unpressurised plane, flying over the Andes at 11,000 feet, above a cloudy ocean of pearls, for Cuzco, where Nicholas found breathing so difficult that I wished we had not come. The wretched state of the peasants deeply troubled him: they seemed still stunned by their fate, yet overtly indifferent to their doom; though a Spanish Peruvian told us that the younger Indios were beginning to demand juster conditions for their race. Four hundred years ago Montaigne in his Essay *On Coaches* wrote: 'They were superior to us on the moral plane, but with regard to their piety, loyalty, devotion, and bounteous liberality, it served us well that we had not so much as they, for by this advantage they lost, sold, undid and betrayed themselves.' How will they be in another 400 years?

To reach the Inca City of Machu Picchu we took a train filled with people of so many different nationalities that the driver called us the 'United Nations'—a four-hour journey covering 4,000 horizon miles of varying vegetation, and ten thousand vertical feet of temperature zones from jungle floor to the limit of plant life. The majesty of mountains, and incomparable citadel architecture, were both overwhelming. Observing Amerindians repairing a wall, we left the 'United Nations' to speak to them, and thenceforth explored on our own. Impressive as this expedition proved, and beyond words beautiful, to behold a once proud race in subjugation and poverty, filled us with what Nicholas called a state beyond pity, beyond compassion, beyond anger, beyond reason.

At the small port of Materani we climbed a steep hill to a white desert, disturbing hawks at a shell-strewn roost, lizards sunning on green serpentine pebbles, and below the cliffs families of jackass penguins chattering. Over the Kümmel Deep I heard as it seemed bells ringing far down, while the ship rode into rafts of pelicans. By night the sky wheeled in glory, Centaur's diamond hoof and knee blazing beside Crux, and Spica rising.

In Antofagasta grew hundreds of those bizarre conifers, *Aracauria Aracana*, reminding me of the friendly monkey-puzzles in my childhood garden: this was *their* nursery. So we reached Valparaiso, sad to quit the *Cuzco* and her crew. A few years later she was scrapped: her phantom will always sail through my memory.

2

The transit over the Andes to Buenos Aires began midst the grandeur of mountains whose moraines drop from terrific crags into stupendous valleys, the train sliding along ledges cut into their shoulders under ridges scarlet and black. Someone in the carriage cried 'Aconcagua! Aconcagua!' and there it was, Father of Mountains, Mountain of Hallucinations, source of thunder and lightning, blizzards and hurricanes. All we saw was a passing glimpse of a golden pinnacle towering above lesser peaks.

A few days later we embarked on the Dutch cargo-liner, *Tegelberg*, with an all Chinese crew, in which we spent most of the next two months. On Easter Day she reached Santos, its harbour heaving with playful dolphins, the air with flapping frigate birds, while down gushed Capricorn's treacly heat. Here we joined an expedition to see Sao Paulo, and a snake farm, where the guide coaxed into his hand an enormous hairy black spider which caused several white South African widows to shriek 'A black widow! A black widow! Don't let it come near *us*!' 'Have no fear, ladies,' laughed the guide. 'If I dare say so, this gentle spider is not half so lethal as yourselves!' And later he told them: 'Only a few miles away in the woods, *wild Indians!*' whereupon they screamed 'Don't let them come near *us*!' Sao Paulo was the most tragic city we saw, until we reached New York.

When the *Tegelberg* dropped anchor off Rio de Janeiro, gunboats were patrolling the bay, and for two or three days it was not permissible to land. Then a notice was pinned up: 'There has been an almost bloodless revolution. President Goulart has been driven out of office. A general strike is going on. It may be possible to dock tomorrow'. The struggle of the Peasant Leagues, or *Campesinos*, the downtrodden masses, had been crushed and their leaders killed or exiled. President Branco was in power.

We splashed through puddles on the *Avenido*, admiring the young people descended from many stocks whose genes have mingled to produce astonishing beauty. On the other hand, people afflicted with dreadful diseases and deformities were peddling trifles on the pavements, including the charms originating in Africa called *figas*, symbolising the 'holding on', the gripping courage, of a once persecuted race, three million of whom over the centuries had been sold into slavery throughout Latin America. Though there are hospitals to care for the sick and old, we were told that they prefer the freedom of the streets where they can earn a few coins and see the world go by. On the foothills huddled the *favelhas*, 'honeycombs', though the cells of these combs are not filled with sweetness. Behind the steaming, proliferating city stretched the forests of the colossal interior, already being ravaged to build highways, from which *Tegelberg*'s crew brought aboard hundreds of macaws, parrots and parakeets destined for the bazaars of Hong Kong and Singapore.

We, who had loved and hated South America, were glad to hear the purser proclaim over the loudspeakers that *Tegelberg* was bound 'for South Africa and the Far East', and 'Anchors Aweigh' was broadcast. Early next morning our cabin steward, Tso Ping-Wing, 'Bee Wing' to us, told us that we were heading back to Rio—a pantry-boy, Poon Chiu, was seriously ill and *Tegelberg* was racing to get him ashore in time to save his life. A South African widow swiftly whipped up a large collection for him as, strapped to a stretcher, he was lowered into a launch sent from the mainland; and the librarian put Debussy's 'Clair de Lune' on the record-player. Several days later, over a cresty sea misting with spray, the first wandering albatross joined us, as if it had brought the good news that Poon Chiu was making a good recovery.

On April 14th a dim, flat-topped giant form rose above the eastern horizon and the South Africans shouted 'Table Mountain! Our land!' A young moon was setting as we tied up in Cape Town Harbour, Crux, Orion and the Pointers gleaming overhead.

Breathtaking was the Cape's beauty, silver trees and wild gazanias blooming, and proteas, the national flower. We spent a morning at the Botanical Gardens, and an afternoon at Cape Point, where two oceans meet and there is a reserve for buck and eland, zebras and baboons. On the coast were seals, penguins and albatrosses and rocks shawled with cormorants. In a steel capsule we ascended Table Mountain, its summit speckled with black lizards and sprinkled with blue and yellow flowers: not a zephyr stirred. A few miles offshore glistened Robben Island where African leaders were incarcerated.

We visited a Shakespeare Quatrocentenary Exhibition in the Public Library, where the sub-librarian showed us Folios and other Editions, in one of which after years of searching I traced the origin of an engraving given to me when *Yellow Sands* was running, depicting sea nymphs on the 'beached verge of the salt flood' singing 'Come unto these yellow sands'—an exquisite picture.

During the coach trek to Durban through the vine-growing valley of the wagon-makers under the Drakenstein Mountains, past the granite dome of Paarl and over Robinson's Pass bordering the Little Karoo, Nicholas surprised the driver and passengers by asking to be put off that he might greet a black family who were waving to us from a shack. Parents and ten children poured out to meet him, smiling, gripping his hands and embracing him. I think some of the white South Africans thought my husband was not only eccentric but quite crazy.

After the Cango Caves and an Ostrich Farm we reached the Transkei Reserve, where distance beyond undulating distance lived more than a million and a half tribesfolk. Smoke drifted from their cooking fires as the sun went down—sundown over Africa, as Nicholas said: 'At this time its soul can be seen and felt.' When the coach stopped, small children whose fathers were slaving in gold and diamond mines ran to welcome us. What would their future be? Discussing apartheid with an elderly man in the coach he said candidly: 'We want this land for ourselves'; and though there must be thousands, and the number increases, we met only one white person who admitted that he disapproved of apartheid and thought it made South Africa the most emotionally, socially, and culturally deprived and depriving of nations, and prevented its citizens from attaining standards common to most of the rest of mankind. Certain it is that the destinies of all South Africans are mingled and their future must be hand in hand.

At Durban we rejoined the *Tegelberg* for Mauritius, a pleasant island with miniature mountains, lagoons and shell beaches, where we played with native children and collected tiger cowries and corals which strewed the sand.

On all our journeys we made lasting friendships, this time with Captain Robert Holden, retired, now of the Master Mariners' Cape Horner's Club, previously Headmaster of the Hong Kong Navigation School, captured in 1941 and imprisoned by the Japanese. Nicholas described him as a 'felicitous joinery of seadog and bookworm', and enjoyed the nightly strolls on deck yarning about ships and books.

So we reached Singapore, with its smell of frangipani, drains and rotting vegetables, where two hundred Chinese emigrants joined the *Tegelberg* for mainland China. Sailing north through the China Seas, every night sheet lightning flared, and northern constellations reappeared. The British doctor took us below to meet the crew— several were trying to teach their parrots Canton Chinese—and the emigrants, amongst whom was a Japanese couple, squashed into a recess half filled with exotic plants and a huge macaw, whose tiny daughter had pneumonia. How anxiously they watched as he sounded her, how joyfully when he pronounced her out of danger. The crew's faces lighted up as they spoke of seeing their families again in Hong Kong, though for but a few days before they left for Japan, and then back to South America.

Every morning we walked round the deck, and for the first time Nicholas mentioned a pain in his right leg which after a turn or two compelled him to rest. He dismissed it as rheumatism, but from that moment a new anxiety nagged at me and instead of five or six months of travel I wished we could go straight home.

In predawn darkness I saw lights outlining Victoria Peak and at 4 a.m. *Tegelberg* anchored in Hong Kong Harbour. Vast quiet graveyards stretch up the island steeps; rackety shanty-towns spread below. The Colony's chief resource is its patient industrious millions, then being increased annually by a hundred thousand births and hundreds of legal and illegal immigrants, who seemed willing to look forward to a time when their ramshackle huts and shops, refugee settlements and skyscraper flats would be cleared, and there would be enough money, houses, education, medical care, food and water for all.

All day *Tegelberg* discharged cargo into sampans and junks, to whose decks were tied babies while mothers cooked, fathers and grandfathers superintended loading and unloading, and grand-mothers lit incense sticks and with hooks on poles fished up tempting objects floating by. In the roadstead lay vessels of all kinds, from aged freighters and an American hospital ship to hydrofoils and elegant Communist craft flying starred oriflammes, laden with water and food.

One morning we met Captain Holden at Blake Pier and accepted his offer to take us to the Chinese frontier, crossing by ferry to Kowloon, where he bargained for a car. We drove through the lush Sha Tin Valley, past ancient villages, Buddhist temples and monasteries, flamboyant trees, and shadow-casting ginkgoes which used to be called scholar-trees and were planted to shade Chinese poets and students working out of doors. Beyond the frontier lay China, shimmering with delicate colours, watery, sun-drenched, remote, enticing the vision on and on to far faint mountains, its innumerable plantations separated by lakes and rivers, where one sensed a presence of multitudes—China, with its marvellous past, amazing present, and hopeful future, destined profoundly to affect mankind.

Captain Holden was stopping in Hong Kong and from *Tegelberg*'s launch we watched sadly as his back disappeared among the crowds on the quay: he was one who does not look back to wave. But he had promised to stay with us at Cobblestones.

For all its superficial prosperity Hong Kong seemed a tragic city, behind whose façade lived at least eighty thousand opium and heroin addicts, whose hard life had driven them to narcotics as the sole relief of compensating dreams before death healed everything.

As we sailed into the North China Sea Typhoon Tess whirled across the Pacific, winds within a hundred miles radius reaching seventy-five knots. Flying-fish were hurled on to the lower deck, the waves boiled, the sky seethed, and our cabin filled with what Nicholas called the chit-chat of the Jinns.

3

The Japanese archipelago was riven by millenniums of volcanic explosions and earthquakes from the mainland, and its first inhabitants were probably ancestors of the Hokkaido Ainus, succeeded by Chinese and Mongols, Malayans and Polynesians, to merge into the Japanese race. When we were there the country was booming, but torn politically and culturally between East and West and one sensed an anguish of spirit. Far more than material harm had been done by those atomic bombs. However, the Japanese have a saying and act on it: Fall down seven times. Get up eight.

Our voyage ended at Yokohama. Tso Ping-Wing stood at the top of the gangway waving madly and calling 'Goodbye. Goodbye! *Write to me!*'—once more the wrench of leaving a new friend. We visited artists' studios, dallied in a garden of water stones, a garden of dwarf trees, a Moss garden and an Iris garden. We meditated in a Zen garden, in Shinto shrines and Buddhist temples. We went to Kyoto, and to the Hakone National Park where giant Sumo wrestlers loomed like figures in a fairy-tale. We took train to Nikko, whose Toshugu Shrine keeps the three famous Monkeys, the sleeping cat, seven thousand volumes of Sutras, and where there are avenues of ancient cryptomeria trees; and to Mount Fuji, concealed behind storms of icy rain so that halfway up we waited in a hut with peasants round a charcoal stove until the downpoor ceased, clouds rolled off the cone and by the time we returned to the station the snow crowned pyramid was unveiled.

The top-gallant day was spent at Kamakura, home of the great bronze Buddha, Amida of Infinite Light, a monument to faith and reason, moulded and cast in 1252 by Ono Goroyemon. Fingertips touching in the attitude of contemplation, for seven hundred years he has reposed there, serene, compassionate, his majestic head inclined downwards as he watches with concern the human generations passing by. How many millions have paid homage, responded to his message, and pursued their ways. How many different Japans he has seen come and go, how many rejoicings witnessed, disasters shared: typhoons, earthquakes, wars, individual tragedies. He will see many more changes himself unchanged. This transcendental Image's most sublime attribute is its conception and creation by man.

One night we were sinking to sleep when the window clattered and slid to and fro, the door burst open, the bed pitched, the building swayed—and the morning paper announced: 'a sharp earthquake rocked the Kanto and Chibu areas for more than a minute at 11.32 p.m.'

We attended a performance by an all Japanese orchestra of Bruckner's Fourth Symphony; and we searched the Jimbocha district for Chamberlin's *Things Japanese* and found an early edition. But the most moving experience was an afternoon at the Jomyoin Temple Children's Cemetery which contains eighty thousand little graves, each attended by a statuette of their Guardian Deity, Jizo Basatsu, some so ancient that their heads had dropped off. Nicholas rescued a head whose body we could not identify and brought it home.

If this were the most touching experience, the most magical was the June Firefly Festival in Chinzan-so, a rolling hillside converted into gardens fit to contain Buddha's Bodhi Tree, the mystical Yggdrasil whose stem upholds the universe, Ailanthus the Tree of Heaven, the Tree of Knowledge and the Tree of Life itself. As the sun sank behind a pagoda and festive children of many nations frolicked together, we were strolling in the twilight when a firefly shone, another and another, until twinkling millions turned Chinzan-so into an inverted bowl of stars. Like flickering emeralds they spangled the dark, colliding with their reflections in a lake and sparkling on a screen like a glittering honeycomb of golden bees. Boys and girls caught and prisoned them in miniature cages.

The time had come for us to leave this land of mysteries and contrasts, beauties and uncertainties, more hidden than revealed. No kinder or more attractive people had we met, yet none we so little knew. On the hotel steps stood Mr Gota, the helpful manager, bowing, shaking hands, saying '*Sayonara*, my English friends. Happy journey!' 'Good luck, Mr Gota! Thank you for everything!' *Sayonara*, Japan!

4

We crossed the Pacific in an American freighter called the *President Taylor*: Nicholas said even the king-posts were stand-offish and the crew dismasted characters. But whatever her drawbacks she had an excellent library, to which I am indebted for the memorable *Tale of Meng Chian* which haunts me still. Two 'goony birds' flew with us as far as the Midway Islands where albatrosses nest. Nearing San Francisco, for six hours a mountainous swell caused every loose object to slide across the cabin floor, the masts to swing like metronomes and the Great Bear to dive up and down into the sea. Then the sun rose over the cliffs of California and threw across our breakfast-table the shadow of the Golden Gate Bridge. I pictured Drake landing in 1579 at 'a faire and good baye' where he was met by those 'Arcadian' Indians he described as 'joyously hospitable and free as birds, their speech like the warbling of birds, their colours like birds' plumage', who cheerfully yielded their domain to the British buccaneer. Their blissful lives continued for two more centuries until a Spanish party, followed by white immigrants from Arizona, reduced them from two hundred thousand free men to a few hundred serfs.

All night we heard the click-clack of tram cables running under Powell Street and Nob Hill to Fisherman's Wharf, and next morning boarded a tram to that pleasant district to explore the *Balclutha*, a square-rigged 'deep waterman' that for a hundred years beat her passage round Cape Horn: now her holds are packed with old sailing gear, figureheads, and faded photographs of bygone windjammers and their bygone crews.

Tiring of the city we spent a day with the giant redwoods of Muir Woods, the loftiest living things, two or more thousand years old, their roots cooled by sword ferns and anemones; and returned for an evening in Chinatown, whose tall metal effigy of Sun Yat-sen gleamed in the moon's rays and stared out of the night.

The Greyhound coaches which carried us across the continent stopped nearly every evening in a different city, of which Los Angeles was the second, where I recall Pershing Square by night, with its pathetic lovers, its rebels, fanatics, visionaries and idealists, religious cranks and lonely old derelicts, weeping, whispering, shouting, gesticulating, while multi-coloured fountains splashed up and down. We explored the Huntington Library and Art Gallery, and the San

Gabriel Mission, founded by Spaniards in 1771. Alas, poor Indians—
only dead and buried in its little *Campo Santo* did they find peace.
Their 'souls were stolen', as they said—their land too, and they willed
to die. (Of their kindred in Peru Benzoni reported: 'They not only
never would believe us to be Christians and children of God, but
not even that we were born on this earth and generated by a man and
born of a woman. So fierce an animal, they concluded, must be the
offspring of the sea'.)

We crossed a roasting desert where scarlet 'dust devils' twirled
among the skeletons of dead ocotillos and tall saguaros seemed to be
semaphoring to each other; where human bones more than 100,000
years old had been unearthed. The purple Vulture Mountains
shimmered in the distance. After a night at Flagstaff, where a
powwow was going on, we took a coach to the Grand Canyon and
lodged in a cabin round which sprawled the Fairy Duster, or
tumbleweed whose feathery seeds foam along the ground like spume.
Our first sight of the tremendous void was of violet and orange light,
gradually disclosing precipices and spired promontories, bluffs and
banded walls—an abyss changing colour as the planet turned. Here
we met Hopi Indians, who, with other Pueblo tribes, are endeavour-
ing, with increasing difficulty, to preserve their ancient identity
with nature, and keep up their mystical celebrations, not only to
entertain the tourists on whom they depend, but for their own sakes—
the Spring Corn Dance, the Cosmic Sun Dance, the Snake Dance,
and in gratitude for its plumage the Eagle Dance. I remember hearing
about an old Indian woman who said 'How can the Spirit of the Earth
like the white man, when everywhere he has touched it it is sore?';
and how my father told me in childhood that the 'Red Indians' were
doomed to extinction and there was no place for them in the modern
world. 'By the time you're grown up they will all be gone,' he said.
Now here they were, telling us about their lives. Part of their tragedy
is that their values were, and many still are, fundamentally opposed
to those of capitalistic, competitive, hierarchical modern society;
for their economy is based not on the accumulation of profits and
usury, but on holding goods in common. Even their all-important
land is held in common, not to be bought and sold, mined, or made
to produce surpluses of often wasted food. For the Indian, land has a
much deeper significance, and is part not only of his life, his culture,
his religion, his society, but of himself; and when it is wrested from
him he loses his identity, and bleeds, sometimes to death.

We were sitting in a wild part of the Canyon when Nicholas put his
hand on a wristwatch someone had left behind and said 'Strange to
find Time here!' Failing to trace the owner we were told to keep it,
but I never felt that it belonged to us. During a coach-trip along the
Canyon rim, above us rosy clouds reflecting the Painted Desert, a

woman sitting behind us said wearily to her neighbour: 'When you've seen it you've seen it and that's that. You can't go *on* looking. It gets boring.' True, the prodigious can fatigue. But we, soon to quit it for ever, clung as long as possible to this stupendous gap—one of those special places most people strike somewhere some-when, which grapple us to Nature's indifferent but compelling bosom—a bond indestructible.

On sped the Greyhounds. At Albuquerque we were close to the secret weapons base at Los Alamos where the nuclear age began. On July 3rd President Johnson signed the Civil Rights Bill, made law in 1965, which brought to millions of people fresh hope and freedom. On—on—to Amarillo, Panhandle's metropolis, across the great plains to Oklahoma carved out of Indian land, to Joplin, Tulsa, the Ozark plateau, and St Louis, where we sat on the bank of the Mississippi beneath James Eads' famous bridge, the first to be cantilevered and built of steel, a monument to Captain Eads, and his brave workmen who died of caisson disease. On the west bank rose the lofty stainless steel arms of an unfinished arch being built to commemorate the city's two hundredth anniversary, at a spot where a couple of French fur traders founded the town, and the pioneers assembled before setting out in covered wagons for the west. When completed it would form an inverted catenary curve—suggested by Galileo as the proper curve for an arch of equilibrium. Its architect, Eero Saarinen, died before his creation was finished, the fate of many brilliant architects and engineers.

On and on, through the woodlands of southern Indiana into Ohio, to Cincinnati, where we rested in another magnificent Library, and while Nicholas looked up his three mentors, Hawker, Powys and Keats, I traced on an illuminated globe the journeys of as many explorers as I could remember. We wound through the sun-filled vales of West Virginia bright with crimson sumachs, and switch-backed over the Allegheny Mountains speckled with flowering rhododendrons, black-eyed Susans, and daisies shining in soaking meadows; through the Shenandoah valley and across the Potomac to Washington, where at Arlington Cemetery we joined the queue waiting to pass the temporary grave of John Kennedy, of whom Nicholas, like millions of others, had hoped so much. 'How death levels,' he said, 'denationalises and is full of honour and peace'. In the superb National Gallery of Art, among works by twenty thousand artists we came across Grünewald's mystical *Small Crucifixion*, Titian's *Venus with a Mirror*, Rembrandt's sublime *Descent from the Cross*, and Donatello's *David*.

On to New York, its environs crowded with storage tanks, chemical plants and marshalling yards, church towers, water towers, radio towers, apartment and office towers, but also with room for waterways, bullrushes and reedy pools, and an avenue of plane trees which might have strayed from an English country town. At the terminal an elderly black lady lost her suitcase and could find nobody to help her until Nicholas dragged it from the underbelly of another Greyhound, and she embraced him with relief.

Amidst the skyscrapers for one surprised moment we saw a windjammer last seen in Valparaiso, the *Esmeralda*—what was she doing in the middle of New York? Our visit had coincided with 'Operation Sail', rendezvous of ships on the Hudson River after their race from Lisbon, so no sooner had we dumped our bags than we sought them, looking oddly small beside the ocean liners berthed on Manhattan wharf, in their turn diminished by the skyscrapers, so-called after clippers' topsails.

After thousands of dry miles water was irresistible and we boarded a Circle boat for a trip round the island. A girl came along selling sweets and postcards of the 'Statue of Liberty', while a small black boy sitting beside us clutching a coin looked first at the sweets and then at the postcards, trying to decide on which to spend it, and finally chose the 'Statue of Liberty', at which he gazed for a long time before putting it in his pocket. Nicholas gave him a packet of sweets, and he grinned with glee. You never know your luck.

To escape the phantasmagoria of the streets we slipped into the gloomy Public Library on 42 Street, where an exhibition was being held of manuscripts on which had rested the hands of Fanny Burney, Walt Whitman, Emerson, Southey and Longfellow: I pictured those hands moving across the pages driven by their remarkable minds. Later, on the night streets—though here there was no true night—raddled derelicts picked over litter and garbage cans, or begged, or were past begging—what tragedies, what suffering we saw. As in book stores, where the scruffiest and most noble works were squeezed together, jostling one another out of doors were the poor and the prosperous, the uppermost and the down-and-outs, startling contrasts common to many big cities, especially so here. Every night, amongst the parade and the masquerade, the screaming police cars and ambulances, we returned to our look-out barrel in the skyscraper hotel, from which I seemed to see New York's tower blocks standing empty, like tombstones in a lifeless necropolis. In all the great cities we had briefly visited one felt powerfully conscious of death, not only of individuals but of civilisations—cities which, like them, must indubitably die. But there were oases of life in this desert: for instance, the Metropolitan Museum of Art, into which are packed so many sublime achievements that they should cheer the most despairing spirit, though not necessarily endow it with hope. For great artistic works bear no relation to great advances in human welfare, and offer no guarantee that human nature will improve enough to enable man to create on Earth the perfection he has dreamed of in Paradise.

5

At length we reached Boston and drove to the old-fashioned Hotel Vendome on Commonwealth Avenue, where Oscar Wilde used to stay. A painting by Utrillo hung in the manager's office. An old grey-haired Negro showed us to a fourth-floor bedroom, its walls hung with prints of steam calliopes and cottage-type animals' vans belonging to Robinson's Circus of long ago. We were soon on the Common, Boston's leaf-green heart—deeded to the populace in 1634 when it was an untouched corner of the pre-Columbian continent—riding in a swanboat on the lake; then we walked to the Public Library to rest in the forecourt on a bench where for many happy and unhappy hours of his youth Nicholas used to sit. America's first free library, of architectural magnificence, it houses thousands of books about New England besides collections connected with Astronomy, Navigation and Mathematics, Spanish and Portuguese literature, Shakespeareana, and musical manuscripts. Outside crouched men and women with heads bowed in pain, shame, despair, who begged for dimes. My husband said: 'It hasn't changed.'

The following afternoon Nicholas's brother Stanley arrived to drive us to his Hingham home, a large colonial clapboard house surrounded by gardens, where his wife Ruth, some of their children and grandchildren, and two aged aunts awaited us, and we cooled off under the trees. Drooping from a pole on the lawn hung the Stars and Stripes, symbolising this vast nation, then menaced by innumerable problems, all as it were wrapped in Old Glory's folds. As the sun set, Nicholas helped his brother to furl the national flag. Our kinsfolk drove us to many interesting places, including Nantucket beaches, Thoreau's Walden Pond, Concord, and Cohasset and Scituate, mother towns founded by the Pilgrims and Puritans where thousands of fine ships had been built, and the Indians, who had helped them to survive the first winter, were dispossessed, massacred, and condemned by certain Christian ministers to Hell.

We spent the last part of our visit in a Quincy Motel, near the apartment of our kind aunts, Olive and Mildred, whose friend Margaret drove us to Falmouth, Plymouth, Duxbury, and Woods Hole, in whose rose garden a golden-haired figurehead in a blue gown smiled across the flowers at a handsome carved Indian chief. (If only they could have met!) Returning in the unremitting heat of evening past steaming cranberry bogs, all of us parched with thirst, Aunt Olive, who had always loved Nicholas, treated us to iced cranberry juice, and bought us boxes of sweet-scented bayberry candles, a craft the first settlers were taught by the Indians.

One day Nicholas took me to the Thomas Crane Public Library

where, under a sizzling roof, we dug out old numbers of the Patriot
Ledger to read his first printed poems, from where we walked to
his birthplace, a little green painted wooden house on Granite Street,
recently designated by the local Historical Society the J. Y. Nightingale House and scheduled as one of Quincy's more-than-century-old
homes. He recalled a garden of lilacs and a buttercup meadow
beyond, through which ran the willow-fringed town brook, famous
for eels, and a Common used by Buffalo Bill's Wild West Shows.
Now the garden was overrun by sumachs, the stream had been piped,
and the Common was covered with bungalows. Everything he
remembered as a child, like childhood had vanished, except slabs
of ice-smoothed granite on which the cottage stood.

Back in Boston we spent hours in its Museum of Fine Arts, for
Nicholas to renew his friendship with El Greco's *Fray Felix Hortensio,
Paravansio Paravicino*, and for me to meet Rembrandt's *Old Man*,
Renoir's *Bal à Bougival*, and Turner's *Slave Ship*. And again we
dallied on the Common, with its Frog Pond near which once stood
the Old Elm, Tree of Hangings, the whipping-post, pillory, and other
punishments meted in the good old days to witches, Indians,
Quakers, and other undesirables. And in the little steamer *Yankee* we
voyaged to Provincetown on Cape Cod to eat fresh clams, steaming
home in the dark, her hot funnel at our backs, fringes of golden light
glittering on Boston's new skyscrapers, black-headed gulls in the
navigation channel perched on piles and buoys. We visited the
Houghton Library with its renowned Keats Collecton, and John
Kennedy's Literary Exhibit, with melancholy relics of a promising
man tragically assassinated. And we met warm-hearted friends of
my husband's youth, including Mrs Phyllis Orcutt, widow of his late
dear friend, Edgar. But time was running out. And as there was no
available cargo-ship sailing from Boston, we booked a passage on the
American Planter, leaving from Brooklyn. Our saddest farewell
was from Aunt Olive, whom we knew we should not see again. Yet,
as we waited on the deserted South station for the midnight 'Owl' to
New York, who should come trotting across the dark platform but
that valiant little woman. 'I couldn't bear not to see you off.' On
quitting his city of both tragic and joyful memories, Nicholas declared
that the reunion had brought some disenchantment but much
liberation, and discovery of 'the most precious ores of human
existence'.

Dockers were swarming down the gangway of the *American Planter*
as we pushed our way aboard. Alongside lay the *African Comet*,
seagulls picking in the bins slung over her bulwarks, evoking in me
a wild, wild desire to transfer to her and sail away to Africa. And I
wondered how often in the future we should crave for the shimmer of
ports dimming over the stern, the swing of a masthead lantern, and

the rising of the Southern Cross.

6

The *American Planter*, launched in 1945 and structurally resembling *Cuzco*, was manned, except for the Malaysian bosun, by grizzled Americans. Our fellow passengers were a Cistercian monk, a Filipino schoolmaster and his wife, and a retired Scottish Merchant Marine engineer with his. The creaky old vessel made heavy weather as she rolled to New Bedford—near which Joseph Slocum built his little *Spray* and began his circumnavigation, tying up three years later in the field from which he launched her, and from which Herman Melville sailed to the Marquesas in the whaler *Acushnet*. We spent a couple of hours at the Whaling Museum on Johnny Cake Hill, and read the *Acushnet*'s crew list with Melville's signature underlined. And there I found a model ship made in 1812 by an American prisoner of war at Princetown gaol, Dartmoor.

Before the *Planter* sailed I rescued from her deck a praying mantis and persuaded it to fly back to land. Mr 'Babbaloo' the black cook told us that he had served in her for eleven years and now she was going to be broken up. And he sighed so deeply that I should not have been surprised if from his large dark eyes had fallen into the Atlantic a tear such as Captain Ahab shed into the Pacific, 'nor did all the Pacific contain such wealth as that one wee drop'. Preceding us out of the harbour bobbed a little fishing-boat called *Moby Dick*.

Off the Grand Banks the groaning *Planter* pitched into a gale, her ropes slapping and whistling, her stem parting huge waters that leapt from below and pelted from above, her keel bumping and grating as if off the backs of whales. A dusky noddy flew over the stern and alighted on the rigging, and a flock of petrels skimmed past, the smallest web-foot, birds of the night and twilight which sailors call Mother Carey's chickens, harbingers of a blast-bestriding witch.

Nearing the Bay of Biscay I thought about our four ships and their crews and captains—amongst them no Lingard, Ahab, or Shotover, no Magellan, Davis or Cook, no Captain Conrad, Captain Slocum, or Captain Kidd, no Queequeg or Robinson Crusoe—yet ours had been a gallant lot. Though we had traversed only a thin swathe of the round world, of all the peoples we had so sparingly but sometimes so lastingly encountered, their differences, their conflicts, seemed insignificant compared to their similarities and agreements. Moreover, their common needs—of peace, stability and enough prosperity not to hunger and drudge and slave, to live without fear—were the same.

The *American Planter* docked at St Nazaire, the Brittany port where in 1942 the Commando raid, Operation Chariot, rammed the dock gate with the destroyer *Campbeltown*, killing for hundred Germans and a hundred and sixty-nine British servicemen. Strolling in the newly built town we came upon a massive structure so ancient that clearly it had nothing to do with today or yesterday, but was a cromlech couched beside a menhir, not even chipped by German missiles or British explosives.

At 2 a.m. the *Planter* sailed into a night of illuminations: Orion shining over the Bassin de Penhoët, Jupiter like a flame near the Pleiades, Venus' reflection wavering on the water, luminescence licking the hull and gleaming in the wash. The air grew colder than we had felt it since February outward bound. Soon we caught the flash of the Needles Lighthouse, and Nicholas recalled another September, in 1820, when the brigantine *Maria Crowther* sailed past the chalk stacks carrying John Keats and Joseph Severn to Italy. One could smell England in the rainy wind, while round us flew kitti-wakes; and like our Liverpool farewell our Southampton welcome came from the herring gulls.

To breathe the long unreplenished air of Cobblestones, break its long silence and disturb its untrodden rooms was like entering Sleeping Beauty's castle. But instead of a slumbering princess we seemed to find ourselves still dreaming of circling the globe. For already the journey was growing dreamlike and we like sleepers awakening in a house we had never left.

The Last Journey

1

The first thing Nicholas made was a small Zen garden, its theme the brotherhood of man. Above it he fixed the Jizo head from the children's burial-ground in Tokyo, and on its bed of sand set particular stones, and scored patterns with special meanings. In 'drear-nighted December' we sat beside it at midnight awaiting a total eclipse of the Moon, whose light glittered on the rimed rocks; crystallised leaves crackled and hoar-frost grew. At one o'clock Earth's shadow touched the Moon's left limb and when its curve became apparent we told each other that we had ringed that rondure. Our satellite looked like a smouldering cornelian. The sky gradually filled with stars, sparkling amongst the branches of the beech. About three o'clock the last coppery shaving slid off the nether rim to reveal the full moon's face, and Nicholas said 'I hope and believe no one will ever get there.'

I was worried, not only about his increasing leg pain but because he was so fretted by the social, racial and political enmities seething over the world. 'All nations should return to or strive after a childlike relationship of simply "We love each other",' he said, and admitted that his depression grew heavier. But when it occasionally dispersed he felt 'as light as thistledown'. He began writing about our travels, but the labour made his head ache, so he set it aside, and resumed copying out his letters from John Powys, which were subsequently bound in several volumes by the monks of St Michael's Abbey at Farnborough.

Summer brought Captain Holden to stay, followed by Henry, while Nicholas's pains in the leg grew more severe and he had palpitations and dizzy spells. So, though he begged me not to, I sent for Dr Blood, who told me that there was nothing wrong with his heart, but the pain was caused by arterial obstruction. He prescribed tranquillisers, and promised to make an appointment at Devonport Hospital for him to see Mr Reilly, a consultant surgeon. This specialist not being available at the time, a Pakistani doctor examined Nicholas and recommended sympathectomy, severing the nerves from the spinal cord to the legs to help dilation of the blood vessels, improve general circulation and keep his feet warm. We waited for another call but none came, and though the delay affected him, little things diverted his mind—like a spider that wove an intricate web in the studio window and spent its time in the centre but caught nothing. He called it the personification of patience and a lesson to him to be calm.

Summoned at last, he was allotted a bed in a ground-floor ward, opposite which lay a young Chinese seaman, Ho Yan-chi, who had been washed overboard from a tanker on her way to Bordeaux, dislocated his shoulder. He reminded us of 'Bee-Wing' on the *Tegelberg*, with whom we were corresponding, he, too, having transferred to a tanker, and I brought Ho a pile of Chinese Pictorials from Peking, to which we subscribed, that delighted him. At night the ward was supervised by a young male nurse who uncannily resembled John Keats, and sometimes he leaned over my husband's bed to see if he were sleeping or needed anything, and in his drugged state he identified the nurse with the real Keats. One night the young man told Nicholas that he had hoped to be a doctor, but the means not being available he trained as a nurse instead. He wrote an account of this strange experience which is one of his most moving works.

As Mr Reilly could not perform both operations then, he suggested that Nicholas should go home for Christmas week and come back afterwards; so he expected to return in seven days. But nearly four months passed and the suspense was like a Damoclean sword. Perceiving how overwrought he was becoming, I begged him to let me arrange a private operation which could be done at any time; but believing that it was unfair he would not consent. I begged Dr Blood to get in touch with Mr Reilly, and he did. On April 25th Nicholas went back to the hospital, where he had a corner bed in Norman Ward on the first floor: that it bore his father's name pleased him. I stopped at a Salvation Army Hostel, where everybody was extremely kind.

Nicholas never betrayed the physical and mental pain he endured; and it was mitigated by the interest he took in other patients, with some of whom he became friends and helped them, they him. I spent the brief visiting-hours with him, and the rest of my time at the hostel, reading a book he had asked me to get: Michael Hamburger's *Beethoven: Letters, Journals and Conversations*—to which I owe more than I can describe.

Many weeks passed before Nicholas gained even a little strength, until in September he felt well enough to visit Stanbury Cove, sure that now he could climb the rocks and walk on the sands without pain. On a 'perfect crystalline day, a happy day for ever', as he called it, we did recapture some of the happiness of former times, yet—I knew that he was suffering and at last nerved myself to ask him. He thought for a moment then said: 'Adelaide, the pain hasn't gone. But I'm sure it will some day.' I was sure that it never would, nor did it, except for one miraculous interlude.

2

On New Year's Eve at midnight we went into the moonlit garden, hoping, as one always hopes of a new year, that 1967 would be a better year for everyone, and Nicholas quoted his favourite lines from Henry Vaughan: 'I saw Eternity the other night / Like a great *Ring* of pure and endless light . . .' and said he was 'supremely thankful to God' for his Christmas happiness. He planned to spend January and February redecorating the cottage, refurbishing the gypsy wagon, and finishing copying the Powys letters. In March he was troubled by the wreck of the *Torrey Canyon*, causing huge oil spillage and death of birds; and he was saddened by the death of John Masefield, whom he had met in Oxford. When our lilacs bloomed he thought of the cottage where he was born, and yearned to be there again, reminding me how my Mother longed for her childhood garden. By June he had repainted the kitchen, bathroom and outside of the house, and was beginning on the wagon and garden when we both felt a passionate urge to revisit Dartmoor, and booked rooms at Riddon Farm, four miles from Widecombe, owned and worked by a widow and her grown-up children, where we arrived during haymaking.

At first, the days were sunny and we sported beside the Wallabrook which ran past the farm, and on an islet of marsh marigolds fringed with water forget-me-nots and bluebells, 'as merry as grigs', where Nicholas in droll mood picked out King and Queen Thistle, Monsieur and Madame Foxglove, and in midstream the Great Presence of Mud, a grotesque granite boulder, and 'meads of enchantment', which he wove into our fairy-tale. On Midsummer Night he planned to go out at midnight to greet the fairies themselves, in whom he believed, and our vegetable and mineral friends; but fearful of disturbing the household we desisted.

One morning we rambled down the river to its confluence with the West Dart, passing a heron and meeting butterflies and damsel flies, mayflies and dragonflies darting over the water, until we reached a flat granite rock covered with pink stonecrop and moss, 'Oberon's platform' to Nicholas, where we spread a meal. Beyond rose a pine wood into which we penetrated as far as a round spot of sunlight, where he recited lines from a John Lyly play:

Pandora: Give me a running streame in both my hands,
             A blew kings fisher, and a pible stone,
             And Ile catch butterflies upon the sand,
             And thou Gunophilia shall clippe their wings.

Stesias: Ile give thee streames whose pible shall be pearle,
             Love birds whose feathers shall be beaten gold,

Musk flies with amber berries in their mouthes,
Milke white Squirrels, singing Popinjayes,
A boat of deare skins, and a floating Ile,
A sugar cane, and line of twisted silke.

And from John Fletcher:

He shall have chariots easier than air,
Which I have invented; and thyself
That art the messenger shall ride before him,
On a horse cut out of an entire diamond,
That shall be made to go on golden wheels,
I know not how yet.

He loved such conceits; much of his own verse resembled them.

Another day we walked over the moor to Postbridge, and spying bog-bean in flower I waded towards it, sank up to my knees and was stuck. I could see Nicholas across the bog, as if in a nightmare, a thousand miles away and inaccessible. But by some magical means —he would have said it was the fairies—he appeared to cause to rise dry hummocks upon which he reached me and pulled me out.

My brother Henry and the family with whom he lived spent a day with us, and as they were leaving, Nicholas clasped his hand and said: 'We look forward to your coming in September.'

Towards the end of our visit we set out in fine mist for Widecombe and on the way found a sheep stuck up to its neck in the Wallabrook, its hooves wedged. We pushed and pulled and at last freed it and shoved it to a gap in the bank, where Nicholas hauled it out. Whether it was the spirit of Dartmoor, which he loved, or a real improvement in his condition I do not know, but during this fortnight he did not once tire and his legs did not pain. He walked easily—'never to be forgotten walks' he called them. In a hut circle he discovered a granite ball, or 'bolus' as he thought it might have been, and a piece of rose quartz, and spoke of 'the old men of the moor', as my father named the Bronze Age farmers with whom he had felt, as Nicholas did, a strong affinity. Many years afterwards I chanced on a sheet of paper where my husband had described our sojourn in the hut circle, and copied a passage from one of Father's books: 'They sleep in night eternal below the roots of the heather. Their tale is told, their short days numbered. But the granite that their hands dragged, sadly to mark a grave, hopefully to build a house, still stands . . . And seeing the stones scattered so harmoniously, so solemnly, and so still, my heart goes out to those vanished shepherds, and I love them across the dark waves of time that roll between their pilgrimage and my own . . .' And I wondered whether my parent might have been glad that the son-in-law he could not bring himself to meet had copied those lines, and whether he would have forgiven us.

The last two days were cold and wet. Damp rose from the parlour's stone floor and crept up the walls. It was too stormy to pay a farewell visit to the outdoor Beings we had adopted; and I felt a foreboding, a shivering fear.

3

Directly Nicholas got home the pain in his limbs recurred as severely as before. The wooden wagon steps having rotted, he began making new ones with breeze-blocks, and said teasingly, 'I'm doing it for you so you shall be safe when I'm not here.' I said he would always be here and he laughed and answered lightly: 'You'll long outlive me.' A flycatcher had built her nest under the studio water-chute and flew back and forth with insects for her single nestling. She would perch on a garden seat and suddenly dart off, twisting in the air, snapping up flies and midges. Nicholas sat in a deckchair when he was tired, watching, and grew attached to the mother bird. Before our moorland visit something had happened deeply to disturb him—the Arab-Israeli War, in which our friend Isaac Rosenberg was fighting. As in Ireland, in the Middle East the past was the enemy of the present, or rather the past and present were one, merged, and both Jews and Arabs regarded Palestine as a gift from their gods. For myself I felt as much Arab as Jew: it was a conflict between brethren, and Britain was partly to blame for having promised too much to each side. Rosie had sent us his annual gift of Jaffa oranges; and while on the moor Nicholas had received a letter from him saying that the Jews had won, and the Rosenberg family were safe, enclosing a copy of the *Jerusalem Post*; and though my husband was thankful for his friend's safety, he was hurt by parts of the journal, and after we got home wrote the following letter: 'Dearest Rosie, We thank all the gods that be, Yaweh, Jupiter, Allah, ALL superhuman beings who are worshipped as having power over nature and human fortunes—that you and your little family are safe and well. In the recent clashes and perplexing events, THIS has concerned us first and most. *It is for you and yours* I have prayed intensely—not the state of Israel or Egypt, because for such events, a perspective on history is required and it is too soon for that comfort to come. One's mind and compassion are torn into so many directions! Charity, or LOVE, requires of us that we accept people how we have experienced them . . . in other words, to allow our thoughts to be guided and controlled by personal experience and not by what we hear and what we read. Even a profound sense of loyalty cannot interfere with that. Yet, it is of the ordinary folk I speak, and not their chosen representatives. (We have never been admirers of General Nasser, but we have always experienced from Arabs and Egyptians the most courteous relationships wherein kindness and understanding were always paramount.

We have many friends in Old Jerusalem.) It is our hope that Old Jerusalem will become a Holy Region, international and independent, free visibly and invisibly, to ALL religions and faiths. The Psychic "side" of History-in-the-long-run, demands it. It should belong to the world with places there for all peoples, including the Chinese. It is there, within its sacred precincts, that troubles of the past could be forgotten once and for all. It was MOST disturbing to read in one of our most reputable newspapers, that before the guns had hardly cooled, Ben Gurion was suggesting that the ancient walls of the city should now be torn down. Of course this may have been a false report as so much else was a few weeks ago, but I have no hesitation in saying that to touch those walls with a view to their destruction would not only be an architectural and archaeological blunder, but a PSYCHIC mistake as well, bound in time to be regretted. The walls are as religiously powerful to other faiths as Herod's wall is to your people. They figure in all the ancient manuscripts and illuminations! St Stephen's Gate is a Shrine of the first Christian martyr. I honestly believe that if YOU were in AUTHORITY in Israel, these things would not be allowed to be done. I refer also to a possible "Americanisation" of the Old City, e.g., the picturesque souks widened and houses flattened to make room for the monstrous cars of rich Americans! It is PEACE everyone wants in the area and the magnanimity of nations is required to bring it about. NOT annexation. No SINGLE nation has a claim on Jerusalem—nor can they ever hope to have, even for a little space of time before the napalm burns again and the crushing tanks waddle into Holy Places, as did happen in the Garden of Gethsemane a few weeks ago. MIGHT is never right! I wonder how many more aeons must pass disastrously before this simple idea and truth dents the skulls of Leaders or so-called Leaders—

'Thank you very much for the copy of *Jerusalem Post*. Some of the articles I like very much and especially the front-page picture of Herod's Wall. But many other things in this paper saddened me. I speak especially of its "tone", which I might almost call a crowing over the fallen, so apt especially in regard of the type of American Newspaper Writing, and the fact that MANY of the Jewish ritualistic words were misspelt, as though the writers had never been into a Holy Synagogue or opened a Liturgical Scroll. (I especially refer to the 'Shekhina'—misspelled thus as you know. The CORRECT English rendering of this holy Jewish thing is AISHAH SCHE-CHINAH. It, as you know, is a sacramental element, a cloudy symbol of the Divine Presence. Elias was the first to experience it and identify it . . . ON MOUNT CARMEL.) And the short article on the almost final page entitled "REALLY, HUSSI, old chap!" was undignified and mistaken. Anointed Kings are worthy of everyone's respect . . . or so I think, regardless of what they do or do not do. I am far from being an admirer of King Hussein, but he is deserving of respect and he HAS TRIED to improve the lot of his people.

'Well, with all this warfare and killing and threats, we felt it best to get away from it all for a little while. So we had two weeks in a lovely region in the South of England called Dartmoor. During this time we hardly saw a paper and did not hear a radio or television set. Our loyalties were torn wide open like wounds. There, in that quiet corner of the countryside we were able to come to terms with those startling events taking place in the Middle East. It was there that I received your letter with your news. It seemed to be an answer to prayer, to hear that you were unscathed and soon to be demobbed. I trust that procedure has now taken place, and that you will no longer be called on to shoulder a gun or leap a barbed wire barricade. You profit much by this latest turn of events and the scope enlarged . . . especially on the land your country has acquired down in the Hebron area, where many prophets are interred. All this new territory will be very interesting to you, as you guide the tourists here and there. One important job I hope your Leaders will immediately pursue, is the rehabilitation of Rachel's Tomb. It was the ONLY shrine we found neglected in Jordan. (It stands filled with rubbish by the side of a lonely road.) Its condition shocked me extremely. Perhaps by now something will have been done to respect it. The Bedouins in that region were always very charming to us and helpful.

'Every day we spoke of you with fear in our hearts—so you can imagine how wonderful it was to have a letter from you. All the wild flowers were at their best, and from the waters every once in a while a trout would bellyflap itself into the sunlight to be saluted by the great variety of bird-life. There were also pre-historic hut circles there, and a clapper-bridge of the Bronze Age. Please give our hearty salaams to Ilse and the family. It must be a great relief to her to have you out of uniform again. I will write again soon. Meanwhile, Ada joins me in sending you our love and every good wish for the future. SHALOM. Nicholas'.

Rosie did not answer and Nicholas feared he had given offence. He continued to work in the garden, and I to feel a nagging dread. On the morning of July 9th he had been reading in a solarium he had built, while I prepared lunch, when he came in sick and giddy. I was going to send for the doctor when he implored me not to, and recovered; but later, watching the flycatcher, his vision distorted and I asked the doctor to come. Unfortunately, Dr Blood, our regular physician and friend, was abroad and another member of the group came, who told me that Nicholas had vascular trouble and high blood pressure and he would prescribe tablets to reduce it. That evening he suffered two more attacks, though he was better in the morning and sat in the garden, looking for the mother flycatcher; but she did not appear and

the nest was empty. 'The baby bird must have been fledged,' he said.
'We shan't see either of them again. Good luck to them! But it leaves
a void.' On looking down I saw the unfledged nestling lying on the
ground dead. Luckily he did not see it. This obscure little tragedy
filled me with quite inordinate sorrow and fear.

He suffered from vertigo but was determined to finish the steps—
the only thing he wanted to do. Every time the doctor came he said
Nicholas would soon be well. One evening he had a bad giddy turn,
followed by a night of cold sweats, vomiting and aching head. At
3 a.m. I ran to the telephone at the end of the street and summoned
a doctor whom I begged to come as soon as possible. Meanwhile I kept
compresses on his head and tried to soothe him, for he was exhausted
and bewildered. Three hours later a young Indian locum arrived.
Nicholas was quite disabled and could not move without help. The
doctor said he would bring another doctor and they would decide
what to do. After more hours he brought a colleague and having
examined my husband said: 'We must get him to hospital tomorrow.
I'll send an ambulance in the morning. I think he has had a slight
stroke.' From that moment I knew the worst, but Nicholas did
not seem worried and asked why I was upset. His mind wandered
and he had hallucinations and delusions. Looking at the eiderdown he
said 'Please give me that book. I can't reach it.' No book was there.

After another terrible night he tried to get up but could not stand
or see straight and wondered why his head still ached. Towards
morning he said, 'I'm getting up now to get your breakfast.' He kept
trying to rise, thinking *I* was ill and needed *his* help. No ambulance
came. In desperation I ran to a near neighbour and begged her to ring
up Stratton Hospital and ask for one immediately. After a long time it
came; and he was put to bed in the hospital.

Early next morning I telephoned for news, to hear that in half an
hour he would be taken to Freedom Fields Hospital at Plymouth.
Leaving everything, I asked someone at the local garage to drive me
to Stratton, which I reached as the ambulance was starting, and I
got in. Nicholas had been drugged and did not know me. At
Plymouth Hospital he was left on a stretcher in the lobby during
another long delay. A baby was screaming somewhere and to my
surprise Nicholas said: 'That poor child. I wish it would stop crying.'
He could not bear to hear children cry. 'You must be tired,' he said,
then relapsed into half consciousness. At last men arrived and
wheeled him to a darkened, silent ward on the ground floor,
containing three other men patients, and a small child with bandaged
head said to be in danger.

I was taken to an office to be interviewed, then waited in a corridor
until I was allowed to see Nicholas, who only half knew me. Later
I found an almoner and asked her for the address of somewhere I

could stay, for I intended to go home that evening, lock up Cobble-stones and return to Plymouth until I could bring Nicholas back. Having booked a lodging I sought a Catholic priest and asked him if possible to visit my husband, which I hoped would comfort him. The man, pressed for time and rather unwilling, said he would try to do so. Then I sat with Nicholas until it was time to get the bus for Bude. Next morning he was no better. I was allowed to feed him, and he thought he was a child and I was his mother. Opposite his bed was another sick husband, whose wife was waiting for him to regain consciousness after an accident. Young parents were bending over the child with the broken skull.

I kept wondering if Nicholas had a tumour on the brain, which someone had suggested, or a stroke, but no one could or would tell me. All the doctor said was: 'He's in the best place.' On the fourth day he seemed more lucid and said: 'I hope that child will get well.' He asked where he was, drank tea, and smiled at the man opposite who was conscious again. For the first time I hoped. On the fifth day he said: 'When are we going home? Who are these people?' And then he said: 'I'm not happy,' and looked at me with a wan smile: 'Old faithful—won't desert the sinking ship.' I hoped. Next day I arrived to find his bed empty, and was told that due to a chest infection he had been moved to a ward where the patients were not on the danger list. I traced him to a large overcrowded place on the top floor of another block where his bed was hemmed in with people who were nearly well, active and noisy, and thought it meant that he too was recovering; but his mind was still clouded and he asked: 'Is Mother asking after me? How did you find me here? I don't know how I got here. Don't let me out of your sight.' I fetched him some water and tried in vain to find a doctor, or even a Sister. When I came in the evening he had been moved into a small anteroom with one other patient, and a member of the Salvation Army watching over them. 'Where have you come from?' Nicholas said, adding, 'Good luck and bad luck knocking together.'

Next day his mind was clear enough to remember the Middle East War and his unanswered letter to Isaac Rosenberg. Fortunately, that morning I had received a letter for him from Rosie which proved that our friend took no offence at what my husband had written, so I read it aloud, but he hardly took it in. During these vigils I tried to appear calm, confident, reassuring, and when Nicholas kept begging me to take him home I explained that he must stay for one or two more days to gain strength, and then I would come and fetch him and he would never leave home again. I tried to see someone in authority, but no one was available. I wanted to find Dr Graham-Wilson, who, I was told, had to do with his case. I asked Nicholas if a Catholic priest had been to see him and he shook his head.

He had been moved back into the restless ward of recovering patients. 'Please take me home. I do want to go home,' he pleaded. He was afraid of dying there. He asked after 'Mother and Dad, and how's my dog?' He put his arms around me, and I gave him some water. Soon the hideous dismissal bell rang. Visiting-time was up. All the visitors trooped out. I waylaid a doctor in a corridor and entreated him to tell me how I could get Nicholas into a private ward. *I would pay anything.* But the man said: 'Impossible—they're all engaged,' and hurried on.

At the next visiting-hour I found Nicholas sitting out of bed and realised how dreadfully he had changed. His face was grey, his eyes were sunken and the bones of his skull stood out. But he was almost completely lucid, though he did say, 'Have you let Mother know?' To my surprise he asked to have Rosie's letter read again, and this time understood it and was relieved by the news. A fog-horn on the Hoe was blowing and he said 'It must be foggy at sea', then 'Will the car come to take me home this evening? . . . I don't know what I'd do without you.' The dreaded bell rang and the other visitors faded away. 'You'll soon be home,' I said and he answered 'Be careful how you go.'

Next morning the landlady came to my room early and said: 'I've got a message for you to ring the hospital at eight o'clock,' and left. I ran downstairs, thinking he was going home that day. A voice said: 'I'm sorry. I'm afraid there's some bad news for you. Your husband died at 3 a.m. this morning, peacefully, in his sleep. Please call here at ten o'clock.' The landlady said: 'You must get in touch with your local undertaker.'

It was July 28th. A hospital official told me where to register the death. Then I waited in a passageway until a doctor arrived and expressed sympathy. I told him that Nicholas had seemed so much better the previous evening and he said: 'Ah, yes—that often happens shortly before a final, massive stroke. You can see him if you like,' and he hurried away to care for the living. From the ward I fetched Nicholas' clothes, his rosary and a gold medal of Our Lady I had given him. A young student nurse was ordered to take me to a building in the grounds. An old man let us in, but the little nurse was reluctant to go into the presence of death. I could understand; however, the old man said 'Go on. You must get used to it. You must wait until the lady is ready to leave'; so, though I would readily have excused her, the poor young thing had to obey. Nicholas lay in a temporary coffin, looking beautiful, young and smiling. Did he really die peacefully in his sleep, or do they always say that? I must believe it. He was at peace now. I placed his medal and rosary in the coffin and kissed him, not to say goodbye. All was well—no more torment, suffering, frustration, pain. I wanted to die too, and most of me did.

Back at Cobblestones I went into the studio. The silence, emptiness, desolation were shattering. I gave Mr Kinsman, the undertaker, Nicholas's wedding-ring to put in the coffin and a small crucifix John Powys had made for him out of two sticks and a rough pewter figure of Christ. Goethe wrote in his Prelude to *Faust* about bliss that touched the verge of pain. My pain ultimately touched the verge of bliss.

On the night before the funeral I felt an impulse to open a desk we rarely used and my purposeless hand strayed to a pigeonhole containing a sheaf of papers I had not seen before—poems I had not read, I presumed by Nicholas. I took one out at random: it was addressed to me. He was a lover of Christina Rossetti's poetry and to begin each verse acknowledged a line of her *Song*.

> *When I am dead, my dearest
> Dance on for I will be
> In Paradise still praying for
> And watching over thee.
> No more the absence of despair
> When time reached for my hand,
> For we shall meet again as one
> for evermore to stand.
>
> *I shall not see the shadows
> Of statues stone and still,
> I shall not feel the stony hearts
> Of men, or their ill-will;
> But delving in God's mine of prayer
> Where intercessions rise
> I'll love thee still my darling till
> We love in Paradise.
>
> *When I am dead, my dearest,
> Remember but our joys,
> Remember every shining song
> Forget Love's broken toys;
> Grieve not and be not lonely,
> Nor fear to love again,
> My heart sweetheart will follow
> And you can spare me pain.
>
> *I shall not see the shadows
> That darken this sad life,
> But only hearts in Paradise
> That beatify a wife.
> Then shed no tears for me, my love,
> When I am gone before;
> Stand ever on Love's threshold sweet,
> Your heart my true tomb door.

*Lines by Christina Rossetti.

Our grave was dug on a grassy slope in view of the *Caledonia* figurehead, Morwenstow Church and the sea. After a service at Bude I was driven there, and the Catholic priest gave me holy water to sprinkle on the coffin. Back in his studio a robin was flying round. Looking about I saw his unfinished work, including the Letters from John Powys, and resolved to finish it. At first it seemed impossible, and my overpowering desire was to be near him. The following morning I walked to his grave, where I felt only love and tenderness for his corpse, and seemed to see him, like a reflection in deep, still water, drawing me to him. Dissolution roused no aversion, corruption no recoil. Grief is a potent reconciler to death, and dying became more and more necessary. There, as near him as possible, was the sole place I wanted to be, and when through the following months and then years this longing for his presence overcame me, this yearning to be in that croft of reunion, I set out on the moment's edge. It was like going home. It was going home, to our port everlasting. One comfort is that though I still belong to diurnal time, he to Earth time, all times pass, and with every hour the time of separation grows shorter. Sorrows are said to destroy us or themselves. But sorrow has other aftermaths.

How shall I visualise our yokèd years?
Not as mere time which headlong speeds away,
Refusing man's impassioned plea to stay,
Mindless of human loves and hopes and fears;
Nor sempiternal our shared life appears—
The conjoined destiny, the linkèd day,
Not subject to mutation and decay,
Indubitable death and parting's tears.

Like waves of light and surges in an ocean
That pulsate onward to infinity;
Like waves of sound that in commingled motion
Beyond the furthest empyrean fly;
And waves from loving spirits whose devotion
Outsoars mortality were you and I.

PART III

PART III

Widow

1

Deep attachments sundered cause deep woe, sometimes despair. Every moment from somebody a loved one is torn, dealing a wound that will never heal, a sorrow never to be rooted out. Every moment someone loses a living treasure dearer than his own life, part of whom dwells on in him, while part of him is buried with the dead. Exceptionally close people live not only their own but each other's lives, and when one dies the other is diminished. For most of us this is our greatest tragedy. Yet however heartbrokenly we rebel there comes the need of acceptance, the sad and often bitter renouncement which has to be made to death. Endless courage is necessary to join with goodwill in that ancient challenge to fate and acquire the resilience to accept death and suffering as in the nature of things, like birth and joy. As each heart knows its own loss, so each must seek its own resolution.

It was long before I could accept my loss. Nothing staunched grief, neither wisdom nor compassion, neither reason nor faith. Courage failed. I could not face the knowledge that my husband had been deprived of so much he hoped to give the world, so much the world still gave. For years I could not listen to his favourite music. But one night I heard the touching trio Smetana composed after the death of his young daughter—a dirge of passionate tribulation, yet with serene and tender interludes that recall her happiness, and one movement which seems to invoke her spirit playing in the netherworld. It spoke directly to my heart, enabling me again to hear Nicholas's most loved musical works. One must dwell on their moments of happiness and fulfilment. Nevertheless, as Abélard wrote, 'To live after thee is but to die.'

Death has inspired every kind of artist; lamentations pervade every sort of art. I read all the elegies I could find, from the Greek Anthology's moving epitaphs to the poems of two world wars. I sought them with feverish agitation and intensity, rifling each appropriate book, one of which was Robert Bridges' *Spirit of Man*, where I found ineffable expressions of fortitude. I re-read Shelley, this time for consolation. As some of the sweetest melodies are composed of the fewest notes, many of the most touching threnodies are the shortest and simplest: 'O rare Ben Jonson'; 'Jane Lister, deare child'; 'Here Philippus laid his twelve-year-old son, his great hope'; 'I am the tomb of a shipwrecked man; but set sail, stranger; for when we were lost, the other ships voyaged on'. I re-read these and many other tributes and laments with increased empathy. But most often I deciphered the living and ever continuing manual of Nature, whose beauty Nicholas beheld with joy.

The dead are only a short distance in front, and I knew that I should soon catch up, and that death is not to be flinched from, or feared, or forgotten; that the passing of one generation gives the next its opportunities. I tried to make myself believe that for those smitten in the fullness of life, with a thousand unfulfilled aims—or, which suffices for most of us, any kind of life to live—death though it be tragic is never evil, not the last enemy but last friend. Missing my husband everywhere, only alone could I tolerate existence, and those meaning to be kind who insisted that I must be lonely, and would not permit me to be alone, made me lonelier. How many of us pity those who do not need our pity and pity not those who do. Nevertheless, it is better to proffer ruth than, fearful of intruding on a private grief, or of being rebuffed, to withhold it. No one should abjure pity, which can comfort the donor, who may be the more pitiable of the twain. None knows better than I the blessing of another's loving-kindness and compassion, the consolation of another's clemency, and the hurt of withdrawal or indifference.

I knew that it is important to have as good a relationship to the dead as to the living, and this I strove to achieve. The Buddhist ideal, which I admire but do not follow, is *not* to grieve, or to overcome grief: 'The giving up of all grief is pleasant'; 'When the sun of suffering has set then arises bliss'. Belief in a future life, in the Supernatural, in ultimate union with the Divine, are necessary to many people and afford deep consolation. But for others the need is more for union with the Nature they know, without faith in eternal existence. Both faith and scepticism, deism and atheism, have inspired humanity to noble aspirations and achievements, and been necessary to its spiritual development. So long as our ideas and practices do not hurt others we should be free, without being the victims of prejudice and persecution, torture and bigotry, to believe what seems to us true, and live as we choose to live. As Sir Thomas Browne wrote in *Religio Medici*: 'No Man can justly censure and condemn another, because no Man truly knows another . . . Further, no Man can judge another, because no Man knows himself.'

2

At the end of that long year I thought about my comrade of the past, Jan Stewart. For long we had not corresponded, but I never ceased to regret the wound I had caused. I resolved to visit her, but on the morning I was going to write and suggest a meeting I heard from her sister that she had died on December 26th. Sometimes it is not our own past tears which in memory-haunted age we most poignantly remember—it is those, long forgotten by the one who shed them, which for the one who caused them will never dry.

Hoping that my death would be soon I prepared for it. I gave Nicholas's Keats Collection and correspondence with his friend Robert Gittings, and other enthusiasts, to Keats House in Hampstead, where the Librarian of the Borough of Camden enthusiastically ackowledged them. I gave our own collections of published and unpublished writings, photographs and other items to the Humanities Research Center, Austin, Texas, to join my father's, in a literary Elysium free from the misunderstandings and uncertainties of personal relationships. While accumulating our scattered scripts I found Nicholas' Mary, Queen of Scots Anthology, over which he had spent years of meticulous research and care. He regarded the John Cowper Powys and Robert Stephen Hawker Collections as part of his provision for me, so I sold them to those who would care for them to the end of time, and where they would be available for study. The Hawker Collection went to the Bodleian Library; the Powys Collection—which included a Shakespeare Diary J.C.P. had made for Nicholas with a quotation for every annual day—joined other Powys material at the Humanities Research Center. Everything of monetary value I gave to Roman Catholic nuns in Leeds who were appealing for funds towards the cost of a Home for sick and old people, and among them included the small carved wooden Byzantine cross that had belonged to Elizabeth Browning, which Wilfred Meynell gave to Nicholas. The Hawker chair that his collateral descendant, Mrs Molly Gibson, had given us stands in the chancel of Morwenstow Church. I asked Patrick Moore, whose talks we had enjoyed, to suggest someone who might like my old telescope, and to fetch it he brought a young friend, Nicholas Tate—a happy occasion for me. He kindly invited me to look through his own telescopes, but though since childhood I had hoped for such a wonderful opportunity, like so much else in life it came too late.

Meantime I completed the excerpts from John Powys' Letters to Nicholas, with a view, as Nicholas hoped, to publication; and when Anthony Rota, the antiquarian bookseller and publisher, our late friend Bertram Rota's son, who had arranged to transfer the Hawker Collection to the Bodleian, came to see me he was eager to publish those Letters. As *Letters to Nicholas Ross from John Cowper Powys*, beautifully produced, and edited by Arthur Uphill, they came out in 1971.

I tried to keep up our little homestead as Nicholas would have kept it, and to many good village friends, from children to the very old, and countless others throughout the world, for their help I am wholeheartedly grateful and wish I could name each one. Indeed, it saddens me that I have had to leave out nearly all that part of my life enriched by friendship—many friends now dead, but many still living, without whom existence would have been a much lesser and less worthwhile adventure. I love and remember them all.

No one was more generous and kind than my brother Henry. For the first time since nursery days we were all in all to each other again. He wrote two or three times every week and we exchanged four visits every year. At last he was able to express the generous and affectionate impulses he used to hide, which had been frustrated. If only our mother could have seen him now—

On the first anniversary of Nicholas's death I felt a strong desire to revisit Dartmoor, which had played a crucial part in our lives, so I took a bus to Okehampton and walked to Belstone. Eastward rose Cosdon Beacon, my father's favourite height. I tramped for miles over the mist-drenched Moor until, late in the day, I was descending a steep hill from the firing-ranges when I came across a derelict house that must have stood empty for many years, its cracked, dusty windows smeared with cobwebs, dead spiders and bluebottles crumpled on the sills, the garden a thicket of overgrown shrubs and weeds, the whole place fallen into desuetude. On the broken gate was printed KLON—klon?—of course, KLONDIKE. This was the house where sixty-five years ago we and Arnold Bennett had stayed! This was the very house. A tall privet hedge now concealed the view of Cosdon across the vale. I pushed through tangled plants, found the back door broken and entered. Bits of decaying furniture lay about. Tattered curtains drooped. The place was dead, like all those people, except Henry and me, and we were on the brink. How desolate that chance discovery left me—a long forgotten place I had not been seeking. Phantoms—But there was one, not of that company, whose spiritual presence was ever beside me, sharing as we shared everything this melancholy episode.

3

One effect of my husband's death was to make time stand still. Hours, days, weeks passed, yet for me time with its becomings, changes, endings, ceased to move. Two or three days every month I walked to our grave. In his Essay, *The Wild*, Thoreau wrote that he had 'met with but one or two persons in the course of my life who understood the art of walking', and describes every walk as a 'sort of crusade'. My walks were more in the nature of a pilgrimage and walking was not an art but a necessity. Gradually time did shuffle on, and the world came slowly back into focus, as if a blinded person were beginning to see. Senses struck insensible revived, and again I felt the wonder of that transit and recovered a vision of life's perpetual renewal. Surrounded by living things coming into being and perishing, I realised how much the living have in common with the non-living, so tenuous is their division, so interdependent are they. For not only at our deaths do we dissolve into new forms and substances, but also during our lives. Ocean is in our blood, rocks are in our bones, plants and animals in our tissues. Our brain-cells contain them all. And however far into space man penetrates, however deeply aware he is of belonging to the whole universe, one of his basic emotions must be consciousness of evolving on this planet. And until, or if, future generations are born, reared and pass their lives on other satellites, men will retain their ability to enter the quintessence of all things terrestrial, from the most insignificant to our fellow humans—until everyone becomes Everyman.

To span the void created by death and purge despair, I resolved to take up writing again, and begin by limning a picture of those walks to our tomb, to preserve a likeness, lamentably dim, of scenes perhaps fated to vanish—for like so much of these islands which has already disappeared this landscape may die—my aim to commemorate one who responded to nature and human nature with a passion of compassion; to weave a coronal of the wild flowers he loved—a wreath of amaranth. As people deprived of one or more faculties often live more intensely than the rest, so people deprived by the loss of loved ones sometimes express themselves in creative mediums, not only to staunch their own wounds but to help others who cannot follow Malcolm's advice to Macduff: 'Give sorrow words.' I had few words, yet determined to offer this pledge to my husband's memory, and to any person stricken by the most universal of sorrows, the death of a beloved.

The passage to Morwenstow church and cliffs and back is roughly ten miles, and every few yards the scene changes, the road vanishing round a bend, the hedges so tall, the path so narrow, that leaning foliage touches the passer-by; and the whole is so sheltered that in coldest winters some creature is active, some plant in bloom. After the first mile one comes upon a pine tree, resembling the tree which grew in our first Torquay garden. It became a friend. One crosses several streams, and I would linger beside fern-fringed pools and lean over the water to note the tiniest creatures which hovered above or lived in the depths. I began to see nature in a new light— impersonal, yet closer than many personalities. Sometimes my father rose to mind and I remembered how he taught me the wild flowers' names, and I recalled the journey with my grandmother to Kingskerswell's primrose banks. Now I met all those blithe flowers again and valued the least hedgling, the smallest insect, the shyest beast and bird. When I reached our grave I felt serene and safe and looked forward to lying there. I wrote my book in the gypsy wagon, from which I could see the sunset and the sea.

Sometimes I reflected on all those artists, in every medium, who have immortalised wild flowers. I sought them in books, and paintings—especially poignant those depicted during the world wars which pushed up on shell-pitted battlefields, amongst the dead, the ghastly trenches and shattered forests of awful landscapes. Even in marble I discovered them: there is an antique *Kore* dating from 640 BC wearing a diadem of daisies, holding to her breast a rose. In music, too, they are to be found: Beethoven, like Bruckner, adored nature and wrote: 'How glad I shall be to wander amidst shrubs, forests, trees, herbs and rocks! . . . Does it not seem as if every tree . . . said to me: Holy! Holy! In the forest, enchantment . . . My unalterable friends, the green shrubs and aspiring trees, the green hedges and bowers . . . O god! What splendour!!! Here there is no envy or competition or dishonesty . . .' When someone asked him for the meaning of his piano sonatas Op. 2 no 2, and Op. 57 he said: 'Read Shakespeare's *Tempest!*' He responded to that in Shakespeare which loved music and could evoke music and the desire for music in others—something which reverberates through nature, from the loftiest sublime to the darkest depths, that nerve attuned to its wonder and mystery. (In all my rovings and vigils, my griefs and joys, I remember those two noble musicians, of the word and of the note, whose music since childhood has sustained me more powerfully than any other, the mere mention of whose names fills my heart with tears.)

Every time I go to Morwenstow I recollect that on our last visit Nicholas said. 'One day you'll be here putting flowers on my grave. But if I have primroses, daisies and buttercups I shall be satisfied.' They soon sprang in the turf, where they tell of everlasting peace. Funebrial garlands have existed since prehistoric days. In an Iraqi tomb dating back sixty thousand years pollen analysis proves that a man, perhaps a Neanderthal man, was buried on a layer of flowers. Flowers were dropped into the mummy cases of Pharaohs. Christopher Smart, when deranged a distinguished poet, indifferent when rational, wrote in *Jubilate Aeno*: 'Flowers are good both for the living and the dead'; and there is a Buddhist aphorism: 'As many kinds of wreaths can be made from a heap of flowers, so, once he is born, can a mortal achieve many good things.' When Chekhov saw students carrying wreaths to a grave he said: 'These are people who are burying the old and bringing fresh flowers and new hopes into the kingdom of death.' Washington Irving's moving Essay on *Rural Funerals* comes to mind at Morwenstow: such rites as he described over a century ago are still performed. And as I loiter among the tombstones I think, with Sir Thomas Browne: 'Who knows whether

the best of men be known? Or whether there be not more remarkable
persons forgot, than any that stand remembered in the known account
of time?'

I chose a granite cross for our headstone. Igneous rock attracted
Nicholas more than rock laid down in water, especially this rugged
crystalline stone compounded of mica, feldspar and quartz. He was
born on New England granite. We met on Dartmoor granite, and
under Cornish granite were buried. Yet it matters not where the dead
lie. Everything passes, and for the grief-stricken grief will pass, if
only when the mourner rejoins the mourned. All's well with the dead.
Our supreme gifts are love and death.

4

My stepmother died, followed by Nicholas's brother Stanley, and in
1970 dear Aunt Olive, after which my bond with the Ross family
broke.

One March foredawn I rose at three o'clock to look for Bennett's
comet, and was astonished by the myriads of stars in the clear spring
sky. Even during Pacific nights in the *Cuzco* the heavens had not been
so thickly stippled with suns. Brilliant under the Milky Way shimmered
the wanderer, wielding its sceptre over Nicholas's 'sparkling spaces'.

I finished *A Wildflower Wreath* and sent it to Edmund Cork, my
kind-hearted literary agent of long ago, who advised me to have a
shortened version printed, and arranged with the Stellar Press,
directed by Mr William Hummerstone, who produced an edition
beyond praise.

Nicholas had intended to take me to Ireland, which he loved, and
to Russia to seek in the Hermitage Art Gallery a portrait of Mary,
Queen of Scots by Labanoff, a copy of which illustrated his unpublished anthology. For his sake I resolved to visit both, and first joined
a coach-tour to Ireland; but while crossing from Anglesey to Dublin I
so missed Nicholas that I blamed myself for coming, and recall little
except Yeats' grave, and as we drove through Donegal, Galway and
the south-west the melancholy of ruined farmsteads and empty
homes.

In May 1970, I booked a cabin on a Russian passenger-trading
vessel called the *Baltika* berthed at Tilbury, bound for Leningrad.
From the train window I sighted the *Cambria*, an old wooden sailing-
barge, slowly crossing the Pool, the last spritsail barge still trading
on the river, and wished Henry could see her. The *Baltika*, moored at
a Tilbury wharf, was old, and though the upper regions seemed
comfortable, my dark narrow berth in the lowest depths, with a port
I could not open and a washbasin with no stopper, smelt of antiquity.
Most of the passengers were jolly, noisy, boisterous East-enders.
With three or four others I joined a Russian language class, but found

it too difficult to master. At meals I sat with two warm-hearted people, mother and son, who refused to let me, as I intended to, follow Plotinus's advice to 'withdraw into yourself and look', but insisted on looking with me. Mrs Alice Smith, in her eighties, was a gallant, vivacious, handsome lady, her son Bob an artist with a deeply sympathetic, suffering nature and the fortitude and humour that sometimes attend it. Who but a curmudgeon could resist their benevolence? We became friends, for the rest of time. The *Baltika* called at Copenhagen, and then sailed up the Gulf of Finland to Tallinn, capital of the Estonian Soviet Republic, whose thirteenth-century castle stands on a lofty Silurian crag called the Domberg, overlooking the port. Rich in Northern Gothic, it is the seat of the Estonian Academy of Arts and Sciences, where every year an open-air festival attended by two hundred thousand people is held in its Field of Song. I walked in its fine park and among aged buildings which created an impression of solemnity.

At the head of the gulf the *Baltika* moved slowly along the ship canal leading to Leningrad and anchored there. Having booked a visit to the Winter Palace Gallery for the following day, without map or plan I set off and tramped for miles along broad avenues until I reached the banks of the Neva, and suddenly all around rose golden domes and palaces, and I knew why Leningrad is called one of the world's most beautiful cities. I dallied for what seemed hours along the embankment, but it was getting late; I was tired, and there was a long slog back to the ship.

Next morning a tour of the city culminated in a visit to the Hermitage, and I looked forward to meeting Mary Stuart, in the Labanoff portrait, sitting in a green velvet chair on whose arms her hands are resting, her eyes, as Nicholas said after studying the reproduction, 'with an exceedingly magical and bewitching expression'. In front of me on the coach sat a woman in a white straw hat, and I noticed another across the gangway wearing a black and white check coat. We passed magnificent Universities, Academies, Institutes, Ministries and Galleries, St Isaac and Kazon Cathedrals, huge squares, bridges and wide prospects, one of which was the famous Nevsky Prospect I had read about in Russian novels. At length we crossed to the Neva's left bank and drew up in a square opposite the almond-green façade of the Winter Palace and entrance to the Gallery. I noted where the coach parked so that I could find it again, and joined our party, led by a young woman guide, which assembled in a crowded hall to await our turn to pass the turnstile. An elderly member of our group felt faint and said she must go to the cloakroom, and as no one offered to accompany her I took her there. She could go no farther and I said I would fetch her when we came back. When I reached the spot where the others had been waiting they had vanished, and I realised with horror that I had missed my chance of getting into the Gallery, for the guide held an inclusive ticket and was nowhere to be seen. I felt stunned; but then a strange thing happened. Invisible hands seemed to swing me round and direct my gaze at a certain point in the mass of people, and propel me to a place from which I spied the white hat I had noticed in the coach. I shoved my way through the mob and arrived as the woman in the hat was moving through the barrier!

A treasure that particularly bemused me was Leonardo da Vinci's adorable little Benois Madonna, of amazing originality. But, alas, lingering was not possible. We were herded along at a spanking pace and swept past the wonders like leaves on a swirling river, unable to resist the current. As to finding Mary, Queen of Scots, I could not even make the guide understand that I wanted to see her. I dared not risk exploring on my own and getting lost; yet later that is what happened. After we returned to the vestibule and I had retrieved the lady from the cloakroom, I detached myself and made my way back to the coach alone. It was gone. My group had disappeared too. I dashed about, panic-stricken, searching in vain. Was I lost in Leningrad for evermore? I tore back to the Gallery—they were not there. Would the ship sail without me? O, that Nicholas were there, he who never lost his nerve, or himself, or me, and got us out of the most difficult quandaries, as he rescued me from the Dartmoor quagmire. But again an odd thing happened, and I was as it were taken in charge, swivelled about, and my vision focused on one particular spot where I saw the black-and-white check coat of the person in the coach, crossing a bridge in the distance. I rushed after her and reached the vehicle, parked on the other side of the river. Was it chance? Coincidence? No doubt it was. But it felt like the concern of one who when we were courting gave me the compass-pendant and said 'Now you are going in my direction!' and was pointing out the right direction still.

On her return voyage the *Baltika* docked at Stockholm, but after Leningrad that city seemed spiritually frozen—or perhaps it was my spirit which was cold. I was confused and already sickening for a bad illness just waiting to strike. All I remember is the seventeenth-century warship, *Vasa*, which in 1628 sank within sight of thousands who had come to cheer the beginning of her maiden voyage. For more than three hundred years she lay seabound, then, in 1956, was discovered and salvaged, towed into dry dock and restored. Now she stands in a specially conditioned maritime museum, her timbers sprayed with chemicals—a weird, sinister-looking hulk.

On the last day of our voyage I felt so ill that it was all I could do to stand in the queue before disembarking at Tilbury. Jammed in the crowd, my limbs ached and I felt so weak that I feared to faint, but got down the gangway and hauled my baggage to a platform, where someone pointed out a train bound for Fenchurch Street. My new friend, Bob, flew over to help me, and vowing to be friends for ever, as we became, I stumbled on to the London platform and was pulled into a carriage as the starting whistle blew. Kind people offered me a seat in their taxi to Paddington, and I just caught a second train, for the West Country, as if Nicholas were propelling me home. The illness was gaining ground and next day I sent for the District Nurse, who proclaimed hepatitis. My travels were over.

I asked if I might have a Home Help for one hour a week, which brought Mrs Doreen Vanstone, interesting, good-hearted and original, to whose visits I looked forward. It was a privilege to know her and her delightful family.

I began re-reading favourite books of long ago, of which Shakespeare and Montaigne provided most pleasure and interest; and like other people I sought links between them. For instance, in his Essay *On Cruelty*, as translated by his contemporary, John Florio, tutor to Shakespeare's patron the Earl of Southampton, Montaigne wrote: 'Yet is there a kind of respect, and general duty of humanity which tieth us not only unto brute beasts that have life and sense, but even unto trees and plants.' Shakespeare read this in Florio's translation, published in 1603, and may have noted that Florio's 'dew-bedabbled hare'—which the humane Montaigne could not bear to hear groaning 'when she is seized by the hounds'—might have been filched from his own *Venus and Adonis*, where he describes the hunting of the 'timorous flying hare', the 'dew-bedabbled wretch'—an echo that may have amused the great dramatist, who himself purloined from another of Montaigne's Essays, *Of the Caniballes*, Gonzalo's Commonwealth speech in *The Tempest*, a passage which like all his ingenious pilferings he borrowed only to embellish. With such mines of inexhaustible riches both splendid artists could afford some plundering.

I had nightmares—of being lost in dark, desolate landscapes where I called at a door to ask the way, only to be shouted at to be gone; of being trapped on a lonely shore by swift incoming waves with no escape from drowning; of being stranded at the foot of steep mountains from which the only outlet was the ascent of a couloir getting perpendicular and ending in nothingness. In other dreams Nicholas returned, Nan reappeared, my father arrived, either young and affectionate, or old and angry when I flung myself at his feet and begged him not to cast me out, and we would be reconciled . . . How little is known about the human psyche! Whatever kind of dream, I woke in anguish: yet it is true, as Strindberg wrote in his preface to the *Dream Play*, 'Sleep, the liberator, often seems a tormentor, but when the anguish is harshest comes the awakening

—which, however painful, is yet a mercy compared with the agony of the dream.' I walked in my sleep, as I used to as a child, to wake standing in darkness, not knowing where I was, on this earth or elsewhere, alive or dead. And during this strange half-life startling hallucinations were frequent, recalling, also, those of childhood. Was this second childhood? Off-balance in every sense I kept falling, but all I got was bruises and a sense of being ridiculous.

I became interested in Survival International, a world-wide society that strives to protect indigenous peoples whose lifestyles, which often work better for them than those of the 'civilised' world do for their members, are threatened, especially those belonging to countries partly or wholly industrialised—peoples who must conform and integrate, or pass unfulfilled lives in shrinking Reserves, in danger of dying out: Amerindians and North American Indians, Eskimos, Australian Aborigines, Polynesians, Ainns, Bushmen, Papuans and others, for whom I feel intensely, to the extent of being one of them, and want to help them. It is a consolation to know that more and more people have their good at heart.

New friends came, among them Professor and Mrs Gordon Lothian, who brought Nicholas's treasured correspondent of many years, Professor G. Wilson Knight, who had lost a beloved mother, and gifted brother, Jackson Knight, and knew the sorrows of parting, though for him death meant a passage to a fuller eternal life. This original thinker, famous Shakespearean scholar and author of many books, including critical-analytical studies of several other writers, Fellow of the Royal Society of Literature, and Commander of the British Empire, was compassionate and understanding—one of the rare people who carry into wise old age the ardour and curiosity of youth, so that they seem ageless. He helped me in many ways.

For nearly four years a spider kept me company. In a corner of the kitchen window it spun a silken tunnel into which it retreated by day, emerging in the twilight, or if an insect got tangled in its trapline. So far as I knew, it never left the window, and even during the night was strolling about the pane or sitting in the entrance to its gossamer bower. Sometimes another spider of the same species approached but I never witnessed a meeting. Once I saw it dart at a blundering bluebottle, stab, enmesh, suck dry and cast down the remains. And one evening I switched on the electric kettle, and watched my spider scampering among its snares. It preferred darkness so I turned out the light and forgot the kettle, until I heard an ominous rattling: the safety device for expelling the flex if it boiled dry had failed, and it was full of red-hot copper globules, the kitchen dense with steam. I thought the spider must be scalded to death, but when the vapour cleared there it was eating a gnat. I grew fond of this diminutive companion; but when returning from a visit to my brother I found no trace, until I examined its nest where curled into a ball it lay dead.

On a September morning I went out early, to find every shrub hung with millions of hammock and wheel webs, several attached to the same points, all sagging with dewdrops. The countryside was over-woven with floss, as if this day was an arachnid festival. An old neighbour said: 'Christmas has come!' A month later three small tortoiseshell butterflies settled on a beam above my bed and hibernated until March, when I watched one wake, stretch its legs, and fly shakily to a flower on the windowsill, where it vibrated its wings. After three cloudy days a sunbeam warmed it and it fluttered into the garden.

On my spring visit to Henry he took me to the site of Eltham: the house, outbuildings and garden were all gone and in their place rose a vast Technical College. For a moment, however, it in its turn vanished and I saw, not my old white-haired brother, but an eager child and his young beautiful mother, a trug on her arm, gathering peonies, preparing to 'do' the flowers indoors which she renewed every day. And there was the pond with its newts and dragonflies, the monkey-puzzles, rockeries, flickering moths and bats, the twilit lawn where from leafy nooks hedgehogs brought their babies to walk, dew settling on the sward, and plants released their savours to scent the dusk. There, too, in the background was the house, which had become a house of mistakes and sorrows, of tragedy, of our mother's poignant death; but also where our father had written all those wonderful books.

Two living things had survived. Near what had been the drive towered the *Magnolia campbellii* I had helped Father to plant when it was no taller than I. Now it soared for forty feet, so magnificent that the authorities had spared it. Every spring it expanded into hundreds of large crimson globes, a triumphant blossoming our father never witnessed. Not far away rose the ginkgo tree which I recalled as a leafless infant swaddled in hessian, being unpacked by my father's long, careful fingers, and planted opposite the drawing-room window. Of that garden which had been my everywhere nothing else was left. But it was pleasant to hear the bustling College of youth.

Another evocative event was a radio revival of *The Farmer's Wife*, fifty years after its first night.

5

When I finished *A Wildflower Wreath* I felt like a spider whose spinnarets are empty. Now that I had cobbled up the loose ends left after Nicholas died I felt stultified, until something happened which led to a new task. It was Easter 1973, and I had come back from taking daffodils to our grave, when a young man knocked on the door, to tell me that he was writing a new life of Robert Stephen Hawker and had been consulting Nicholas's Hawker Collection at the Bodleian Library. It was Dr Piers Brendon, Cambridge lecturer in Ecclesiastical History, a literary critic and author, his aim to scotch the inaccuracies of a previous Life, that gives a false impression of Hawker the poet, mystic and priest. With Dr Brendon's humour and insight into human nature, including the baffling nature of a complicated person like the Cornish parson, coupled with a sympathetic imagination and amazing capacity for meticulous research, he was the right man to undertake this task. For over a hundred years his family had been associated with the Falcon Hotel in Bude, where Hawker had visited and Tennyson stayed. We kept in touch, and as he completed his chapters he sent me copies. I was delighted as a portrait of the real Hawker emerged, with an evocative re-creation of the Victorian period as it affected the remote setting of Morwenstow, and a fine description of its dangerous promontories, tumultuous seas and terrible shipwrecks.

Hawker of Morwenstow, Portrait of a Victorian Eccentric was published by Jonathan Cape in 1975, the centenary year of Hawker's death, when celebrations were held at Morwenstow which aroused interest beyond this small corner of the British Isles, for it extends farther than the regional, into the mystical sphere of the poet's extraordinary mind. To my pride and pleasure the author dedicated his book to the memory of my husband and to me, my sorrow being that Nicholas was not here to enjoy his company, his book, the honour of its dedication, and to share my gratitude. Piers Brendon encouraged me to write some reminiscences, and thus I began this book.

Here I had intended to conclude it. But life and time went on and the end is a little delayed.

6

In 1975, during Henry's summer change to Cobblestones, we spent peaceful days in the garden watching collared doves feeding and perching in the beech tree; and he told me that he was surprised and gratified to have lived for eighty years. But when he came for Christmas he seemed much aged and I felt worried. During our long concurrent lives we had never exchanged a caress; and as we were parting I thought: Suppose we died without a single endearment, and I kissed him for the first time. I did not see him again until my May visit to the bungalow, where he lived with Mrs Maude Briault, now widowed. In a recent letter he had mentioned influenza but said he had recovered. I found him pale and despondent; and when Mrs Briault told me he had not had influenza but had grown increasingly silent and melancholy I feared a return of the depressive illness which darkened his earlier years. But though there had been recurrences, my visits had hitherto dispelled them. This time he did not respond and I saw that he was more than mentally ill. Maude naturally blamed him for refusing to consult a doctor, or to let her do so, and I tried in vain to persuade him. Like our mother, but very unlike our father, he hated having to resort to medical help. He was so upset by our insistence, that, unwilling to spoil our meeting, I decided not to summon assistance until later. When we were out together he walked unwontedly slowly, but pooh-poohed any suggestion of illness: 'It's just old age.'

Visible from the living-room grew a white-flowering cherry tree which during my spring visits was always in full bloom: we admired it together and Henry's face lit up when he looked at it. This year something had gone wrong: it had budded but now its young leaves were shrivelling and the buds turning brown. The tree was dying. I sensed Henry's anxiety though when I mentioned its sickness he silently turned away. The fate of this hitherto jubilant tree filled me with more than dismay; it struck me cold with foreboding.

Every day I hoped Henry would recover the happiness which until now had graced our reunions, but he grew more uncommunicative, inarticulate, totally unable to express what was on his mind, though I knew that he wanted and expected me to help him to tell me. One day he was sitting bowed before the fire when suddenly he said: 'I don't think I shall get through this year . . . I feel so *lonely*.' Before I could answer, Maude came in and declared that if he died she would be blamed for not summoning a doctor. I could bear no more. Telling them that I was going to get one, I rushed out of the house. Henry was registered with a husband-and-wife team who lived half a mile from the bungalow, to whose house I ran and asked if the woman partner, whom he knew, could come to see him as soon as possible. In a quarter of an hour she was there. Henry was relieved that at last he was *obliged* to see her, and willingly submitted to an examination. She said there was no cause for alarm but she would take a blood sample and let us know the result. 'There's nothing to worry about. He seems a little anaemic.' She wrote a prescription which Henry and I went into town to have made up. Then he took me to a bookshop to choose a parting gift, as it had been arranged for me to leave in the morning. He had already marked down two books he knew I would like; The Penguin *Book of the Natural World* and *Book of the Physical World*, and he bought me a bottle of lavender water, and fruit. His gloom had lifted. I promised to come back soon and fetch him for as long as he liked to stay.

After I left, Henry wrote to say he was better, and the doctor wrote: 'He seems a lot improved.' But a few days later she told me that his blood count revealed extensive anaemia and he was to see a specialist. Then came a letter mentioning a 'severe anaemia of an unusual type, with a deficiency of both red and white cells', and she thought the possibilities were 'kidney failure or perhaps a malignancy somewhere in the body'. I prepared to return and just before starting had a telephone message that my brother had been taken to Torbay Hospital. I had to wait until the evening visiting-hour before seeing him, and found him in the men's medical ward receiving a blood transfusion. Smiling and calm he was relieved to be there.

The hospital was only a mile from the bungalow and I could walk there in a quarter of an hour. Visiting-hours were restricted to one hour a day. For a week I was told nothing definite about Henry's illness; everyone was evasive. The Sisters and nurses grew very fond of him and he of them, and he missed them when he was transferred to a single room far away in Turner Wing, and charged me to get a parting gift for each. When I asked a Sister why he had been elected to solitude she said that his bone marrow could no longer make red and white blood cells, so he had no defence against even a minor infection and had been moved for his own good. At first he missed the other patients, for whom he felt close sympathy, but later admitted that the quieter environment was better. Like Nicholas he never complained. During those broiling drought days he accounted for his weakness by the unusual heat and we assured each other that he would soon be better. His mind often dwelt on the past and one day he said: 'Do you remember our picnics at Jordan on the Ball? I'd love to go there again.' I resolved to take him there.

Most of my time was free so I not only thought about the past, I wandered in it. On my way to the hospital I passed the cemetery where Grannie and Uncle Mac had lain under their slab for half a century, and one afternoon I went in to find their grave, approached by a weedy path once nicknamed 'Park Lane', bordering which lay the skeletons of those wealthy Torquegians who used to throng to Mother's parties. Their villas had long since been converted into flats, hotels and nursing-homes, and their once grand monuments, with elaborate inscriptions and angels, were weather-stained and overgrown, some lolling askew, vaults broken open, their denizens long forgotten. Grannie's grave was crowded in among others at some distance from 'Park Lane', but I traced it and found its once radiant marble splotched and chipped, the kerbs smashed, someone else's cross pitched atop it and a vigorous ash sapling pushing out of a crack like a crooked limb. The lettering, too, had been damaged but I made out: Adelaide Phillpotts. Born 19 September, 1843. Died 1 November 1921; and on the opposite kerb was inscribed: Herbert Macdonald Phillpotts 1865–1912. At the foot of the plot was: In Hope of Eternal Life; at the head: BELOVED. Round about flourished a forest of horsetails, the only agreeable beings in that enclosure.

One evening I passed the site of Eltham, and visited those Rocks where Nan took us to play. All that remained unbuilt on was a small grassy waste and the deserted lime-kiln whose mysteries and dangers had once allured me. The thyme-scented terraces with their glittering insects had gone. And though the slaughterhouse where screaming pigs were stuck had also vanished, Jenkins, the more than a century-old marble works, still operated, driven by electricity. Windmill Hill was covered with houses, but in one garden a single stump had been preserved.

I strolled along the Victorian Rock Walk, with its crystal-lined grotto of fossils and stalactites that once enthralled me, and its eucalyptus trees that bewitched Henry. Only one, battered and scrawny, remained. Beyond stretched Torre Abbey sands, where at low tide the old cobbler used to build sandcastles while we aimed pennies at his cap. Driven by a morbid longing to be where we had been together, I went to the harbour shop where Henry took me for coffee, trying to convince myself that before long we should for-gather there again. But in my mind's eye I kept seeing the spectral cherry tree. So I left and sought another of our haunts, Haldon Pier, where the hulk *Success* had anchored, and Henry and I had often watched ships come and go. To my astonishment there lay an old tan-sailed Thames barge, like those he loved. During the next visiting-hour I told him about it, feeling sure he would be thrilled, but he showed no interest, and with acute misery I realised that ships mattered to him no more.

My final retracement led to Chapel Hill, less altered than the other ancient places: hundreds of ilex oaks still strewed the ground with leaves, and the same old seats were occupied by courting couples. I walked up and down the path where Father used to take his constitutional, and sat on the bench overlooking Torre Station where Nan sat, and Henry watched Mr Pack wielding his shunting hook.

On my next hospital visit the Senior Sister summoned me to meet Dr McGill, in charge of Henry, and took me to an ante-room where he stood surrounded by students in white coats. 'I don't know if you have been told that your brother has a severe *leukaemia*,' he began. 'There was a possibility of trying some new treatment, but this might have made him feel rather ill, and at his age it is not likely to benefit him. So we decided against it. I am afraid there is no more we can do. Don't worry. He will be all right.' Stunned, I asked how long he might live, hoping it would be for a few years, with the remissions leukaemia patients have. He replied matter-of-factly: 'Two or three weeks perhaps, but some infection could carry him off at any time—like that!' and he snapped his fingers. The shock overwhelmed me. The doctor said the best thing would be to get Henry into a good nursing-home, and I realised that they needed his ward for a patient whose life might be saved. So I told the doctor to move him and I would find a home. Dr McGill and his troupe thanked me and left: I heard and

saw them no more. He had done his best for Henry and I was grateful.
The Sister said she would get in touch with the Social Service
Organiser, who arranged for Henry to be transferred to a local nursing
home, and meanwhile he was shifted into a ward occupied by an old
man on his deathbed.

I wrote to tell Henry's friend of the past, Ray Eddy, about his
illness—they had lost touch and she was living in retirement at
Plymouth. She immediately came to see him, which gave him
pleasure, and for which I was intensely grateful.

At the nursing-home one of the first things the Superintendent said
was: 'I hope your brother won't expect to mingle with our other
residents. You see, they don't mix here. They have their own single
rooms and visitors.' My heart slumped, not because of non-mingling,
but because of the attitude. However, all Henry needed was skilled
nursing and kindness, peace of mind, protection and safety, and these
he had. He was not told what had struck him or that he could not
recover, and was spared mental and physical pain. I rarely left him.

On the fifth day he welcomed me as usual, and had not his
breathing been so shallow and his pulse hardly perceptible I should
have thought he was improving. About one o'clock a nurse came in
and asked me to come back after lunch. Henry nodded, smiled and
waved as I stood at the door. I returned to Mrs Briault, for whom I
felt very sorry, for she was upset by Henry's illness, and uncertainty
about the future, and had been good in letting me stay at the
bungalow. She gave me a meal, and I returned to the nursing-home. A
nurse met me at the front door, took me to a chair in the hall and said:
'Your brother died at twenty minutes to two, very peacefully.'

After a long wait the Superintendent appeared and said: 'Now you
can come and say goodbye to your brother', and led me to his room . . .
He was cremated, and his ashes left in the garden of remembrance.

7

In March 1975, the Professor of English and Philosophy at Lock
Haven State College in Pennsylvania, Dr James Dayananda, Indian
by birth, had written to Henry and me seeking our help for his project
of writing a Critical Study of Eden Phillpotts for Twane's World
Authors Series: a survey of World Literature—a firm for which he
had already published a Critical Study of the Life and Work of the
Indian writer, Manochar Malgonkar, besides contributing articles on
the history, theory and practice of literary criticism, especially of
twentieth-century American and British literature, to international
Journals and Reviews. 'Eden Phillpotts is the most unjustly neglected
English novelist,' he wrote. 'Any information you could give me
would be most appreciated,' adding that he hoped to visit Britain in
the summer of 1976 to meet people associated with our father. A

correspondence ensued and he arranged to see me at Cobblestones. When this date approached, Henry had just died and I was still in Torquay, so I deflected him to the bungalow. Not knowing that Henry was dead, he arrived two days after the funeral. A handsome, vigorous man, full of friendly greetings and kind gifts, but saddened to hear about my brother's death, he showed me a photograph of himself and his beautiful young wife, Vanitha, and their two little daughters, Priya and Soumya. Then he unpacked a talking machine which recorded my answers to questions.

The following day I showed Professor Jim the site of Eltham, where he photographed the magnolia and the ginkgo trees, and I wished *they* could have recorded their impressions of my father. Before we parted I knew that this warm-hearted man would succeed in his project.

8

Though aware since nursery days of Henry's fantasy world, I knew only that there he found the desirable objects and beings he failed to find—where most of us find them if we find them at all—in the world of every day; but he shared with none his imaginary country, whose delectable forms and characters remain for ever beyond my knowledge, though I glimpsed them in the wonderful pictures, now lost, he painted before the First World War. I shared to the full, however, his sympathy for animal and human suffering and like him could not endure to see a fish caught, a beast hunted, a man, woman or child assaulted. When violence appeared on television Henry closed his eyes. Few people understood, appreciated or penetrated to the heart of him, and fewer loved him. Like me only more so he was a loner, and if ever artist hid his light he did. He had little ambition, yet latterly was pathetically touched if anyone admired the pictures which still endured—all of which I now possess—and bothered to tell him so. Though I had always been close to him in spirit, even when our lives were widely separated, now, with only each other left, we had become still more attached, and I had tried to make his old age the best period he had known.

Having outlived all my loved ones, no one would be close to me again, and it was eerie for the first time to be quite alone. Often thinking about the past—often at Eltham, a ghost in a ghost-house— I recalled how in childhood I had once saddened Nan by choosing on a certain afternoon to be alone instead of having tea with her, that I might play fancy games with my fancy family and call up my beloved poets to a fancy feast; and later how I stole a day, consecrated to friends, to walk alone on the Quantock Hills. Now, destined always to be alone, with all the time but no longer the desire for fantasies, what would I not have given to retrieve that selfish afternoon, that schemed for day, and spend them with my dead while they still lived.

I worked in the wagon, and sometimes felt there a mysterious return of youth's vitality, passion, love; and remembered how at eighty-eight my father said he felt no older 'inside' than he did at twenty—which I have also heard other old people say. One morning I placed the watch Nicholas had picked up in the Grand Canyon on the wagon table and returned briefly to the cottage for a book. When I came back it had gone—purloined by magpie, jackdaw, jay? Strangely found, it as strangely disappeared again. I had never felt that it belonged to us. As to the garden, when Nicholas, who made it, died it went on making itself—I let it do what it liked—and ultimately most of it returned to the wild.

I continued to walk to our grave, and one day seated there, not far from servicemen killed in war, how mad seemed our mutual hatreds, fears, piling up of infernal armaments, our terrors and rivalries. These are for the day. Death is for ever. And I trusted with my heart and soul that one day all nations, still in splendid diversity but conscious of being one family, would look back on us with compassion, and wonder how we survived, if we do survive. Should those descendants be born, they could owe their existence to our renouncement of war. But whether for good or ill, whether leading to a better world or culminating in life's extinction—life, which got on well without us for two thousand million years—nothing will stop such an adventurous being from delving deeper and deeper into all that is, because his curiosity is part of his humanity. Long may he continue to contemplate the mysterious universe, to speculate, experiment, and wonder. And long may he quest inside his own self, and aspire to spiritual truths expressed in religion, art and philosophy; for there are many sorts of truth, and some people have moments of insight, understanding, revelation, and make profound discoveries that penetrate the murk through which most of us, like astronomers with earthbound instruments, view the cosmos, and bring us closer to reality. Except to some, nature may seem indifferent and the universe purposeless, but we can endow collective and individual lives with any purpose we choose, from the humblest to the most sublime, one of the nobler being the search for beauty, love and joy. If we do not destroy it, planet Earth may last for thousands of millions more years, until it reaches some inexorable conclusion, and long before then life will have ceased. But the human venture may not be quite over: there could be satellites whirling round other planets where a new adventure might begin.

Another year passed—a moist violet spring. Had Nicholas lived we should have been celebrating the hundred and fiftieth anniversary of Beethoven's death in his fifty-seventh year. In that comparatively short life, like Shakespeare's still shorter one, what marvels he bequeathed to humanity. As he wrote his compositions did he ever surmise how they would echo through the centuries to the end of time, to enchant millions yet unborn? Music was one of my stronger passions; and if human lives can be likened to symphonies—the tunes of childhood recurring in the minor key during old age—those themes-with-variations repeated in my life, as in many other people's, were Love, Nature, and Art.

'So much,' says Socrates in *Phaedrus*, 'by way of tribute to Memory, whose revival of our yearning for the past has led us far afield.' I yearn for the past no more. Every life is but a Hail and Farewell, and my transit to oblivion will soon be over. As one looking for a last time at a well-known landscape, a familiar view never to be seen again, I have taken too long a look at my bygone journey, about which I have told 'Nothing but the truth', yet not nearly 'the whole truth', which no one tells. Death stills the loudest and the softest voices, and silence is more precious than sound. (Perhaps I should have remained silent.) Out of my silence and solitude came to me in my reveries these voices from the past.

Index